CW0644564

A
Treatise
on the Law
and the Gospel

A Treatise on the Law and the Gospel

by
John Colquhoun

Introduction by Joel R. Beeke

Edited by Don Kistler

Reformation Heritage Books
Grand Rapids, Michigan

Reformation Heritage Books
3070 29th St. SE
Grand Rapids, MI 49512
616-977-0889
e-mail: orders@heritagebooks.org
website: www.heritagebooks.org

This edition of *A Treatise on the Law and the Gospel*, in which
spelling, grammar, and formatting changes have been made,
is © 1999. It was adapted from the first American edition
printed in New York in 1835 by Wiley and Long.
A new publisher's introduction was added © 2009.

Reprint 2022

ISBN # 978-1-60178-968-6

*For additional Reformed literature, both new and used, request a
free book list from Reformation Heritage Books at the above address.*

Contents

Publisher's Introduction

John Colquhoun (ka-hoon) was a minister in the Church of Scotland and a prolific writer. He was born in the parish of Luss (Dunbartonshire) in 1748 and was led to conversion as a teenager by the answer to the Shorter Catechism's question, "What is effectual calling?" He immersed himself in the writings of Thomas Boston, then studied at the University of Glasgow. He was ordained as minister of St. John's in South Leith in 1781, where he served for 46 years. He died in 1827.

Colquhoun was a Reformed experiential preacher. His sermons and writings reflect those of the Marrow brethren, whose theology was more like that of the Secession churches than like that of Colquhoun's fellow evangelicals in the Church of Scotland. Though Colquhoun was not allowed to recommend Fisher's *Marrow of Modern Divinity* as a Church of Scotland minister, because the General Assembly had condemned it, he felt free to recommend Thomas Boston's notes.

Colquhoun's writings are theologically astute and intensely practical. He wrote on the core doctrines of the gospel, particularly on experiential soteriology. He wrote *A Treatise of Spiritual Comfort* in 1813, then, three years later, *A Treatise on the Law and the Gospel* (hereafter referred to as *Law and Gospel*). He also wrote books on the covenant of grace (1818), the covenant of works (1821), saving faith (1824), the promises of the gospel (1825), and evangelical repentance (1825). Then, too, he wrote a catechism for young communicants (1821) and a volume of sermons that was published posthumously (1836) with a brief memoir.

To whet your appetite for *Law and Gospel*, I provide a summary of it below, and then provide some practical applications drawn from Colquhoun that you can glean from it.

Chapter One: The Moral Law
The opening chapter of *Law and Gospel* provides a three-part theological overview of the moral law. The first section shows that the law was "inscribed on the heart of man in his creation." Colquhoun says that that law is sometimes called *the law of creation* because it is the will of the sovereign Creator revealed to man as His creature and made in His image, owing "all possible subjection and obedience to God as his benign Creator" (p. 6).

Sometimes this is called *the law of nature* because it was founded in the holy and righteous nature of God, its author, and was woven into the nature of man who is justly subject to that law. Sometimes it is called *the moral law* because it reveals the will of God as man's moral governor. God uses this moral law, summarized by the Ten Commandments, as the standard and rule of man's moral qualities and actions. Both God and man are bound to this law by their very nature and relationship, a relationship between "God the Creator, Proprietor, Preserver, Benefactor, and Governor of man; and man the creature, the property, and the subject of God" (p. 7).

In the second section, Colquhoun explains how the law was given to Adam under the form of the covenant of works. That covenant includes a precept, promise, and penalty, Colquhoun says: "a precept requiring perfect, personal, and perpetual obedience as the condition of eternal life; a gracious promise of the continuance of spiritual and temporal life and, in due time, of eternal life; and a penal sanction, an express threatening of death: spiritual, temporal, and eternal" (pp. 11–25).

In the final section, Colquhoun teaches how the law functions in the Mediator's hands as a rule of life to believers. After establishing that the law in Christ's hands is not a new perceptive law but the old law issued to believers under a new form, Colquhoun explains that this law must be given to believers in and through the Mediator. Otherwise, the law could only terrify and destroy. Colquhoun writes, "It was requisite that a Mediator should interpose both between the offended Lawgiver and the sinner, and also between the violated law and the sinner, who, by satisfying the justice of the one and by not answering the demands of the other, might obtain free access for the guilty criminal to both" (p. 29).

God did not give the law through Christ to His people for their justification, for that is complete in Christ alone, but for their sanctification, that the law may "direct and oblige them to walk worthy of their union with Christ, of their justification in Him, of their legal title to and begun possession of life eternal, and of God Himself as their God in Him" (p. 32). In words reminiscent of Luther, who described the law as a stick that God first uses to beat a sinner to Christ, then is used by the believer, saved at the cross, as a cane to help him walk the Christian life, Colquhoun writes, "The precept of the law as a covenant is 'Do and live,' but the command of the law as a rule is 'live and do.' The law of works says, 'Do or you shall be condemned to die,' but the law in the hand of Christ says, 'You are delivered from condemnation; therefore do'" (p. 32).

The law initially metes out the rewards and punishments of judgment, but in the hands of Christ, it offers the rewards and paternal chastisements of grace. To keep believers from disobedience and sin, the Lord warns as their Father that "although He will not cast them into hell for their sins, yet He will permit hell, as it were, to enter their consciences" in the form of afflictions, the greatest being the withdrawing of His favorable and sensible presence in the soul. Colquhoun concludes that to distinguish clearly between "the law as a covenant and the law as a rule of life is, as Luther said, 'the key which opens the hidden treasure of the gospel'" (p. 40).

Chapter Two: Covenant and the Law
In this chapter, Colquhoun explains how the Ten Commandments were published from Sinai in the form of a covenant, then how the Sinaic transaction contained aspects of both the covenant of grace and the covenant of works.

The covenant of grace was promulgated from Mount Sinai. That is evident from the following:

- The Ten Commandments are rooted in the gracious prologue "I am the LORD thy God, which have brought thee out of the land of Egypt, out of the house of bondage" (Ex. 20:2);

- The people with whom the Lord covenanted at Sinai were "the people of God" upon whom He was to have mercy;

- God commanded that the two tables of the covenant on which He had written the Ten Commandments were to be placed in the ark of the covenant and covered by the mercy seat;

- After Moses read the book of the covenant, he sprinkled the people with the blood of sacrifices and said, "Behold, the blood of the covenant which the LORD hath made with you concerning all these words" (Ex. 24:8);

- The ceremonial law, which referred exclusively to the

covenant of grace, was an important part of the transaction at Sinai; and

- Circumcision and the Passover, the two sacraments of
  the covenant of grace made with the patriarchs, were
  added to the transaction at Sinai (John 7:22–23; Deut.
  16:1–8; pp. 47–55).

The Ten Commandments were also displayed to the Israelites at Sinai in the form of a covenant of works, Colquhoun
says. God did not do this to renew that broken covenant with
His people. Rather, in subjection to the covenant of grace,
He displayed the covenant of works before His people so that
they would see "how impossible it was for them as condemned
sinners to perform that perfect obedience" which the law by
its very nature requires.

The covenant of works at Sinai is evident in the following:

- The thunderings and lightnings, the noise of the trumpet, the smoking mountain, the thick darkness, and
  the awful voice of the living God are all symbols of divine justice and wrath;
- Paul's reference to the Ten Commandments given to
  Moses on Sinai as "the ministration of death, written
  and engraven in stones" (2 Cor. 3:7) implies a covenant of works, for only this type of covenant includes
  the penalty of death;
- Christ's command to the rich young ruler to keep
  the Ten Commandments if he would earn eternal life
  (Matt. 19:17–19) implies a covenant of works;
- The New Testament presentation of law and grace in
  contrast to each other (e.g., "The law was given by Moses, but grace and truth came by Jesus Christ," John
  1:17) implies a covenant of works, for if the law only

included the covenant of grace, grace would not be contrasted with grace.

The Israelites at Sinai could not have been placed under the covenants of works and grace at the same time. As Colquhoun explains, "The believers were internally and really under the covenant of grace and only externally under that terrible display of the covenant of works as it was subservient to that of grace, whereas the unbelievers were externally, and by profession only, under that dispensation of the covenant of grace, but were internally and really under the covenant of works" (pp. 63–64).

Furthermore, Colquhoun teaches that a national covenant between God and the Israelites was added to the covenant of grace. That is evident because the moral law was given in the context of ceremonial and judicial laws that related to the blessed entrance of Israel into Canaan. This national covenant with Israel, which is embedded in the moral law, is a secondary and subservient dimension to the primary emphasis of Scripture, however, which is that the moral law underscores the covenant of grace.

Chapters Three and Four: Properties and Principles of the Moral Law

In chapter 3, Colquhoun offers a traditional Reformed understanding of the properties of the moral law, saying that the moral law is universal, perfect, spiritual, holy, just, good, and perpetual (pp. 76–84). In chapter 4, he offers several principles for rightly understanding the Ten Commandments. Some of these principles, such as the following, are standard Reformed fare:

- That which is forbidden requires the opposite duty, and a required duty forbids the opposite sin.

- A required duty implies that every duty of the same kind is required; a forbidden sin means that every sin of the same kind is prohibited.
- No sin may be committed to prevent a greater sin.
- Obedience should aim for God's great goals: His own glory and our holiness.
- Love is the beginning, summary, and end of all the commandments.

Some of Colquhoun's principles are quite innovative, however, such as:

- That which is forbidden is forbidden always; that which is required is to be done only when the Lord affords opportunity.
- We are obliged to persuade others around us to be, do, or forebear whatever the law commands us to be, do, or forebear.
- The commandments of the second table of the law must yield to those of the first when they cannot both be observed (pp. 85–98).

Chapters Five and Six: The Uses of Gospel and Law
In chapter 5, Colquhoun introduces the concept of the gospel as good news, or glad tidings of salvation "to lost sinners of mankind" through the Savior, Christ the Lord (Luke 2:10–11). The gospel includes all the promises of grace as well as God's gracious offers and invitations of His Son to sinners (pp. 102–110). Colquhoun concludes this chapter by stressing that if a reader wants to know if he is truly experiencing the grace of the gospel, he should ask himself such questions as:

1. Do I know spiritually, and believe cordially, the doctrines of this glorious gospel?

2. Do I heartily comply with the invitations and accept the offers of the gospel?

3. Do I frequently endeavor to embrace and trust the promises of it, and do I place the confidence of my heart in the Lord Jesus for all the salvation which is offered and promised in it?

4. Do I so love the gospel that I delight in reading, hearing, and meditating on it?

5. Do I find that under the transforming and consoling influence of the gospel that I, in some measure, delight in the law of God after the inward man and run in the way of all His commandments? (pp. 116–117).

In chapter 6, Colquhoun says that the primary purposes of the gospel are to reveal:

• How the believer is reconciled with God in Christ,

• The covenant of grace and how that gives sinners a right, or warrant to trust in Christ for complete salvation, and

• The grace of Christ to elect sinners by the Spirit, using the gospel as a means to effect a supernatural change of their nature and state. This is the instrument by which the Holy Spirit plants saving faith in the soul and continues to apply Christ to believers for their sanctification and comfort so they may glorify God before men and angels (pp. 118–124).

The moral law is subservient to the gospel. It reveals to sinners the holy nature and will of God, informs them of their duty to God and neighbor, restrains sin and promotes virtue, convinces sinners of their sinfulness and misery and utter inability to recover themselves from this tragic state, and especially shows sinners their dire need of Christ and of His righteousness. It drives them to Him and serves believers as a rule of life (pp. 124–31).

A faithful preacher cannot preach the gospel faithfully unless he preaches the law in subservience to the gospel, Colquhoun concludes. He must press the demands of the law upon the consciences of his hearers, particularly on secure sinners and self-righteous formalists. He must "tear away every pillow of carnal security on which they repose themselves" (p. 136) and show "how great is the misery, and how intolerable will the punishment be, especially of those under the gospel who obstinately continue in their unbelief and impenitence" (p. 138).

Colquhoun goes on to say, "Suppose that sinners reject the gracious offer (of Christ) a thousand times; they are a thousand times greater sinners than they were when He began to be offered to them—and according to the greatness of their sin will their punishment be" (p. 139).

Chapter Seven: The Difference Between Law and Gospel

Those who do not know the difference between law and gospel are prone to mix bondage with freedom of spirit, fear with hope, and sorrow with joy, Colquhoun says. They are prone to misunderstand both justification and sanctification, thus diminishing Christ in the soul and promoting self-righteousness. Some souls will be discouraged from coming to Christ for salvation but will instead look in vain for something to bring with them to recommend themselves to Christ (pp. 141–45).

The major differences between the law and the gospel are these:

- The law proceeds from the very nature of God; the gospel, from His love, grace, and mercy, or His good will to men.

- The law is known partly by the light of nature, but the gospel is known only by divine revelation.

- The law regards us as creatures who are capable of yielding perfect obedience; the gospel regards us as sinners who have no strength to perform perfect obedience.

- The law shows us what we ought to be but not how to become holy, whereas the gospel show us that we may be made holy through communion with Christ and by the sanctification of His Spirit.

- The law says, "Do and you shall live"; the gospel says, "Live, for all is already done, believe and you shall be saved."

- The law promises eternal life for man's perfect obedience; the gospel promises eternal life for Christ's perfect obedience.

- The law condemns but cannot justify a sinner; the gospel justifies but cannot condemn a sinner who believes in Jesus Christ for salvation.

- The law, by the Spirit, convicts of sin and of unrighteousness; the gospel presents the perfect righteousness of Christ to justify a sinner before God.

- The law shows the sinner that his debt is infinitely great and he can make no payment toward that debt; the gospel tells the sinner that, by Christ's obedience as his divine Surety, his debt is paid to the last penny.

- The law irritates the depravity of the sinner and hardens his heart; the gospel melts the sinful heart and subdues depravity.

- The law, when obeyed, prompts boasting; the gospel discourages all boasting because of the law of faith (Rom. 3:27) (pp. 146–54).

Chapter Eight: Harmony Between Law and Gospel

In this chapter, Colquhoun teaches how law and gospel are harmonious. First, the commanding and condemning power of the law harmonizes with the gospel, for both law and gospel seek to lead the sinner to Christ. The law does so indirectly; the gospel, directly. As Colquhoun explains, while the law is our schoolmaster that teaches us our absolute need of Christ, the gospel presents Christ as the end of the law for righteousness to everyone who believes (p. 165).

The gospel is the law immersed in the blood of Jesus Christ. The good news of the gospel is that for lawbreakers, Christ took upon Himself their nature, and bore the law's curse and paid the law's penalty for them as their Mediator and Substitute. Christ not only satisfied the moral and punitive claims of the law, however; on the basis of His finished work on the cross, He transforms lawbreakers into lawkeepers. And thus the good news of the gospel is that Jesus Christ has been made unto us justification (having satisfied the claims of the law) and sanctification, guaranteeing our restoration as image-bearers of God and as keepers of His law.

Second, the law and gospel harmonize in being a rule of life for believers. What the law requires as duty is offered as a privilege by the promise of the gospel. "The commands of the law reprove believers for going wrong, and the promises of the gospel, so far as they are embraced, secure their walking in the right way," Colquhoun says. "The former show them the extreme folly of backsliding; the latter are the means of healing their backslidings and restoring their souls."

The law requires true holiness of heart and of life, and the gospel promises and conveys this holiness. Thus, as Colquhoun says, "The gospel dwells richly in none but in such as have the law of Christ put into their minds and written on their hearts.

The law cannot be inscribed on the heart without the gospel, nor the gospel without the law" (pp. 167–68).

Finally, the law and the gospel have the same friends and enemies. It is impossible to be a friend of the gospel and an enemy of the law, for both the law and the gospel are transcripts of the moral perfections of God, and those perfections are loved by true believers. Law and gospel, therefore, are not to be seen in opposition to each other (pp. 170–73).

Chapter Nine through Twelve: The Believer's Response to the Law

In chapter 9, Colquhoun stresses how the gospel establishes the law. As Paul says, "Do we then make void the law through faith? God forbid: yea, we establish the law" (Rom. 3:31). Believers, by the doctrine of faith, establish the law especially as a rule of life, Colquhoun says. This helps prevent licentiousness, promotes holiness, condemns legalism, and exposes sin in its heinousness (pp. 186–92).

In chapter 10, Colquhoun shows (in a detailed manner reminiscent of Ralph Erskine) how the believer becomes dead to the law as a covenant of works. Dying to this covenant of works includes being delivered from anxiety about being justified by works, he says. Justification by faith alone sets believers free from the commanding, condemning, and irritating power of the covenant of works. Redeemed sinners are divorced from the law, their first master, enabling them to be married "to him who is raised from the dead." The goal of this remarriage, as the apostle says, is that believers "should bring forth fruit unto God" by living unto Him (Rom. 7:4). Living unto God is a holy, humble, and heavenly life, Colquhoun says. It involves living in close communion with the Triune God and the inestimable blessings of salvation.

In chapter 11, Colquhoun focuses on why believers must

yield obedience to the law as a rule of life. This obligation is grounded in God's nature as the sovereign and supremely excellent Jehovah: in being our Creator and Provider and we being His dependent creatures; in being our redeeming, covenantal God; in His holy, revealed will, which commands obedience; and in the great blessings that come to us when we pursue holiness.

Obedience to God is honorable, delightful, and pleasant. Believers, therefore, should make spiritual and moral vows of gratitude to God, voluntarily covenanting and dedicating themselves and all that they are, have, and do to the Lord.

In chapter 12, Colquhoun addresses the nature, necessity, and desert of good works. "Good works are such actions or deeds as are commanded in the law of God as a rule of life," he writes. Such works must be performed in obedience to God's holy will as expressed in His law. They must be motivated by evangelical principles and obedience and based on sound doctrine, especially the glorious doctrine of justification by faith in Christ alone. They must be done out of evangelical graces such as faith, hope, and love, which flow out of the heart. And they must have evangelical goals, which are to glorify God in Christ, to conform heart and life to our great Redeemer, and to prepare for the full enjoyment of God in glory as our infinite portion.

Such good works are necessary as just acknowledgments of God's sovereign authority over believers, as acts of obedience to His righteous commands, as inevitable fruits of God's election of believers, and as the great design of the gospel and of all God's providential leadings of His people. They are also essential expressions of gratitude to God for His great salvation. They are the ordained way that leads to heaven, as confirming and assuring evidences of the faith of the saints, as sources of comfort that help maintain the Spirit's peace and

joy in believers, as adornments of the doctrine of God our
Savior that promote God's glory before a watching world, as
requisites to close the mouths of unbelievers and to prevent
offense, and as sources of edification and comfort for fellow
believers.

The good works of believers cannot procure the smallest
favor at the hand of God, much less eternal life, Colquhoun
teaches. They have no merit in themselves. This teaches us
several important lessons:

- That we are dependent for all the good works we do as
  believers upon Christ alone.
- That no unregenerate person outside of Jesus Christ
  can ever perform even the slightest good work.
- That millions today in the visible church are deceiving
  themselves for eternity when they base their salvation
  in any measure on their own works.
- That our good works, instead of contributing to our
  salvation, are evidences of our salvation.
- That believers receive rewards of grace, not rewards of
  debt, for good works, and even then, these rewards are
  all for Christ's sake.

Colquhoun's *Law and Gospel* helps us understand the pre-
cise relationship between law and gospel. He excels in showing how important the law is as a believer's rule of life without
doing injury to the freeness and fullness of the gospel. By im-
plication, he enables us to draw four practical conclusions:

1. *The law shows us how to live.* Colquhoun shows how both the
Old and New Testament teem with expositions of the law that
are directed at believers to help them in the ongoing pursuit of
sanctification. The Psalms repeatedly affirm that the believer
relishes the law of God in the inner man and honors it in his

outward life (see especially Psalm 119). One of the psalmist's greatest concerns is to understand the good and perfect will of God, then to run in the way of His commandments.

Likewise, the Sermon on the Mount and portions of Paul's epistles in the New Testament are prime examples of the law being used as a rule of life. The directions contained in these portions of Scripture are intended primarily for those who are already redeemed, to encourage them to combine a theology of grace with an ethics of gratitude. In this ethics of gratitude, the believer finds his life in Christ and follows in the footsteps of his Savior, who was Himself the Servant of the Lord and Law-Fulfiller, daily walking in all of His Father's commandments throughout His earthly sojourn.

2. The law combats faulty understanding. The law as a rule of life combats both antinomianism and legalism. Antinomianism, meaning anti-law, teaches that Christians have no obligation toward the moral law because Jesus has fulfilled it and freed them from it. Paul strongly rejected this heresy in Romans 3:8, as did Luther in his battles against Johann Agricola, and New England Puritans in their opposition to Anne Hutchinson.

Likewise, Colquhoun teaches that antinominians misunderstand the nature of justification by faith, which, though granted apart from works of the law, does not preclude the necessity of sanctification. One of sanctification's most important elements is grateful obedience to the law. As Colquhoun writes, "When the law as a covenant presses a man forward, or shuts him up to the faith of the gospel; the gospel urges and draws him back to the law as a rule."

Antinomians charge that those who maintain the necessity of the law as a rule of life for the believer fall prey to legalism. It is possible, of course, as Colquhoun warns us, that abuse of the law can result in legalism. When an elaborate code of con-

duct is developed for believers to follow, little freedom is left
for believers to make personal decisions based on the principles of Scripture. In such a context, man-made laws smother
the divine gospel, and legalistic sanctification swallows up gracious justification. The Christian is then reduced to bondage
like that of the medieval monks of Roman Catholicism.

The law offers us a comprehensive ethic but not an ex-
haustive application. Scripture provides us with broad principles and illustrations, not the particulars that can be applied to every circumstance. Daily the Christian must bring
the law's broad teaching to his particular situation, carefully
weighing all matters according to the "law and testimony"
(Isaiah 8:20), praying all the while for a growing measure of
Christian prudence.

Legalism and thankful obedience to God's law are totally
different, Colquhoun says. They differ as much from each
other as compulsory, begrudging slavery differs from willing,
joyous service. Sadly, too many people confuse law with legalism. They do not realize that Christ did not reject the law
when He rejected legalism. Legalism is indeed a tyrant, but
law is our helpful and necessary friend. Legalism is a futile
attempt to attain merit with God. Legalism is the error of the
Pharisees; it cultivates outward conformity to the law without
regard for the inward attitude of the heart.

The law as a rule of life steers a middle course between antinomianism and legalism. Neither antinomianism nor legalism are true to the law or the gospel. Antinomianism stresses
freedom from the law's condemnation at the expense of the
believer's pursuit of holiness. It accents justification at the
expense of sanctification. As Colquhoun points out, antinomianism fails to see that abrogation of the law's condemning
power does not abrogate the law's commanding power.

By contrast, legalism so stresses the believer's pursuit of

holiness that obedience to the law becomes something other than the fruit of faith. Obedience becomes a constitutive element of justification. The commanding power of the law for sanctification suffocates the condemning power of the law for justification.

Legalism denies in practice, if not in theory, the Reformed concept of justification. It stresses sanctification at the expense of justification. The Reformed concept of the law as a rule of life helps the believer safeguard, both in doctrine and in practice, a healthy balance between justification and sanctification. Justification leads to and finds its proper fruit in sanctification. Salvation is by grace alone and cannot help but produce works of grateful obedience.

3. The law shows us how to love. As 1 John 5:3 says, "For this is the love of God, that we keep his commandments: and his commandments are not grievous."

God's law is evidence of His tender love for His children (Psalm 147:19–20). It is not a cruel taskmaster for those who are in Christ. Rather, in giving His law to His own, God is like a farmer who builds fences to protect His cattle and horses from wandering into roads and highways.

This became clear to me when I witnessed a horse belonging to a farmer break through a fence and wander across a highway. The horse was struck by a car. Not only the horse, but also the 17-year-old driver were killed immediately. The farmer and his family wept all night. As broken fences can cause irreparable damage, so can broken commandments. But God's law, obeyed out of Spirit-worked love, will promote joy and rejoicing, Colquhoun says. Let us thank God for His law, which fences us in so we may enjoy His Word.

In Scripture, law and love are friends rather than enemies. Indeed, the essence of the law is love. As Scripture teaches:

"Thou shalt love the Lord thy God with all thy heart, and...
thou shalt love thy neighbour as thyself. On these two commandments hang all the law and the prophets" (Matt. 22:37–
40; cf. Rom. 13:8–10). As a loving subject obeys his king, a
loving son obeys his father, and a loving wife submits to her
husband, so a loving believer yearns to obey the law of God.

4. The law promotes true freedom. Today there is widespread
abuse of the idea of Christian liberty, which is only an excuse
for freedom to serve the flesh. But true Christian freedom is
both defined and protected by the law of God. When God's
law limits our freedom, it is only for our greater good, and
when God's law imposes no such limits, the Christian enjoys
freedom of conscience from the doctrines and commandments of men. In matters of daily life, true Christian freedom
consists of willing, thankful, and joyful obedience to God and
Christ. As Calvin wrote, true Christians "observe the law, not
as if constrained by the necessity of the law, but that freed
from the law's yoke they willingly obey God's will" (*Institutes*
3.19.4).

God's Word binds us to Him as believers. He alone is
Lord of our consciences. We are truly free in keeping His
commandments, for freedom flows out of grateful service. We
were created to love and serve God above all and our neighbor as ourselves in accord with God's will and Word. Only
when we realize this purpose do we find true freedom. True
freedom is a free servitude and a serving freedom. True freedom is obedience. Only those who serve God are free. Such
liberty is used to promptly and readily obey God.

This, then, is the only way to live and to die.

—Joel R. Beeke

Author's Introduction

The subject of this treatise is, in the highest degree, important and interesting to both saints and sinners. To know it experimentally is to be wise unto salvation, and to live habitually under the influence of it is to be at once holy and happy. To have spiritual and distinct views of it is the way to be kept from verging towards self-righteousness on the one hand and licentiousness on the other; it is to be enabled to assert the absolute freeness of sovereign grace, and, at the same time, the sacred interests of true holiness. Without an experimental knowledge of and an unfeigned faith in the law and the gospel, a man can neither venerate the authority of the one nor esteem the grace of the other.

The law and the gospel are the principal parts of divine revelation; or rather they are the center, sum, and substance of all the other parts of it. Every passage of sacred Scripture is either law or gospel, or is capable of being referred either to the one or to the other. Even the histories of the Old and New Testaments, as far as the agency of man is introduced, are but narratives of facts done in conformity or in opposition to the moral law, and done in the belief or disbelief of the gospel. The ordinances of the ceremonial law, given to the ancient Israelites, were, for the most part, grafted on the second and fourth commandments of the moral law; and in their typical reference they were an obscure revelation of the gospel. The precepts of the judicial law are all reducible to commandments of the moral law, and especially to those of the second table. All threatenings, whether in the Old or New Testament, are threatenings either of the law or the gospel; and every promise is a promise either of the one or the other. Every prophecy of Scripture is a declaration of things obscure or future, connected either with the law or the gospel, or with both. And there is not in the Sacred Volume one admonition, reproof, or exhortation but what refers either to the law or the gospel or both. If then a man cannot distinguish aright between the law and the gospel, he cannot rightly understand so much as a single article of divine truth. If he does not have spiritual and just apprehensions of the holy law, he cannot have spiritual and transforming discoveries of the glorious gospel; and, on the other hand, if his view of the gospel is erroneous, his notions of the law cannot be right.

Besides, if the speculative knowledge which true believers themselves have of the law and the gospel is superficial and indistinct, they will often be in danger of mingling the one with the other. And this, as Luther in his commentary on Galatians well observes, "doth more mischief than man's reason can conceive." If they blend the law with the gospel or, which is the same thing, works with faith, especially in the affair of justification, they will thereby obscure the glory of redeeming grace and prevent themselves from attaining "joy and peace in believing." They will, in a greater degree than can be conceived, retard their progress in holiness as well as in peace and comfort. But on the contrary, if they can distinguish well between the law and the gospel, they will thereby, under the illuminating influences of the Holy Spirit, be able to discern the glory of the whole scheme of redemption, to reconcile all passages of Scripture which appear contrary to each other, to try whether doctrines are of God, to calm their own consciences in seasons of mental trouble, and to advance resolutely in evangelical holiness and spiritual consolation. In

order, then, to assist the humble and devout reader in study-
ing the law and the gospel, and in learning to distinguish so
between them as to attain those inexpressibly important objects, I shall, in humble dependence on the Spirit, consider:

First, the law of God in general;

Second, the law of God as promulgated to the Israelites
from Mount Sinai.

Third, the properties of the moral law;

Fourth, the rules for understanding rightly the Ten
Commandments;

Fifth, I shall endeavor to explain the gospel;

Sixth, I shall point out the uses of the gospel, and also of
the law in its subservience to the gospel;

Seventh, it will be proper to consider the difference between the law and the gospel;

Eighth, the agreement between them;

Ninth, the establishment of the law by the gospel, or the
subservience of the gospel to the authority and honor of the
law;

Tenth, the believer's privilege of being dead to the law as
a covenant of works, with a necessary consequence of it;

Eleventh, I shall consider the great obligations under
which every believer lies to perform even perfect obedience
to the law as a rule of life.

Twelfth, and last, the nature, necessity, and reward of
good works.

Advertisement

The immediate design of the following treatise is to promote conviction of sin and misery in the consciences of sinners, and true holiness in the hearts and lives of saints.

There can be no evangelical holiness, either of heart or of life, unless it proceeds from faith working by love; and no true faith either of the law or of the gospel unless the leading distinctions between the one and the other are spiritually discerned. Though in the external dispensation of the covenant of grace the law and the gospel are set before us as one undivided system, yet an immutable line of distinction is drawn between them so that the works of the law cannot pass over to the gospel as a proper condition of the blessings promised in it, nor can the grace of the gospel pass over to the law as a recompense for the works of men therein prescribed. To blend or confound them has been a fatal source of error in the Christian Church, and has embarrassed many believers not a little in their exercise of faith and practice of holiness. Troubled consciences cannot ordinarily be quieted unless the doctrine of the gospel is rightly distinguished from that of the law.

Though to some readers there may appear in several passages of the following work a redundance of words and too frequent a recurrence of the leading sentiments, and even of the same modes of expression; yet the author cannot but hope that to others these will, in some degree, serve to make my meaning more obvious and determinate.

As it has been my constant endeavor to render my subject easy and intelligible to candid and devout readers even of the lowest capacity, so it is my unfeigned desire that this feeble attempt to promote the faith and holiness of believers may obtain the gracious approbation of the Divine Redeemer and, by His blessing, be made subservient to the glorious cause of evangelical truth and vital godliness.

John Colquhoun
September 11, 1815

Chapter 1

The Law of God, or the Moral Law in General

The term "law" in Scripture is to be understood either in an extended or in a restricted sense.

In its extended or large acceptance, it is used sometimes to signify the five books of Moses (Luke 24:44), at other times all the books of the Old Testament (John 10:34), sometimes the whole Word of God in the Scriptures of the Old and the New Testament (Psalm 19:7), in some places the Old Testament dispensation as distinguished from the New (John 1:17), in others the Old Testament dispensation, as including prophecies, promises, and types of Messiah (Luke 16:16; Hebrews 10:1) and in several the doctrine of the gospel (Isaiah 2:3 and 42:4).

In its restricted or limited sense, it is employed to express the rule which God has prescribed to His rational creatures in order to direct and oblige them to the right performance of all their duties to Him. In other words, it is used to signify the declared will of God, directing and obliging mankind to do that which pleases Him, and to abstain from that which displeases Him.

This, in the strict and proper sense of the word, is the law of God; and it is divided into the natural law and the positive law. The natural law of God, or the law of nature, is that necessary and unchangeable rule of duty which is founded in the infinitely holy and righteous nature of God. All men, as the reasonable creatures of God, are, and cannot but be, indispensably bound to it. The positive law of God comprises those institutions which depend merely upon His sovereign will, and which He might never have prescribed and yet His nature always continued the same; such as the command not to eat of the forbidden fruit; the command during the period of the Old Testament dispensation to keep holy the Sabbath of Jehovah, the seventh day of the week, which under the New Testament is altered to the first day; the ceremonial law given to the Israelites which prescribed the rites of God's worship, together with many of the precepts of their judicial law; and the positive precepts concerning the worship of God under the gospel.

The dictates of God's natural law are delivered with authority because they are just and reasonable in their own nature previous to any divine precept concerning them, inasmuch as they are all founded in the infinite holiness, righteousness, and wisdom of His nature (Psalm 3:7–8). On the contrary, the dictates of His positive law become just and reasonable because they are delivered with authority. The former are "holy, just, and good," and therefore they are commanded; the latter are commanded, and therefore they are "holy, just, and good." Those commandments of God which are founded in the holiness and righteousness of His nature are unalterable and perpetually the same; whereas these which are founded on the sovereignty of His will are in themselves alterable, and He may, by His own express appointment, alter them whenever He pleases. But till He Himself alters them, they continue to be of immutable obligation (Matthew 5:18).

Although the positive precepts of God are capable of being changed by Him, yet our obedience to them is built upon a moral foundation. It is a moral duty, a duty of perpetual obligation, to obey in all things the revealed will of God. It was upon a moral ground that Christ as Mediator proceeded when He changed the seals of the covenant of grace, altered the Sabbath from the seventh to the first day of the week, and instituted new ordinances of worship and government for His Church. And it is upon the same ground that we are bound to obey the positive commands of Christ respecting those ordinances.

The law of God strictly taken in the aspects which it bears on mankind is to be considered in a threefold point of view: first, as written on the heart of man in his creation; second, as given under the form of a covenant of works to him; and third as a rule of life in the hand of Christ the Mediator to all true believers.

Section 1. The law as inscribed on the heart of man in his creation

God, in creating the first man, made him after His own moral image (Genesis 1:27). This image, as the Apostle Paul informs us, consists of knowledge, righteousness, and true holiness (Colossians 3:10; Ephesians 4:24). God, then, created man in His own moral image by inscribing His law, the transcript of His own righteousness and holiness, on man's mind and heart. The law of God is to be taken either materially, as merely directing and obliging the rational creature

to perfect obedience, or formally, as having received
the form of a covenant of works. Now it is the law not
formally, but materially considered, that was inscribed
on the heart of man in his creation. Man, therefore, as
the creature of God, would have been obliged to perform perfect obedience to the law in this view of it,
though a covenant of works had never been made with
him. This law, and sufficient power to obey it, were included in the image of God, according to which He
created man (Ecclesiastes 7:29). Although the law, in
this view of it, contained no positive precepts, yet it required man to believe everything which God should
reveal, and to do everything which He should command (Deuteronomy 12:32).

Since the first man, on whose heart his Creator had
inscribed this law, was not confirmed in rectitude of nature and life, and so was fallible; it implied a sanction
of eternal punishment to him, as the just recompense
of his disobedience, if he should at any time transgress
it (Romans 1:32 and 6:23). I say, it implied this sanction, for as it was never designed by God to be in that
simple form either a rule of duty to man or of judgment to himself, and as Adam was not permitted to
transgress till after the covenant of works was made
with him, there does not seem to have been any express threatening of eternal punishment annexed to it.
But though it implied a penal sanction, and though
disobedience to it would deserve even eternal death,
yet there is no ground from the Scripture to conclude
that a penal sanction or a threatening of eternal wrath
is inseparable from it. For glorified saints and confirmed angels in heaven are all naturally, necessarily,
and eternally bound to perform perfect obedience to it

as the law of creation; but to affirm that they have a threatening of eternal punishment annexed to it would be rash and unscriptural. The truth is, there is no place for a penal sanction where there cannot be a possibility of sinning. Besides, if a threatening of eternal punishment was inseparable from the law of creation, true believers, who are and always must be under this law, should inevitably remain under that threatening. Although their justification for the righteousness of Jesus Christ, received by faith and imputed by God, is perfect and irrevocable, yet if, even in that state, they committed but a single sin, it would lay them afresh under condemnation to eternal wrath. And that would be contrary to these consoling passages of Scripture: "He that heareth My Word, and believeth on Him that sent Me, hath everlasting life, and shall not come into condemnation" (John 5:24). "There is therefore now no condemnation to them which are in Christ Jesus, who walk not after the flesh, but after the Spirit" (Romans 8:1). Indeed, if a penal sanction were inseparable from the law of creation, believers would at once be both justified and condemned. For as all men, considered as creatures of God, are subject to the law of creation (Romans 2:15), so this law cannot but forbid the smallest degree of sin, and cannot but require perfection of obedience from all believers as well as all unbelievers. It may be proper here to remark that no mere man, even by perfect obedience to the law in that simple form, could ever have merited from God eternal life. It therefore implied no promise of eternal life, even no promise that mankind should ever be confirmed under it as a rule of life. It was only when it received the form of the covenant of works that a promise of life eternal and, consequently, of confirmation in holiness and happiness, was annexed to it.

The law, as written on the heart of the first man, is often called the law of creation, because it was the will of the sovereign Creator, revealed to the reasonable creature, by impressing or engraving it on his mind and heart. To this law, so inlaid in the mind and heart in creation, as to the natural instinct and moral rectitude of the rational creature, every person, as a reasonable creature, is indispensably bound. It obliges to perfect and perpetual obedience in all possible states of the creature, whether he be on earth, in heaven, or even in hell. Since man is the creature of God, and since, in his creation, he was made in the image of God, he owes all possible subjection and obedience to God, considered as his benign Creator.

The same law is also called the law of nature because it was founded in the holy and righteous nature of God, and was interwoven with the nature of the first man; because it corresponds both to the nature of God who is the author of it, and to that of man who is subjected to it; because to act according to this law is the same as to act naturally and reasonably; because writing it on the heart of Adam was so distinct, and the impression of it on his nature was so deep, that they were equal to an express revelation of it; because the dictates of this law are the very same that the dictates of natural conscience in the first man were; and, because the obligation to perform perfect obedience to it proceeds from the nature of God and lies on the nature of man. The knowledge which man in innocence had of this law was cemented with his nature.

It is sometimes called the moral law, and is so

called because it was a revelation of the will of God as his moral governor to the first man, and was the standard and rule of all the man's moral qualities and actions; because, while it was manifested to his reason, it represented to him the moral fitness of all his holy inclinations, thoughts, words, and actions; because while it regulates the manners or morals of all men, it is of perpetual obligation; and because it is summarily comprehended in the ten commandments, which are usually called the moral law. The Ten Commandments are the sum and substance of it. There is, however, this difference between it and them: in it there is nothing but what is moral, but in them there is something that is positive.

The obligation of the law of nature results both from the nature of God and the nature of man; and from the relation between God the Creator, Proprietor, Preserver, Benefactor, and Governor of man, and man the creature, the property, and the subject of God. The immediate ground of the obligation of the natural law upon man is the sovereign authority of God, or His absolute right to command the perfect obedience of man. This sovereign authority of the Lord flows from the infinite supereminence or supreme excellence of His nature above the nature of man; from His being the Creator of man and man's being His creature; from His being the Preserver and Benefactor of man, and man's being dependent upon Him for life and all the comforts of life; and from His being, therefore, the sole Proprietor and sovereign Ruler of man, and man's being His property and in absolute subjection to Him.

The obligation of the natural law upon mankind,

then, as resulting from the nature of God and from the relations between God and man, is such that even God Himself cannot dispense with it. It cannot cease to bind so long as God continues to be God and man to be man—God to be the sovereign Creator and man to be His dependent creature. Since the authority of that law is divine, the obligation flowing from it is eternal and immutable. It must continue forever without the smallest diminution, and that upon all men, whether saints or sinners; at all times, from the moment of man's creation before the covenant of works, under the covenant of works, under the covenant of grace, and even through all eternity. Man has no being, no life, no activity without God. So long, therefore, as man continues in existence, he is bound to have no being but God, and no activity but such as is according to His will.

That fair copy of the natural law which had been transcribed into the nature of the first man in his creation was, by the fall, much obliterated; and it continues still to be, in a great degree, defaced and even obliterated in the minds of all His unregenerate offspring. And, indeed, if it was not in a great measure obliterated, what need could there be of inscribing it anew on the hearts of the elect? What occasion would there be for such a promise as this: "I will put My laws into their mind, and write them in their hearts" (Hebrews 8:10)? What necessity could there be of writing it in the Sacred Volume in order to make it known to men in all generations? Indeed, so obliterated was it that the Lord saw it necessary to make it known to His people by both external and internal revelation. But although this natural law inscribed on the heart of Adam

was much defaced by the Fall, yet it was not wholly
obliterated. Some faint impressions or small relics of it
remain still in the minds of all men. Indeed, with respect to its general principles and the immediate conclusions obviously deducible from them, it is not and
cannot be totally effaced; but with regard to such conclusions as are more or less remote, it is, by the darkness of the mind and the depravity of the heart of man,
wholly perverted (Romans 1:21, 32). The general principles which, in some measure, are still inscribed on
the minds of men, even where they have not the benefit of the written law, are such as these: there is a God;
that God is to be worshipped; that none are to be in-
jured; that parents ought to be honored; that we
should do to others what we would reasonably wish
that they would do to us; that such general principles
as these are, still in some degree, engraven on the
minds of all men, is evident from these words of an
apostle: "The Gentiles, which have not the law, do by
nature the things contained in the law." This shows the
work of the law written in their hearts, their conscience
also bearing witness, and their thoughts the meanwhile
accusing or else excusing one another (Romans 2:
14–15). The same is also manifest from the laws which,
in countries destitute of the light of revelation, are
commonly enacted for encouraging virtue and discouraging vice, and for preserving the rights of civil society. Men in heathen countries can have no standard
for those laws but the relics of natural law, which all
the descendants of Adam bring with them into the
world.

The remains of the law of nature in the minds of
men are commonly called the light of nature, some-

times the light of reason. They are the dictates of natural conscience, and they contain those moral principles respecting good and evil which have essential equity in them. The law of nature, as engraven on the heart of Adam in his creation, should always be distinguished from the light of nature as now enjoyed. The former is uniform and stable, of universal extent, and of perpetual obligation; the latter, being that knowledge of the nature of God, and of their own nature, as well as of the duties resulting from the relations between them which men since the fall actually possess, is greatly diversified in its extent and degree, according to their different opportunities, capacities, and dispositions. In some parts of the world, where the light of nature is not assisted by the light of revelation, it does not appear superior to the sagacity of some of the inferior creatures. How far, then, must it be from being sufficient to guide men to true virtue and happiness; or to afford them in their present depraved state proper views of the wisdom, power, justice, goodness, and mercy of God!

So much for the law of nature, which is the law of God in its primitive, simple, and absolute form.

Section 2. The law as given under the form of the covenant of works to Adam

The law of creation, or the Ten Commandments, was, in the form of a covenant of works, given to the first Adam after he had been put into the garden of Eden. It was given him as the first parent and the federal representative of all his posterity by ordinary generation. An express threatening of death, and a gracious promise of life, annexed to the law of creation, made it to Adam a covenant of works proposed; and his consent, which he as a sinless creature could not refuse, made it a covenant of works accepted. As formed into a covenant of works, it is called by the Apostle Paul "the law of works" (Romans 3:27), that is, the law as a covenant of works. It requires works or perfect obedience on pain of death, spiritual, temporal, and eternal; and it promises to the man who performs perfect and personal obedience life, spiritual, temporal, and eternal. In the law, under the form of a covenant of works, then, three things are presented to our consideration: a precept, a promise, and a penal sanction.

1. A precept requiring perfect, personal, and perpetual obedience as the condition of eternal life. The law of creation requires man to perform perfect obedience, and says, "Do." But the law as a covenant of works requires him to "do and live"—to do, as the condition of life; to do, in order to acquire by his obedience a title to life eternal. The command to perform perfect obedience merely is not the covenant of works; for man was and is immutably and eternally bound to yield perfect obedience to the law of creation, though a covenant of works had never been made with him. But the form of the command in the covenant of works is perfect obedience as the condition of life. The law in this form comprised not only all the commandments peculiar to it as the law of nature, but also a positive precept which depended entirely on the will of God. "The Lord God commanded the man, saying, 'Of every tree of the garden thou mayest freely eat; but of the

tree of the knowledge of good and evil thou shalt not eat of it; for in the day that thou eatest thereof, thou shalt surely die" (Genesis 2:16–17). This positive precept was, in effect, a summary of all the commands of the natural or moral law: obedience to it included obedience to them all, and disobedience to it was a transgression of them all at once. The covenant of works, accordingly, could not have been broken otherwise than by transgressing that positive precept. The command requiring perfect obedience as the condition of life bound Adam, and all his natural posterity in him, not only by the authority of God his sovereign Lord and Creator, but by his own voluntary consent, to perform that obedience.

The natural law, given in the form of a covenant of works, to Adam and all his natural descendants, required them to believe whatever the Lord should reveal or promise, and to do whatever He should command. All divine precepts, therefore, are virtually and really comprehended in it. "The law of the Lord is perfect" (Psalm 19:7). But if any instance of duty owed by man to God, in any age of the church, were not either directly or indirectly commanded in it, it would not be a perfect law. But since it is perfect, all duties and, among others, the duties of believing and repenting of sin are virtually commanded in it; they are required in its first commandment (see the *Westminster Larger Catechism,* Question 104). Adam, it is true, was not actually obliged by it to believe in a Redeemer till, after he had sinned, a Redeemer was revealed to him. But the same command that required him to believe and trust the promise of God his Creator required him also to believe in God his Redeemer as soon as He should be revealed and offered to him. Nor was Adam required to repent of sin before sin was committed. But the same law that obliged him to abhor, watch against, and abstain from all appearance of evil bound him also to bewail and forsake sin whenever he found that he was guilty of it. Since the holy law is a perfect rule of all internal as well as external obedience, it cannot but require faith and repentance as well as all other duties. Without them, no other performances can please God (Hebrews 11:6). Our blessed Lord informs us that faith is one of "the weightier matters of the law" (Matthew 23:23), and the Apostle Paul says that "whatsoever is not of faith is sin" (Romans 14:23). Unbelief, which is a departing from the living God, is evidently forbidden in the first commandment of the law. Faith, then, as I said already, is required in the same command (Isaiah 26:4 and 1 John 3:23). And with regard to repentance, though neither the covenant of works nor of grace admits of it as any atonement for sin or any ground of title to life, yet on the supposition that sin has been committed it is a duty enjoined in the first and, indeed, in every other precept of the moral law.

Although the law in its covenant form requires of all who are under it since the fall perfect obedience as the condition of life, and full satisfaction for sin in their own persons; and at the same time, upon the revelation and offer of Christ in the gospel as Jehovah our Righteousness, commands them to believe in Him as such; yet, as is the case in various other instances of duty, it requires the one of these only on supposition that the other is not performed. The law as a covenant of works requires that all who are under it present to it, as the conditions of eternal life, perfect obedience and complete satisfaction for sin, either in their own persons or in that of a responsible surety. So long then as a sinner, unwilling to be convinced of his sin and his want of righteousness, cleaves to the law as a covenant, and refuses to accept and present in the hand of faith the spotless righteousness of the adorable Surety, that sinner continues "a debtor to do the whole law" (Galatians 5:3). He keeps himself under an obligation to do, in his own person, all that the law in that form requires, and also to suffer all that it threatens. The righteous law, accordingly, goes on to use him as he deserves. It continues to proceed against him without the smallest abatement of its high demands, requiring of him the complete payment of his debt both of perfect obedience and of infinite satisfaction for his disobedience. As it accepts no obedience but that which is absolutely perfect or fully answerable to all its demands (Galatians 3:10–11), so the acceptance of a man's person as righteous according to it will depend on the acceptance of his obedience (Matthew 5:18; Romans 10:5).

In consequence of God's having proposed the law in its covenant form to Adam, and of Adam's having, as the representative of all his natural descendants, consented to it, all the children of men, while they continue in their natural state, remain firmly, in the sight of God, under the whole original obligation of it— even those who, as members of the visible church, are under an external dispensation of the covenant of grace remain under all its obligation (Romans 9:31–32). For though the law in its covenant form is broken, yet it is far from being repealed or set aside. The obligation of this covenant continues in all its force, in time and through eternity, upon every sinner who is not released from it by God, the other party. The awful consequence is that every unregenerate sinner is bound at once to perform perfect obedience, and also to endure the full execution of the penal sanction. The preceptive part of that divine contract continues to bind, both by its original authority and by man's consent to it; which consent is no more his to recall, unless he is freed from his obligation by the other contracting party. And now that the curse of the covenant has, in consequence of transgression, become absolute, it binds as strongly as even the precept.

The law, then, as a covenant of works, demands in the most authoritative manner, from every descendant of Adam who is under it, perfect holiness of nature, perfect righteousness of life, and complete satisfaction for sin. And none of the race of fallen Adam can ever enter heaven unless he either answers these three demands perfectly in his own person, or accepts by faith the consummate righteousness of the second Adam, who "is the end of the law for righteousness to everyone that believeth" (Romans 10:4).

2. In the law as a covenant of works there is also a promise, a gracious promise of the continuance of spiritual and temporal life and, in due time, of eternal life. This promise, which flowed solely from infinite benignity and condescension in God, was made, and was to have been fulfilled, to Adam and all his natural posterity, on condition that he as their representative perfectly obeyed the precept. That a promise of life was made to the first Adam, and to all his natural descendants in him, on condition of his perfect obedience during the time of his probation is evident; for

the Lord Jesus said, "If thou wilt enter into life, keep
the commandments" (Matthew 19:17). Again, "This do
and thou shalt live" (Luke 10:28). The Apostle Paul
also says, "Moses describeth the righteousness which is
of the law, that the man which doeth those things shall
live by them" (Romans 10:5). The promise of life to
Adam as the representative of his posterity was implied
in the threatening of death. When the Lord said to
him, "In the day that thou eatest thereof, thou shalt
surely die" (Genesis 2:17), it implied, "If thou eat not
of it, thou shalt surely live." Besides, the tree of life,
which was one of the seals of that covenant, serves to
evince the same thing. It sealed the promise of life to
Adam as long as he continued to perform perfect
obedience.

It is evident that the infinitely great and sovereign
Creator could be under no obligations to man, the
creature of His power, but such as arose from the wisdom, goodness, and faithfulness of His own nature. It
was therefore free to Him whether He would still, by
absolute authority, command man to obey Him, or enter into a covenant with man for that purpose; whether
after perfect obedience to His law He would give man
eternal life or annihilate him; and whether, if it should
please Him to give it, He would bestow it on condition
of man's obedience, or make a free grant of it to him,
and confirm him in the eternal enjoyment of it, as He
has done elect angels. It depended solely upon the will
of God whether there would be a covenant at all con-
taining a promise of eternal life to man, and, if a
promise of it, whether that promise would be absolute
or conditional. The promise of eternal life upon man's
perfect obedience, then, flowed entirely from the good

pleasure and free grace of God. Had Adam fulfilled the condition of life in the first covenant, the Lord, instead of having been a debtor to him for his obedience, would have been a debtor only to His own grace and faithfulness in the promise. It is manifest, then, that there could have been no real merit in the perfect obedience of man, nor so much as the smallest proportion between it and the promised reward. If Adam had performed the condition of that covenant, he could not have expected eternal life upon any ground except this: that God had graciously promised it on that condition.

The peculiar form of the covenant of works, or that which distinguishes it from every other contract, does not consist in the connection between the precept and the promise; but, in the manner of that connection. Obedience to the precept is made to give a contractual title to the life promised. Eternal life is made so to depend on personal and perfect obedience, that without this obedience, that life cannot be obtained; it cannot be claimed on any other ground. But if the obedience be performed, the life promised becomes due, in virtue of the covenant. This being the manner of the connection, between the precept and the promise, of the first covenant; when this covenant was broken, that connection was as far as ever, from being dissolved. Eternal life, according to the covenant, will still follow upon perfect, personal, and continual obedience. It still continues true, "That the man who doeth those things shall live by them." But since no such thing as perfect obedience, is to be found now, among any of the sons of men; no man can have a title to life, according to the promise of that covenant. Thus, the law has become weak, not by any change in itself; but because men have not yielded perfect obedience to it. The reason why it cannot now justify a man in the sight of God or satisfy him with eternal life is because he cannot satisfy it with personal and perfect obedience.

Although eternal life was, in the covenant of works, promised to Adam and his posterity on condition of his perfect obedience, and that only, yet a man is to be counted a legalist or self-righteous if, while he does not pretend that his obedience is perfect, he yet relies on it for a title to life. Self-righteous men have, in all ages, set aside as impossible to be fulfilled by them that condition of the covenant of works which God had imposed on Adam, and have framed for themselves various models of that covenant which, though they are far from being institutions of God, and stand upon terms lower than perfect obedience, yet are of the nature of the covenant of works. The unbelieving Jews who sought righteousness by the works of the law were not so very ignorant or presumptuous as to pretend to perfect obedience. Neither did those professed Christians in Galatia who desired to be under the law, and to be justified by the law, of whom the apostle therefore testified that they had "fallen from grace"(Galatians 5:4), presume to plead that they could yield perfect obedience. On the contrary, their public profession of Christianity showed that they had some sense of their need of Christ's righteousness. But their great error was that they did not believe that the righteousness of Jesus Christ alone was sufficient to entitle them to the justification of life; and therefore they depended for justification partly on their own obedience to the moral and ceremonial law. It was this, and not their pretensions to perfect obedience, that the apostle had in view when he blamed them for cleaving to the law of works, and for expecting justification by the works of the law. By relying for justification partly on their own works of obedience to the moral and ceremonial laws, they, as the apostle informed them, were fallen from grace; Christ had become of no effect to them. And they were "debtors to do the whole law" (Galatians 5:3–4). By depending for justification partly on their imperfect obedience to the law, they framed the law into a covenant of works, and such a covenant of works as would allow for imperfect instead of perfect works; and by relying partly on the righteousness of Christ, they mingled the law with the gospel and works with faith in the affair of justification. Thus they perverted both the law and the gospel, and formed them for themselves into a motley covenant of works.

The great design of our apostle, then, was to draw them off from their false views of the law; to direct them to right conceptions of it in its covenant form in which it can admit of no personal obedience as a condition of life, but such as is perfect—and so to destroy their legal hope as well as to confute their wrong notions. By the reasonings of the apostle upon this subject, it is manifest that every evangelical, as well as every legal, work of ours is excluded from forming even the smallest part of a man's righteousness for justification in the sight of God. It is evident that even faith itself as a man's act or work, and so comprised in the works of the law, is thereby excluded from being any part of his justifying righteousness (see the *Confession of Faith* XI:I). It is one thing to be justified by faith merely as an instrument by which a man receives the righteousness of Christ, and another to be justified for faith as an act or work of the law. If a sinner, then, relies on his actings of faith or works of obedience to any of the commands of the law for a title to eternal life, he seeks to be justified by the works of the law as much as if his works were perfect. If he depends, either in whole or in part, on his faith and repentance for a right to any promised blessing, he thereby so annexes that promise to the commands to believe and repent as to form them for himself into a covenant of works. Building his confidence before God upon his faith, repentance, and other acts of obedience to the law, he places them in Christ's stead as his grounds of right to the promise; and so he demonstrates himself to be of the works of the law, and so to be under the curse (Galatians 3:10).

3. Last, in the law as a covenant of works, there is moreover a penal sanction, an express threatening of death: spiritual, temporal and eternal. This dreadful threatening was annexed to the positive precept not to eat of the tree of the knowledge of good and evil, as comprehending all the precepts of the natural or moral law. "Of the tree of the knowledge of good and evil, thou shalt not eat of that: for in the day that thou eatest thereof, thou shalt surely die" (Genesis 2:17). "The soul that sinneth, it shall die" (Ezekiel 18:4). Seeing the natural law was promulgated to Adam—who though a holy creature was yet a mutable creature, and liable to fall away from God—not only was a promise of eternal life in case of obedience, but a threatening of eternal death in case of disobedience, added to it. Thus it was turned into a covenant or law of works, of which the law of the ten commandments was, and is still, the matter. Accordingly, in its covenant

form, it not only says to every man who is under it, "Do this and live," but, "Do this or die; do this on pain of death in all its dreadful extent." This law of works has a twofold power: a power to justify persons if they yield perfect obedience, and a power to condemn them if in the smallest instance they disobey. It said to Adam, and it says to every descendant of Adam, "If you offend but in one instance, dying you shall die." It is to every sinner the ministration of condemnation and of death. That awful sanction is founded in the justice of God, and is as much according to His mind and will as the precept of the law itself. His mind and will are unchangeable; consequently, no sooner did man become a sinner than he became subject to the first and the second death which divine justice and faithfulness were bound to see inflicted upon him. One single transgression has forever cut him off from all possibility of attaining life by the law. And since all have sinned, consequently, "by the works of the law shall no flesh living be justified." The law of works has pronounced all the race of Adam guilty, has condemned them to eternal punishment, and has not made the smallest provision for their deliverance.

That penal sanction annexed to the law of the covenant was most reasonable. There were indeed many other motives which might have induced Adam to continue obedient, but as he was naturally a mutable creature, and as yet was only in a state of probation, his Creator had sufficient reason to be jealous of him. The Lord, therefore, in order to guard His grace and condescension from being despised and trampled on, annexed such a penalty to His righteous law as, if duly considered, should serve to terrify man from violating

His gracious covenant. Death, especially spiritual and eternal death, could not but appear to Adam, whose knowledge and holiness were perfect, to be of all objects the most horrible. Nothing could appear better calculated to deter him from transgressing the covenant than the awful consideration that, as he was already bound by the precept to perform perfect obedience, so he should, if he disobeyed, be as firmly bound by the curse to suffer endless punishment. Besides, the punishment of death in all its dreadful extent and duration is no more than the smallest sin against the infinite Majesty of heaven justly deserves. It is due to the sinner; and immutable justice requires that every man should have all that is due to him. "The wages of sin is death " (Romans 6:23).

It is evident, then, that the promise of life in case of obedience, and the denunciation of death in the event of disobedience, annexed to the law of creation, made it to Adam a covenant of works proposed. Nothing further was necessary to complete this covenant with him, as the head and representative of his natural posterity, than his consent to each of those articles. Since he was created in the image of God, he could not but discern clearly the equity and advantage of that divine covenant, and so approve and consent to it. His consenting to it, accordingly, is hinted in these words of Eve to the serpent: "We may eat of the fruit of the trees of the garden; but of the fruit of the tree which is in the midst of the garden, God hath said, 'Ye shall not eat of it, neither shall ye touch it, lest ye die' " (Genesis 3:2–3). Adam then consented to the precept, promise, and threatening of the first covenant. And in his consent to it, as well as in God's approbation of the tenor of it, the formal obligation of it consisted; so far as that was added to the previous obligations under which he lay, by the law of creation. In consenting to the precept, he bound himself to perfect obedience as the condition of eternal life to himself and his posterity, as well as to believe whatever God should afterwards reveal, and to do whatever He should command. By consenting to the promise, he agreed that he would have eternal life on no other condition than that of personal and perfect obedience; and that he would never have eternal life unless he performed and persevered in such obedience. In consenting to the threatening in case of disobedience, he bound himself to renounce, in that event, all his pretensions to life by that covenant; and he obliged himself to suffer the full execution of the penalty denounced. By thus approving of and consenting to that proposed contract, the form of it was completed; and the obligations of it became so firm that the one contracting party could not retract without the consent of the other.

Since Adam, in consenting to the penal sanction of the first covenant, bound himself and his natural posterity never to have eternal life but on condition of his perfect obedience; and since he failed in this obedience, and so fell with all his natural descendants under the begun execution of the penalty, no sinner under that broken covenant is bound by it to seek eternal life by his own performances. The penalty of the covenant to which Adam, as the representative of his posterity, consented is by his transgression now become absolute; the penalty binds the unregenerate sinner as firmly as does the precept itself. Instead, then, of obliging him to seek eternal life for his obedience, it binds him to

suffer eternal death for his disobedience. His consent
in the first Adam to the penalty, he is not at liberty to
recall unless he is released by God, the other contracting party. He is therefore as firmly bound, according to
the constitution of the covenant, to endure the full execution of the penalty, unless God Himself delivers
him from it, as to yield perfect obedience to the command. The curse of the law is so bound upon him that
it would be a second breach of the covenant, to seek to
elude the execution of it, so long as he desires to continue under that covenant. But to seek eternal life by
his own righteousness is to try to elude that execution.
No obligation therefore lies on a sinner under the
covenant of works to seek eternal life for his own obedience: on the contrary, it is utterly unlawful for him to
attempt this. That very contract which afforded man,
while innocent, a prospect of life, now that he is guilty
debars him from all expectation of it. The covenant of
works left innocent man at liberty to expect life upon
his perfect obedience, but did not oblige him to seek it
on that ground, but only on the ground of the faithfulness of God in the promise in which He graciously
annexed eternal life to perfect obedience (Matthew
19:16–17). And if it did not oblige innocent man to
seek life on the ground even of perfect obedience, how
can it bind guilty man to seek it on the account of imperfect obedience? The law as a covenant, indeed,
leaves the sinner at liberty, nay, it commands him to
receive the righteousness of the second Adam offered
to him in the gospel, and to seek as well as to expect
eternal life on the ground of this consummate righteousness. But so long as he continues to reject this
righteousness the law continues its obligation on him,

both to perform perfect obedience and to suffer the infinite execution of the curse. The connection established by the covenant between perfect obedience and life, and between the smallest instance of disobedience and death, is immutable and eternal. And therefore no sinner can otherwise be delivered from the bond of that covenant than by receiving and presenting to the law of it the perfect and glorious righteousness of the second Adam, which answers fully all its high demands (Romans 10:4 and 7:6). If he labors to escape the death threatened, and to procure the life promised in it, by his own righteousness, his labor is to no purpose but to increase his guilt and aggravate his condemnation (Romans 9:30–32).

Before I conclude this section, it may be proper to remark that the moral law, in the revelation which is given of it in Scripture, is almost constantly set forth to us in its covenant form as proposed to the first Adam. And it appears that the infinitely wise and holy Lord God has left it on record in that form in order that sinners of mankind might be convinced by it not only of their sinfulness and misery under the dominion of it, but of the utter impossibility of their ever obtaining justification and eternal life by any righteousness of their own (Romans 3:20).

Section 3. The law in the hand of Christ the blessed Mediator as a rule of life to all true believers

The authority and obligation of the law of nature, which is the same as the law of the Ten Commandments, being founded in the nature of God, the

Almighty Creator and sovereign Ruler of men, are necessary, immutable, and eternal. They were the same
before the law received the form of a covenant of
works; that they are, after it has received this form; and
that they are, and will continue to be, after it has
dropped this form. It is divested of its covenant form to
all who are vitally united to the last Adam, who have
communion with Him in His righteousness, and who
are instated in the covenant of grace. But though it is
to them wholly denuded of its covenant form, yet it has
lost nothing of its original authority and obligation.
Now that it is taken in under the covenant of grace,
and made the instrument of government in the spiritual kingdom of Christ, it retains all the authority over
believers that, as a covenant of works, it has over unregenerate sinners. It is given to believers as a rule to direct them to holy obedience. It has the sovereign and
infinite authority of Jehovah as a Creator as well as a
Redeemer to afford it binding force. His nature is infinitely, eternally, and unchangeably holy; and therefore His law, which is a transcript of His holiness, must
retain invariably and eternally all its original authority
(Leviticus 11:44; 1 Peter 1:15–16). The law as a rule,
then, is not a new preceptive law, but the old law,
which was from the beginning, issued to believers under a new form.

  This law issues to true Christians from Christ, the
glorious Mediator of the New Covenant, and from God
as their Creator, Proprietor, Benefactor, and covenant
God. It proceeds immediately from Jesus Christ, the
blessed Mediator between God and men. It is taken in
under the covenant of grace, and, in the hand of
Christ, the Mediator of that covenant, it is given to all

who believe in Him, and who are justified by faith, as the only rule of their obedience. The Apostle Paul accordingly calls it "the law of Christ" (Galatians 6:2). It is a law which Christ has clearly explained, and which He has vindicated from the false glosses of the scribes and Pharisees; His new commandment which He has given and enforced by His own example, and whose obligation on the subjects of His spiritual kingdom He has increased by His redemption of them from their bondage to sin and Satan. It is a law which He, according to the promise of His gracious covenant inscribes by His Holy Spirit on their hearts; a law too which He calls His yoke, and which, in comparison to the law of works, is a light and easy yoke (Matthew 11:29–30).

While the law as a rule of life to believers is issued forth immediately from Christ to them, it proceeds at the same time from God as their sovereign Lord, their Creator, Proprietor, and covenant God. God the Father said concerning Messiah, "Behold I have given Him for a witness to the people, a leader and commander to the people" (Isaiah 55:4). All the sovereign authority of the Father, the Son, and the Holy Spirit is, according to the everlasting covenant, vested in Him as God-man, Mediator, and King of Zion. In Exodus 23: 21, Jehovah gives this solemn charge to the Israelites, in reference to Messiah, the uncreated Angel of the covenant: "Beware of Him and obey His voice, provoke Him not; for My name is in Him." It is as if He had said, "My essence, My sovereignty, My authority, My law, are in Him, yea, all the fullness of the Godhead is in Him; and in Him only will obedience to My law be acceptable to Me." The name of the Father is so in Him that His voice in the law is the Father's voice, for it follows in verse 22, "But if thou shalt indeed obey His voice, and do all that I speak." To the same purpose the Apostle Paul said of himself that he was "not without law to God, but under the law to Christ" (1 Corinthians 9:21). To be "not without law to God" can mean no less than to be under the law of God. Therefore, to be under the law of Christ is the same as to be under the law of God. Believers, by being under the law as a rule in the hand of Christ, or, which is the same thing, by being under the law to Christ are under the law of God. When they are under the law of the Ten Commandments as the law of Christ, they are under it as enforced by all the sovereign authority of God. The original authority of the moral law is not in the smallest degree lessened by the believer's reception of it not as the law or covenant of works, but as the law of Christ standing in the covenant of grace. Its original obligation proceeding from the infinite authority of the adorable Trinity is inseparable from it, and cannot possibly be in the least impaired, by its being conveyed to believers by and from the Lord Jesus. For He, equally with the Father and the Holy Spirit, is, in His divine nature, the eternal Jehovah, "the Most High over all the earth." He is God over all, and the Creator of "all things . . . that are in heaven, and that are on earth, visible and invisible" (Colossians 1:16). He is also in the Father, and the Father is in Him (John 14:11). As God's authority to judge is not lessened by His having committed all judgment to the Son, so His authority to command is not, and cannot be, in the least diminished by His having given Christ for a commander to the people.

That the holy law of God should be given to believ-

ers in and through the Mediator, and not immediately
by God Himself, is necessary. When the divine law was
at first given to man, he was the friend of God, and so
he could receive the law immediately from Him in a
manner consistent both with the honor of God and the
safety of his own soul. But now that man has sinned
against the Lord and has become an object of His infinite wrath, and that God has assumed the character of
an offended Sovereign and an avenging Judge; now
that the law as a covenant of works has become the
dreadful instrument of divine indignation on account
of sin, the guilty sinner cannot regard either God or
His righteous law but as an object of the greatest terror
to him. It was requisite, then, that a Mediator should
interpose both between the offended Lawgiver and the
sinner, and also between the violated law and the sinner who, by satisfying the justice of the one, and by answering the demands of the other, might obtain free
access for the guilty criminal to both.

Outside of Christ the blessed Mediator, a holy God
cannot, with the safety of His honor, have any dealing
with a sinful creature; but in and by Christ He can,
consistent with His own infinite honor, and that of His
holy law, issue forth His commandments to believers
and receive their sincere obedience. Accordingly, the
great Mediator, having admitted believers to communion with Himself in His surety-righteousness, writes by
His Spirit the law on their hearts, and in His Father's
name makes it the instrument of His government of
them and the rule of their duty to Him. And as the
same law is called "the law of nature," because in His
creation it was inlaid in the nature of the first man, so
it may be called "the law of renewed nature" because in

the hand of Christ, and as standing under the
covenant of grace, it is interwoven with the new nature
of all who are "created again in Him to good works."
Since it is only in Christ, then, that the offended
Majesty of heaven can give His holy law to a sinner,
and since it is only in Christ that a sinner can with
safety receive and obey such a law, it may well be called
"the law of Christ." Considered as the law of Christ's
justified, sanctified, and peculiar people, it is not the
law of an absolute God, or of God out of Christ, but
the law of God in Christ. Were believers to keep the
moral law only as the law of nature, and without any relation to the Mediator, their obedience would be but
natural religion; were they to obey it merely as a
covenant of works their obedience would be but legal
righteousness; but when they obey it in its relation to
Christ and the covenant of grace, their conformity of
heart and life to it is true holiness, acceptable to God
by Jesus Christ (1 Peter 2:5).

The precepts of the law as a rule of life to true
Christians are the same with those of the law as a
covenant of works, and they require the same perfection of obedience. The Ten Commandments are the
precepts of the divine law, both as a covenant of works
to the unregenerate and as a rule of duty to the saints.
But while they are issued to believers with all the
sovereign authority that originally belonged to them,
the obligations under which believers lie to yield obedience to them are greatly increased by the grace of
the Redeemer and the mercies of redemption. If the
saints are obliged as creatures, they are still more
firmly bound as new creatures to keep those commandments. If they were formerly under firm obliga-

tions to obey them in their covenant form as the precepts of God out of Christ, they are now under additional obligations to yield obedience to them as the commands of God as their own God and Father in Christ. Does the grace displayed in the first covenant oblige all who are under that covenant to perform perfect obedience? The exceeding riches of grace in the second covenant lay all who are instated in it under additional ties to give perfect obedience. If sinners under the covenant of works are bound to yield perfect obedience for life; believers within the bond of the covenant of grace are under still higher obligations to perform perfect obedience from life, and for the glory of Him who, by fulfilling all the righteousness of the law in its covenant form, has merited eternal life for them. The law as a rule, then, enforced by all the sovereign authority of God, both as Creator and Redeemer, requires believers to perform not sincere obedience only, but perfect and perpetual obedience. The great Redeemer gives this high command to all His redeemed: "Be ye therefore perfect, even as your Father which is in heaven is perfect" (Matthew 5:48). Accordingly, real believers, instead of resting satisfied with sincere obedience to that law, consider their want of absolute perfection in obedience as their sin, and bewail it as such.

True Christians, and none else, are under the law as a rule in the hand of Christ. The Apostle Paul exhorted the brethren in the churches of Galatia thus: "Bear ye one another's burdens, and so fulfill the law of Christ" (Galatians 6:2). The endearing relations in which believers stand to Christ, and to God in Him, as well as the inestimable blessings of salvation conferred

on them, and the exceeding great and precious
promises given them, all require and enforce their
obligation to abound in holy obedience to the law as a
rule (1 Peter 2:4 and 5:9; Titus 2:11–14; 2 Corinthians
7:1). Believers, before the incarnation of Christ, were
as much under the binding force of it as believers now
are (Luke 1:73–75).

The great design of God in giving this law in the
hand of Christ to His people is not that by their obedience to it they may procure for themselves a right to
eternal life, but that it may direct and oblige them to
walk worthy of their union with Christ, of their justification in Him, of their legal title to and begun possession of life eternal, and of God Himself as their God in
Him. Their conformity of heart and life to its commands, instead of procuring their title to salvation, is a
principal part of their salvation already begun, and a
necessary preparative for the consummation of it
through eternity (Hebrews 12:28; 1 Peter 2:9).

The law as a rule of life to believers, especially in
this view of it, is very different from the law as a
covenant of works. The precept of the law as a
covenant is "Do and live," but the command of the law
as a rule is "live and do"; the law of works says, "Do or
you shall be condemned to die," but the law in the
hand of Christ says, "You are delivered from condemnation; therefore do." The command of the former is
"Do perfectly that you may have a right to eternal life,"
but that of the latter is, "You already have begun possession of eternal life, as well as the promise of the
complete possession of it, therefore do in such a manner as to advance daily toward perfection." By the former, a man is commanded to do in his own strength;

but by the latter he is required to do in the strength that is in Christ Jesus. The Lord Jesus says to every believer, "My grace is sufficient for you; My strength is made perfect in weakness; therefore do." The commandments of the law, both as a covenant and as a rule, are materially, but are not formally, the same.

Although the law as a rule of duty to believers requires perfect obedience from them; yet it admits of God's accepting their sincere obedience performed in faith, though it is imperfect. It admits of His accepting this obedience, not indeed as any part of their justifying righteousness, not as the foundation of His acceptance of their persons as righteous, but as the fruit and evidence of their being vitally united to His beloved Son as Jehovah, their Righteousness, and of their being already accepted in Him (Ephesians 1:6; Hebrews 13:16).

Since true believers are already irrevocably interested in the covenant of grace, in the righteousness of Christ, and in the favor of God; and since they have in Christ, and on the ground of His righteousness imputed to them, a complete security against eternal death and a full title to eternal life; the law as the law of Christ has no sanction of judicial rewards or punishments. It has no promise of eternal life or threatening of eternal death annexed to it. The form of the covenant of works, indeed, is eternally binding on all who live and die under that violated covenant, but because Christ, as last Adam, has answered all the demands of it for believers, they are delivered from the law in that form (Romans 7:4–6).

The law which believers are under is the law of Christ, and of God in Christ, which has no promise of eternal life to them for their obedience to it. The promise of eternal life to the saints is the promise of the covenant of grace or the gospel, and not of the law, as a rule of duty. Eternal life is promised to them not in consideration of their sincere obedience to the law as a rule of life, but on account of Christ's perfect obedience to it as a covenant of works received by faith and imputed by God. It is promised to them not as a reward of debt for their sincere obedience, but as "the gift of God through Jesus Christ our Lord" (Romans 6:23). The righteousness of Jesus Christ imputed to them gives them a perfect title to life; they are already heirs of it, "and joint heirs with Christ." They have begun possession of it, and have the gracious promise of the gospel that they shall, in due time, attain the perfect and everlasting possession.

There is therefore no need that a promise of eternal life should be annexed to the law as a rule of duty, to be fulfilled to believers on the ground of their obedience to that law. And, indeed, it cannot be annexed to it; for since the law as a rule cannot require less than perfect obedience, and since believers cannot in this life yield perfect obedience to its precepts, it cannot justify them or promise life to them for their obedience. Neither can they begin to perform even sincere obedience to it until, in union with Christ, they are already justified and fully entitled to life eternal. Accordingly, we are informed in Scripture that believers are justified by grace, and by no law or work of a law, whether it is of the law as a covenant or the law as a rule. "That no man is justified by a law in the sight of God, it is evident" (Galatians 3:11), and "Christ is become of no effect unto you, whosoever of you are justified by a law" (Galatians 5:4). "Therefore we conclude that a man is justified by faith, without the deeds of a law" (Romans 3:28—the original word used for "law" in these passages, I have taken liberty to translate literally so that the apostle's meaning may appear more clearly). No promise of life, then, is made to the sincere obedience of believers to the law of Christ; otherwise their title to life would be founded not entirely on the righteousness of Christ imputed to them, but partly, if not wholly, on works done by themselves.

As no promise of eternal life belongs to the law as a rule of duty to believers, so no threatening of eternal death belongs to it. Not that the law considered as a covenant of works is stripped of its sanction; the penal sanction of it in that form, is eternal and must be eternally endured by all who die under it. But because the whole penal sanction of it was wholly endured by Christ—the Surety of those who believe on Him, and because His infinite satisfaction for all their sins is placed to their account—that law, being satisfied, cannot now condemn them. And as the law in its covenant form cannot condemn them, or require from them a double payment for the same debt; neither can the law, in the hand of Christ, as a rule. No divine law can condemn them. "There is now no condemnation to them who are in Christ Jesus" (Romans 8:1). Believers are perfectly and irreversibly justified; and therefore, though their iniquities deserve eternal wrath, yet they can no more make them actually liable to that wrath. It is the peculiar privilege of believers only, who are already justified, and so set forever beyond the reach of condemnation, to be under the law in the hand of Christ. But were a threatening of eternal death an-

nexed to the law as a rule in His hand, every time that
the believer transgressed this law it would lay him anew
under condemnation; and as he every moment falls
short of perfection in his obedience, he must inevitably
be every moment under condemnation to eternal
wrath. But, instead of this, he always continues in a
state of justification and "never comes into condemnation." "Whom God did predestinate, them He also
called; and whom He called, them He also justified;
and whom He justified, them He also glorified. . . .
Who shall lay any thing to the charge of God's elect? It
is God that justifieth; who is he that condem-
neth?" (Romans 8:29–30, 34). "Their sins and their iniquities, will I remember no more" (Hebrews 8:12).
Though the law as a rule of duty, then, standing under
the covenant of grace as the instrument by which the
Lord Jesus rules the subjects of His spiritual kingdom,
has lost nothing of its original authority to direct and
bind them, even to perfect obedience, yet it has no
promise of eternal life to them for their obedience,
and no threatening of eternal death for their disobedience. Therefore, as the law in its covenant form can
neither justify nor condemn believers, so neither can
the law as a rule of life (Larger Catechism, Question
97).

But though the law as a rule of duty to believers has
no sanction of judicial rewards and punishments, yet it
has a sanction of gracious rewards and paternal chastisements. A promise of gracious rewards, or rewards of
grace, to believers in the way of their obedience is annexed to the law in the hand of Christ. In order to dispose and encourage them to obedience, God promises, on Christ's account, gracious rewards to them, such

as the light of His gracious countenance, sensible and comfortable communion with Him, peace and joy in the Holy Ghost, the assurance of their personal interest in Christ, freedom from trouble of mind, hope in their death, and degrees of glory in eternity, corresponding probably to the degree of their holy activity in time (Psalms 19:11; 2 Corinthians 1:12; 2 Timothy 4: 7–8).

To the law as a rule in the hand of Christ belongs also a threatening of paternal chastisements. In order to deter believers from disobedience, as well as to promote in them the mortification of sin, the Lord threatens that, although He will not cast them into hell for their sins, yet He will permit hell, as it were, to enter their consciences; that He will visit them with a series of outward afflictions; that He will deprive them of that sensible communion with Him which they sometime enjoyed; and that He will afflict them with bitterness instead of sweetness, and with terror instead of comfort (Psalms 89:30–33; 1 Corinthians 11:30–32; Hebrews 12:6–11). These chastisements are, to a believer, no less awful, and much more forcible restraints from sin than even the prospect of vindictive wrath would be. A filial fear of them will do more to influence him to the practice of holiness than all the slavish fears of hell can do. A fear, lest he should be deprived of that sweetness of communion with God with which he is favored, will constrain him to say to his lusts, as the fig-tree in Jotham's parable, "Should I forsake my sweetness, and my good fruit, and go to be promoted over you? Shall I leave the spiritual delight which I have had in communion with my God and Savior, and have fellowship with you?" Or if, for his iniquities, he is

already under the dreadful frowns of his heavenly
Father, his recollection of the comfort which he formerly enjoyed, and of which he is now deprived, will
make him say, "I will go and return to my first husband; for then was it better with me than now" (Hosea
2:7).

It is plain that no sanction but this is suitable to the
happy state of believers. They, in union and communion with the blessed Redeemer, are justified, adopted,
sanctified, and instated in the covenant of grace, in
which they "shall never perish, but have everlasting
life." So long, indeed, as they are imperfect in holiness,
and their temper and practice subject in change, such
promises and threatenings are necessary. But it is manifest that their necessity is occasioned by the remain-
ders of sin in the saints, who require to be treated as
children under age. It is necessary in their state of imperfection that they be influenced to obedience by the
promises and threatenings of the law of Christ; for
though their being excited to obedience by these
promises and threatenings is neither servile nor slavish,
yet it is childish. It is not suitable to the state of one
who has "come to the measure of the stature of the
fullness of Christ." When believers become perfect,
they will perform obedience as freely as the angels in
heaven do, without being in the least influenced to it
by promises or threatenings. And the nearer they come
to perfection in holiness, the more free and disinter-
ested will their obedience be. But as long as they are in
a state of imperfection, it is their duty, in order to advance in holiness, to have respect in their obedience to
what the law of Christ promises and threatens to them.
Promises of gracious rewards, and threats of paternal

chastisements, properly belong to the covenant of grace, which has no proper penalty rather than to the law as a rule. They are implied in the blessings promised in that covenant, or at least are means of accomplishing the promises of it. But, seeing the law as a rule is received into the covenant of grace as the instrument of Christ's government of His spiritual subjects, those promises and threats may be said, though not with strict propriety, to belong or be annexed to the law in that form.

It appears evident from what has been said that though the Ten Commandments are the substance of the law of nature, yet they do not contain the whole of this law. The law of nature, inscribed on the heart of man in his creation, had a penal sanction. Although a penal sanction, as is evident from the case of glorified saints and confirmed angels, who are and who will remain eternally under the law of nature, is not inseparable from that law, yet such a sanction belongs to it.

The devout and attentive reader may hence discern the difference between heathen morality, pharisaic righteousness, and true holiness. Heathen morality is external obedience to the law of nature, and may be termed "natural religion." Pharisaic righteousness is hypocritical obedience to the law as a covenant of works, and is usually called "legal righteousness," or "the works of the law." True holiness is spiritual and sincere obedience to the law as a rule of life in the hand of the blessed Mediator, and is commonly called "evangelical holiness," or "true godliness." True believers are the only persons who obey the law in its relation to Christ and to the covenant of grace; and their acts of obedience are the only spiritual sacrifices ac-

ceptable to God by Jesus Christ (1 Peter 2:5). The holy
Lord God does not account Himself glorified by any
obedience from the sons of men unless that which they
perform to Him is in Christ. For it is the will of the
Father, the Almighty Creator and sovereign Ruler of
the world, that all men should honor the Son, even as
they honor Himself; and that "every tongue should
confess that Jesus Christ is Lord, to the glory of God
the Father."

It may be justly inferred from the preceding doctrine that the distinction of the divine law, especially
into the law as a covenant of works and as a rule of life,
is a very important distinction. It is, as the attentive
reader has seen, a scriptural distinction; and it is necessary in the hand of the Spirit to qualify believers for
understanding clearly the grace and glory of the
gospel, as well as the acceptable manner of performing
every duty required in the law. To distinguish truly and
clearly between the law as a covenant and the law as a
rule is, as Luther expressed it, "the key which opens
the hidden treasure of the gospel." No sooner had the
Spirit of truth given Luther a glimpse of that distinction than he declared that he seemed to be admitted
into Paradise, and that the whole face of the Scripture
was changed for him. Indeed, without a spiritual and
true knowledge of that distinction, a man can neither
discern, nor love, nor obey acceptably the truth as it is
in Jesus. Nay, if the law as a covenant were not to be
distinguished from the law as a rule in the hand of the
Mediator, it would inevitably follow that believers are
still under the law as a covenant of works; that they
ought still to regard God not as their gracious God and
Father, but as their angry and avenging Judge; and that

their sins are still to be considered as transgressions only of the covenant of works, and as rendering them, notwithstanding their justification, actually subject to the curse and revenging wrath of God—contrary to Scripture (Romans 6:14, 7:1–6, and 8:1–2) and to our *Confession of Faith* (XIX:1, 6).

As an evidence that all unregenerate persons are under the dominion of the law as a covenant of works, the natural bent of their hearts in all their views respecting the means of salvation is to the way of that covenant. They all desire to be under the law of works. All who have embraced either one or another of the false religions that are in the world agree at least in this principle: It is by doing that men are to live. Hence, when the Lord opens the eyes of a man to see that horrible gulf of sin and misery into which the first Adam plunged him, he is strongly inclined to exert himself for deliverance in the way of the covenant of works. He struggles hard to forsake his sins and to perform his duties, hoping that by his own performances he will become so righteous as to pacify the wrath of God and to procure for himself eternal life. Ah, ignorant, proud, vain attempt! This, however, he resolutely persists in doing until he is made to despair of ever being able to procure salvation for himself in the way of that covenant. Indeed, this natural bent of the depraved heart toward the way of the law as a covenant, together with deep ignorance of the high demands of the law in that form, is the source of all the self-righteousness that is in the world. To take sinners off from this to a cordial reliance only on the righteousness of the second Adam for all their title to salvation, is a special part of the Holy Spirit's work in conviction and conversion; and to do it requires a greater exertion of His almighty power than even to create a world.

From what has been said, we may also see that there are two sorts of sinners who offend more especially against the law in its covenant form, namely legalists and antinomians. Legalists, on the one hand, transgress against it by seeking to be justified by their own pretended obedience to it. Antinomians, on the other hand, offend against it by despising the divine authority and obligation of it. The former transgress against the form of the law as a covenant by depending on their own obedience for justification; the latter offend against the matter of it, or the Ten Commandments, as vested with all the infinite authority which belongs to it, by disregarding that high authority. Legalists contend that believers are under the law even as it is the covenant of works; antinomians, on the contrary, assert that believers are not only not under it as a covenant, but not under it even as a rule of duty. These two assertions are not more contrary to one another than they both are to the truth as it is in Jesus. In the Scriptures, we are informed that, believers are delivered from the law as a covenant of works, but that they are under it, and delight to be under it, as a rule of life. Indeed, to affirm that they are freed from it in its covenant form implies that they are under it in another form.

Does the law in its covenant form command every sinner under it who hears the gospel to believe and repent? Then it is of inexpressible importance to every sinner to believe that it does. If the law as a covenant of works does not require of every sinner under it who hears the gospel faith and repentance, it will follow that faith and repentance, as acts or works, cannot be excluded from being grounds of a sinner's justification in the sight of God, since on that supposition they cannot be denominated works of the law. Under this character, all the sinner's works of obedience are, in Scripture, excluded from being causes of his justification before God (Galatians 2:16). Doubtless, if the moral law, or law as a covenant, taken into the administration of the covenant of grace, does not require faith and repentance, then there must be a new law to command them. Besides, if faith and repentance, which, as some have said, contain all that is necessary to salvation, are commanded only by a new and gospel law, then the moral law is unnecessary—and so a wide door will be opened to gross antinomianism. Sinners, then, are commanded by the moral law as a covenant, and by no other law, to believe and repent; and saints are commanded by the moral law as a rule of life, and by no other, to advance in the exercise of faith and repentance.

To conclude, is it so that the moral law has lost nothing of its original authority and obligation by being, to believers, divested of its covenant form? Then the supposition that the sovereign authority of God in it is laid aside, or that the original obligation of it is, in the least degree, weakened by its being issued to believers as the law of Christ is utterly groundless. Such a supposition reflects great dishonor on the glorious Mediator; for is not our Lord Jesus, equally with the Father and the Holy Spirit, "Jehovah, the Most High over all the earth?" Does not all the fullness of the Godhead dwell in Him bodily? Is not the name or infinite authority of God in Him? Is it not by Him that all

things were created, and that they all consist? How
then is it possible that the original and infinite authority of the divine law can, in the smallest degree, be
lessened by its issuing to true believers from Him who
is God over all, the great God our Savior?

Chapter 2

The Law of God as Promulgated to the
Israelites from Mount Sinai

After the Israelites, the peculiar people of God had, during their long continuance and grievous bondage in Egypt, become grossly ignorant of the precepts and penalties of His righteous law, He graciously condescended to reveal it to them in express terms, and with awful solemnity, from Mount Sinai.

In this publication of His law to them, He summed it up in ten commandments; and therefore it is commonly called "the law of the Ten Commandments." While it is largely set forth and explained in the whole Word of God, it is briefly comprehended in ten words or commandments (Deuteronomy 10:4). It was God in the person of the Son who, from the top of Mount Sinai, spoke these words. For we read that the Prophet whom Jehovah was to raise up to the children of Israel of their brethren like unto Moses, was "the angel who spake to him in the Mount Sinai"(Acts 7:38). And the Apostle Paul said, "See that ye refuse not Him that speaketh," namely "Jesus the Mediator of the New Covenant, for if they escaped not who refused Him that spake on earth, much more shall not we escape if we turn away from Him that speaketh from heaven" (Hebrews 12:25–26). After the Son of God had, in the hearing of all the assembly of Israel, spoken those

commandments out of the midst of the fire, He wrote
them on two tablets of stone. Moses informs us that
"the tables were written on both their sides; that, on
the one side and on the other, they were written"
(Exodus 32:15). They were filled with writing on both
sides in order, perhaps, to teach us that when this law
is written on the hearts of believers they are sanctified
wholly (1 Thessalonians 5:23), and that nothing must
be either added to the words of the law or taken away
from them. It is remarkable that the Ten Commandments were, by the finger of God, written on tables of
stone twice.

After the first two tables had been broken by Moses
beneath the mount, the Lord was graciously pleased to
write on two other tables the same words that He had
written on the first (Exodus 34:1). His writing of the
law twice, without the smallest variation, and that on
tables of stone, was doubtless intended to represent to
us, as well as to the Israelites, the immutable authority,
and eternal obligation of that law. When the moral law
was promulgated to Israel from Mount Sinai or Horeb,
we are informed that it was given them in the form of a
covenant. Moses said to them, "The Lord our God
made a covenant with us in Horeb" (Deuteronomy
5:2). "Take heed unto yourselves, lest ye forget the
covenant of the Lord your God, which He made with
you" (Deuteronomy 4:23). Hence, the tables of stone
are called "the tables of the covenant," and the words
engraven on them "the words of the covenant."

The Ten Commandments, accordingly, were published from Sinai in the form of a covenant, or federal
transaction. The Sinaic transaction was a mixed dispensation. In it, the covenant of grace was repeated and

published; the covenant of works was awfully displayed in subservience thereto; and a national covenant between God and the Israelites was also made as an appendage to the covenant of grace. Accordingly, the law of the Ten Commandments was thence promulgated by the Son of God, the glorious Mediator, as a rule of life to believers in a manner suited to the covenant of grace. The same law was repeated and displayed to the Israelites in the form of the covenant of works; and it was published to them as the matter of a national covenant, or covenant of peculiarity, between God and them. I shall endeavor briefly to consider the moral law in each of these views.

Section 1. The Covenant of Grace, and of the Ten Commandments, as the rule of duty to believers according to it, as published from Mount Sinai

The covenant of grace, both in itself and in the intention of God, was the principal part of the Sinai transaction. It was therefore published first, as appears from these words in the preface to the commandments: "I am the Lord thy God." These gracious words, in which Jehovah exhibited Himself to the Israelites as their God, were spoken to them as His peculiar people, the natural seed of Abraham, and as typical of all His spiritual seed (Galatians 3:16–17). To this gracious offer or grant, which Jehovah made of Himself to them as their God and Redeemer, the Ten Commandments were annexed as a rule of duty to them as His professed people, and especially to true believers among them as His spiritual seed. In virtue of His having en-

gaged to answer for them all the demands of the law as
a covenant of works, He repeats and promulgates it to
them as a rule of life in the covenant of grace. Instead
of saying to them, "Keep My commandments, so that I
may become your God," on the contrary He said to
each of them, "I am the Lord thy God, therefore keep
My commandments."

This is not the form of the law as it is the covenant
of works, but the form of it only as the law of Christ,
and as standing in the covenant of grace. But more
particularly that, in the Sinaic transaction, the
covenant of grace, with the law annexed to it as a rule
of life, was repeated and delivered to the Israelites appears evident to me from the following considerations:

1. The Ten Commandments are founded on these
words of the preface: "I am the Lord thy God, which
hath brought thee out of the land of Egypt, out of the
house of bondage" (Exodus 20:2). The inestimable
privilege here exhibited is made the foundation of the
duty required. Jehovah, the Son of God, and the
Messenger of the covenant of grace, spoke those words
to the members of His visible church, the natural posterity of Abraham. He declares that He is their God by
virtue of this covenant made with Abraham: "I will establish My covenant between Me and thee, and thy
seed after thee, to be a God unto thee, and to thy seed
after thee" (Genesis 17:7). He also affirms that He is
their God who has brought them out of the land of
Egypt, according to the promise He made to Abraham
when, in the most solemn manner, He renewed the
covenant with him. "Afterwards shall they come out
with great substance" (Genesis 15:14). He first avouch-
es Himself to be their God and Redeemer, and then

commands them to perform all their duties to Him. This was the very form of His covenant with Abraham. "The Lord appeared to Abram, and said unto him, 'I am the Almighty God; walk before Me, and be thou perfect' " (Genesis 17:1). It is as if He had said, "I am a God all-sufficient for you, both to uphold and protect you, and to provide all good things for you. Walk therefore before My face and be perfect." But the covenant made and renewed with Abraham, and also with Isaac and Jacob, was the covenant of grace—a covenant to be believed and embraced by faith. When the covenant made with the Israelites at Sinai was afterwards renewed with them in the land of Moab, we are told it was in order "that the Lord might be unto them a God, as He had sworn to their fathers, to Abraham, to Isaac, and to Jacob" (Deuteronomy 29:12–13). The covenant of grace, then, which had been made with Abraham was the very covenant that was expressed in the preface to the Ten Commandments, and repeated from Mount Sinai to the Israelites. Besides in the Sinai transaction, Jehovah exhibited Himself to Israel not only as their God and Redeemer, but as a God who promised to forgive iniquity (Exodus 34:7), to circumcise the heart to love Him (Deuteronomy 30:6), to take them for His inheritance, to lead them, instruct them, and keep them as the apple of His eye (Deuteronomy 32:9–10), and to dwell and walk among them (Exodus 29:45–46; Leviticus 26:12). These clearly are promises of the covenant of grace.

2. They with whom Jehovah covenanted at Sinai are called in Scripture "the people of God," upon whom He was to have mercy (Hosea 2:23), a peculiar treasure

to Him above all people (Exodus 19:5), His firstborn, precious in His sight and honorable (Exodus 4:22), and the seed of Abraham, to whom the promises were made (Galatians 3:16). These descriptions of ancient Israel, given of them as a people in covenant with God, refer evidently to the covenant of grace.

3. God commanded that the two tables of stone on which He had written the Ten Commandments a second time be laid in the ark. Accordingly, after the first two tables—which had been hewn as well as engraven by God Himself—had been broken beneath the mount, the second tables, which were hewn by Moses, the typical mediator, were deposited in the ark (Deuteronomy 10:3, 5). This represented that after the divine law as a covenant of works had been broken, it was to be fulfilled by Christ the true Mediator, and to be laid up as fulfilled and honored in Him (Isaiah 42:21). Because the fulfilling of the law written on those tables, by obedience and suffering, was the proper condition of life in the covenant of grace made with the second Adam, as the representative of His spiritual seed (Matthew 3:15), they are called "the tables of the covenant," and the ark in which they were deposited is called "the ark of the covenant" (Hebrews 9:4). And because the law as a rule of life, in which Jehovah testified His will to His people, was written on them, and also because they were a testimony of His gracious covenant with that people, they are called "the two tables of testimony" (Exodus 31:18), and the ark into which they were put is called "the ark of the testimony" (Exodus 25:22).

Moreover, the tables of the law in the ark were covered and hidden by the mercy seat or propitiatory cover. This prefigured that the violated law should be so covered by the divine Surety, who was to fulfill all the righteousness of it for believers, so as never to appear again to condemn them (Romans 8:33–34). It was after the Lord had renewed the covenant of grace with the believing Israelites that He said to Moses, "Come up to Me into the mount, and be there; and I will give thee tables of stone, and a law, and commandments which I have written, that thou mayest teach them" (Exodus 24:12). It was after that, too, that He commanded Moses to make the ark and the mercy seat in order not only to keep the tables safe, but to cover and remove the form of the covenant of works which had been engraved upon the commandments so that believers would no longer perceive it. And it was also after that solemn transaction that Moses was enjoined to lay up the tables in the ark and under the mercy seat. This signified that as the ark with the mercy seat was an eminent type of Christ, so the law is in Christ to believers, and in His hand is issued forth as from the mercy seat to them, or from God as pacified toward them. It is manifest, then, that the covenant of grace, with the law annexed to it as a rule of life, was published from Mount Sinai.

4. The same also appears evident if we consider that the covenant made with the Israelites at Sinai could not be the covenant of works. God could not consistently, either with His own honor or with the nature of the covenant of works, renew or make again that covenant with persons who, by breaking it in the first Adam, had already subjected themselves to the penalty of it. He could, indeed, display it in its terror before condemned sinners, but could not again make it with

them. Neither could He renew it with the Israelites in particular without disannulling the covenant of grace made with Abraham in which He graciously promised to be a God to him, and to his seed after him; for a future covenant of works made with the seed of Abraham would annul the former covenant of grace made with him as their representative. But this covenant was not, and could not be, annulled by the transaction at Sinai; for the Apostle Paul says that "the covenant that was confirmed before of God in Christ, the law, which was four hundred and thirty years after, cannot disannul, that it should make the promise of none effect" (Galatians 3:17). Since the covenant made with the Israelites at Sinai, then, did not and could not so disannul the covenant of grace made with Abraham and his seed, especially his believing seed after him, as to make the promise of no effect, it could not be the covenant of works. It was, therefore, the covenant of grace that was repeated and offered to his posterity on that solemn occasion; and it was the law, standing in that gracious covenant as the rule of their obedience, that was promulgated to them.

5. That in the transaction at Sinai the covenant of grace was published to the Israelites is also evident from this: that after Moses had taken the book of the covenant and read it in the audience of the people, he took half of the blood of the sacrifices, which had on that solemn occasion been slain, and sprinkled it on the people and said, "Behold, the blood of the covenant, which the Lord hath made with you, concerning all these words" (Exodus 24:8). An apostle informs us that Moses, on that great occasion, sprinkled the book of the covenant with the blood as well as all

the people (Hebrews 9:19). It would seem that he laid the book on the altar before he sprinkled the altar with the other half of the blood. Now according to the same apostle, it was the first Testament, or Old Testament dispensation of the covenant of grace that was thus dedicated with the blood of the sacrifices (Hebrews 9:18–20). It was therefore the covenant of grace, according to the Jewish dispensation of it, that was delivered from Mount Sinai. Moreover, the blood sprinkled by Moses typified the blood of Christ; and the sprinkling of that, both on the altar and on the people, was figurative of the sprinkling of this: both on the altar of His divine nature for the satisfaction of justice, and on His people for the justification of their persons and the sanctification of their natures. But it was the New Testament dispensation of the covenant of grace that the blood of Christ confirmed, which is therefore called "the blood of the everlasting covenant" (Hebrews 13:20), and it is according to the covenant of grace, and that only, that the blood of Jesus is sprinkled, either for pardon or for purification.

6. The promulgation of the ceremonial law formed a part of the transaction at Sinai; and that law had no reference but to the covenant of grace. When it was enacted to regulate the worship of the Israelites, it was so framed as to prefigure the Messiah in His obedience and suffering, and also the privileges and duties of believers in every future age, according to the covenant of grace (Colossians 2:17; Hebrews 10:1). The sacrifices enjoined by that law did not make atonement for sin in any other point of view than as types of the sacrifice of Christ. Hence the burnt sacrifice is said to have been "an offering of a sweet savor," or "for a savor of

rest to the Lord" (Leviticus 1:9). But it could not be a
sacrifice of a grateful odor to Him from any value or
virtue in itself, but only from its being a figure of the
sacrifice of Christ with which, as an atonement for the
sins of His people, God is infinitely well pleased
(Hebrews 9:9–14 and 10:4). The sacrifices which the
Israelites were enjoined to offer had indeed influence
to remove typical or ceremonial guilt and prevent
temporal punishment; but they had not the smallest efficacy to remove real or moral guilt from the conscience. But though they themselves could procure
only a figurative pardon, they served to prefigure our
great Redeemer who "by one offering hath perfected
forever them that are sanctified" (Hebrews 10:14). And
it was only when an Israelite presented his sacrifice in
the faith of the great atonement to be according to the
covenant of grace, made by the sacrifice of Christ, that
he received a real and full remission of sin.

7. Last, circumcision and the Passover, the two
sacraments of the covenant of grace as formerly made
with Abraham, Isaac, and Jacob, were appended to the
transaction at Sinai (John 7:22–23; Deuteronomy 16:
1–8). They were added to it as seals of the covenant of
grace in order to confirm the interest and the faith of
believers in that covenant; and by a divine appointment they continued to be the signs and seals of it during the whole period of the Jewish dispensation. But
the sacraments of the covenant of grace could not, as
sealing ordinances, be appended to any other
covenant. The covenant of grace, then, with the moral
law standing in it as a rule of life to believers, was promulgated from Mount Sinai to the Israelites, and was,
both in itself and in God's intention, the principal part

of the transaction at Sinai.

It will be proper here to observe that, although believing and unbelieving Israelites in the Sinai transaction were under the covenant of grace, yet they could not both be under it in the same respects. The believers among them were internally and really under it, and under the moral law as a rule of life, as all true believers in every age are (Romans 6:14; 1 Corinthians 9:21). But the unbelievers were only externally, in respect of their visible church-state, under it (Romans 9:4), and under the law as a rule of duty.

Section 2. The moral law in the form of a covenant of works as displayed to the Israelites on Mount Sinai

The violated covenant of works, as I observed above, was not, and could not be, made or renewed with the Israelites at Sinai; for it was a broken covenant, and besides, it was a covenant between God and man as friends, whereas now man has become the enemy of God. But though it was not renewed with them, yet it was, on that solemn occasion, repeated and displayed to them. It was not proposed to them in order that they might consent, by their own works, to fulfil the condition of it; but it was displayed before them in subservience to the covenant of grace that they might see how impossible it was for them as condemned sinners to perform that perfect obedience which is the immutable condition of life in it. Although the Lord knew well that they were far from being able to yield perfect obedience, yet He saw proper to set forth eternal life to them upon these terms (Leviticus 18:5; Deuteronomy 27:26), and so to speak to them in a strain adapted to their self-righteous temper. For previous to the giving of the law to them at Sinai, they were so ignorant of the perfection and vast extent of that holy law, as well as of their own utter inability to perform the smallest acceptable obedience to it; and, at the same time, they were so full of self-confidence as to say to Moses, "All that the Lord hath spoken we will do" (Exodus 19:8). God therefore displayed on Mount Sinai the law of the Ten Commandments as a covenant of works in subservience to the covenant of grace. He displayed it in that form in order that the people might, by contemplating it, see what kind and degree of righteousness it required as the condition of eternal life; and that by means of it, finding themselves utterly destitute of perfect righteousness, they might be impelled to take hold of the covenant of grace in which the perfect righteousness of the second Adam is provided and exhibited for the justification of all who believe.

That the law of the Ten Commandments as a covenant of works was repeated and displayed on Mount Sinai in subservience to the covenant of grace appears evident:

1. From the thunderings and lightnings, the noise of the trumpet and the mountain smoking, the thick darkness and the voice of the living God, speaking out of the midst of the fire on that awful occasion (Exodus 20:18; Deuteronomy 5:22–26). These terrible emblems signified the vindictive and tremendous wrath of God which is due to all the race of Adam for their breach of the covenant of works, by transgressing the law of that covenant (Galatians 3:10). They represented also the

extreme danger to which every sinner who continues under the law in its covenant form is exposed as being liable, every moment, to the eternal execution of its dreadful curse. This awful display of the law as a covenant of works, though it was not the principal part, yet it was the most conspicuous part of the Sinaic transaction; for "the people saw the thunderings and the lightnings, and the noise of the trumpet, and the mountain smoking." And so terrible was the sight that Moses said, "I exceedingly fear and quake" (Hebrews 12:21). Now the covenant of works was displayed in this tremendous form before the Israelites in order that self-righteous and secure sinners among them might be alarmed, and deterred from expecting justification in the sight of God by the works of the law; and that, convinced of their sinfulness and misery, they might be persuaded to flee speedily to the blessed Mediator, and to trust in Him for righteousness and salvation. That terrible display, accordingly, contributed in some measure to humble them, to lessen that self-confidence which they had formerly discovered, and to show them their need of the divine Redeemer, and of union with Him by faith, in order to their being qualified for performing acceptable obedience. This appears from their own words to Moses after the dreadful sight which they beheld: "Speak thou unto us all that the Lord our God shall speak unto thee, and we will hear and do." Standing afar off, they do not say, as they did before the publication of the law at Sinai, "All that the Lord hath spoken, we will do," but "We will hear and do. We will first hear or believe, and then do." For speaking in this strain, the Lord commended them thus: "They have well said all that they have spoken. Oh, that there

were such an heart in them" (Deuteronomy 5:27–29).
Hearing applies to the words of the gospel as well as to
those of the law. They said well in that they made hearing or believing the principle of acceptable obedience
(Hebrews 11:6). The law then, as it is the covenant of
works, entered at Sinai "that the offense might
abound," not in the life by the commission of it, but in
the conscience by conviction (Romans 5:20); it entered
that it might be their schoolmaster to bring them unto
Christ, that they might be justified by faith (Galatians
3:24).

2. That the law as a covenant of works was displayed
on Mount Sinai appears also from this: the Ten
Commandments, written on tables of stone, and so
given to Moses on Sinai, are, by the Apostle Paul,
called "the ministration of death, written and engraven
in stones" (2 Corinthians 3:7). Now it is manifest that
these commandments are no otherwise the ministration of death than as they are in the form of the
covenant of works. In this form they were delivered to
Moses to be deposited in the ark in order to prefigure
the fulfilling of them by Messiah, "the Surety of a better covenant," and the concealing of that form, or the
removal of it from them, to all who should believe in
Him.

3. The moral law, as it was delivered from Mount
Sinai is in Scripture expressly called a covenant. These
are the two covenants: the one from Mount Sinai
(Galatians 4:24). The law, in that promulgation of it,
was such a covenant as had the appearance, through
misapprehension of its design, of disannulling the
covenant of grace made with Abraham. "The
covenant," says the Apostle Paul, "that was confirmed

before of God in Christ, the law, which was four hundred and thirty years after, cannot disannul, that it should make the promise of none effect" (Galatians 3:17). The law included a way of obtaining a title to the heavenly inheritance, typified by that of Canaan, so very different from that of the promise made to Abraham as to be incompatible with it. "For if the inheritance be of the law, it is no more of promise"; but God gave it to Abraham by promise (Galatians 3:18). The covenant of the law from Mount Sinai, then, was the covenant of works; which contains a method of obtaining the inheritance inconsistent with that of the promise, but which cannot disannul the promise or covenant of grace. Besides, Moses, speaking of that law under the denomination of a covenant, affirms that it was not made with the Patriarchs, or displayed publicly before them. "The Lord our God made a covenant with us in Horeb; the Lord made not this covenant with our fathers, but with us" (Deuteronomy 5:2–3). This covenant displayed on Sinai, then, was not the covenant of promise made with the fathers of the Israelite people.

4. The covenant of works is, in the New Testament, introduced and illustrated from the law as given by Moses. Our blessed Lord, in replying to one who asked Him what good thing he should do that he might have eternal life, said, "If thou wilt enter into life, keep the commandments"; namely Thou shalt do no murder, Thou shalt not commit adultery, Thou shalt not steal, Thou shalt not bear false witness, Honor thy father and thy mother. . ." (Matthew 19:17–19). These being some of the commandments promulgated from Mount Sinai, our Lord repeats them to him in the form of the

covenant of works. And the Apostle Paul, when men-
tioning the promise of the covenant of works, says,
"Moses describeth the righteousness which is of the
law, that the man which doeth those things shall live by
them" (Romans 10:5). In expressing also the penal
sanction of that covenant, he says, "As many as are of
the works of the law are under the curse; for it is written (Deuteronomy 27:26), 'Cursed is every one that
continueth not in all things which are written in the
book of the law to do them' " (Galatians 3:10). That a
conditional promise (Leviticus 18:5), then, and a
dreadful curse (Deuteronomy 27:26) as well as the Ten
Commandments were published to the Israelites is
plain; and it is no less evident that, according to our
apostle in the passages cited above, they are the *form* of
the covenant of works.

5. That the law in the form of a covenant of works
was displayed on Mount Sinai appears, likewise, from
the opposition between the law and grace often mentioned and inculcated in the New Testament. We there
read that, "The law was given by Moses, but grace and
truth by Jesus Christ" (John 1:17), and that, "The law is
not of faith; but the man that doeth them shall live in
them" (Galatians 3:12). But it is in its covenant form
only that the law in Scripture is contrasted with grace.

6. In the Sinaitic transaction, the hewing of the latter tables of stone by Moses, before God wrote the Ten
Commandments on them, might be intended to teach
sinners that they must be convinced of their sin and
misery by the law as a covenant of works before it can
be written legibly on their hearts as a rule of life.

7. Last, the same also appears from these words of
the Apostle Paul cited above, "These are the two

covenants; the one from the Mount Sinai, which gendereth to bondage" (Galatians 4:24). The covenant which genders to bondage is the covenant of works, made with Adam as the head and representative of all its natural posterity, and displayed on Mount Sinai to the Israelites. This covenant genders to bondage for, according to the apostle, the children of it, or they who are under it, are excluded from the heavenly inheritance, as Ishmael was from Canaan the typical and earthly inheritance. "Cast out the bondwoman and her son; for the son of the bondwoman shall not be heir with the son of the free woman" (Galatians 4:30). The generating of bondchildren, excluded from the heavenly inheritance, is a distinguishing property of the covenant of works; and it cannot be a property of the covenant of grace under any of its dispensations. It is the covenant of works only that has a tendency to beget a servile and slavish frame of spirit.

It is evident, then, that the covenant of works was displayed on Mount Sinai. It was there displayed, together with the covenant of grace, in order to subserve the latter, and particularly to represent to the Israelitish church that the discharging of the principal and penalty of the covenant of works was to be required of Messiah, the Surety of elect sinners, as the proper condition of the covenant of grace.

Although the Sinaic transaction was a mixed dispensation, yet the covenant of grace and the covenant of works were not blended together in it. The latter, as well as the ceremonial law, was added to the former, and was added to it in order that the Israelites might be so convinced of their sinfulness and misery as to see their extreme need of embracing the promise, or covenant of grace. God, says the Apostle Paul, "gave it [the inheritance] to Abraham by promise. Wherefore then serveth the law? It was added because of transgressions, till the seed should come to whom the promise was made" (Galatians 3:18–19). The promise made to Abraham and his seed we have found in the preface to the Ten Commandments. To this promise or covenant of grace, then, was the law or subservient covenant of works added. It formed no part of the covenant of grace, which had been a covenant entirely to the Patriarchs before that was added to it at Sinai; and it is a covenant entirely to believers under the gospel after that is removed from it. For our Apostle says, "It was added till the seed should come."

Accordingly, the Ten Commandments as promulgated from Mount Sinai must be considered at least in a two-fold point of view, namely as the law of Christ, or the law as a rule of life to believers, and as the law as it is the matter of a covenant of works to unregenerate sinners. This, I humbly apprehend, is intimated to us by their having been twice written on tables of stone by God Himself (Exodus 32:16 and 34:1), and by the double accentuation of them in the sacred original.

In the Sinaic transaction, then, the promise or covenant of grace was published to the Israelites, and the law or covenant of works also as subservient to it. The former was and still is a covenant to be believed or embraced by faith; the latter was a covenant to be done or fulfilled. The Apostle Paul, accordingly, contrasts the one with the other thus: "The law is not of faith; but the man that doeth them shall live in them" (Galatians 3:12). The covenant to be embraced by faith was given to the fathers of the Israelites as well as to themselves; but concerning the covenant to be done Moses said to them, "The Lord made not this covenant with our fathers, but with us" (Deuteronomy 5:3). And again, "The Lord spake unto you out of the midst of the fire . . . and He declared unto you His covenant, which He commanded you to perform, even Ten Commandments" (Deuteronomy 4:12–13). Although the same covenant of works that was made with Adam was displayed from Mount Sinai, yet it was for a very different purpose. God's design in making this covenant with Adam was to have that righteousness which was due to Him from man; but His great design in displaying it to Israel at Sinai was that they, by contemplating it, might see what kind and degree of righteousness it was by which they could be justified before God, and that, finding themselves wholly destitute of that righteousness, they might be excited to take hold of the covenant of grace in which a perfect righteousness for justification is graciously provided.

QUESTION. The attentive reader might now ask, "Seeing the covenant of grace, and also that of works, were both repeated from Mount Sinai, were not the Israelites under both these covenants at one and the same time?"

ANSWER. They could not be under both at the same time and in the same respects. The believers among them, as I hinted above, were internally and really under the covenant of grace, and only externally under that terrible display of the covenant of works as it was subservient to that of grace (Galatians 3:24); whereas the unbelievers were externally, and by profession only, under that dispensation of the covenant of grace (Romans 9:4), but were internally and really under the covenant of works (Romans 4:14).

Section 3. The law promulgated from Mount Sinai to the Israelites as the matter of a national covenant between God and them

When we consider God as delivering to the Israelites at Mount Sinai not only the moral law, but the ceremonial and judicial laws as appendages to it, and as requiring them to perform obedience to these as the condition of their happy entrance into Canaan, and especially of their peaceful and continual residence in it as a nation; we are to regard those laws, as the matter of a national covenant, or covenant of peculiarity, between Jehovah and them. To consider Jehovah, the Son of God, as the King or Sovereign of Israel as a nation or political body is perfectly consistent with our viewing Him likewise as their God and Redeemer. And to regard His law, promulgated from Mount Sinai to them, as the rule of their obedience considered as a nation is consistent enough with viewing it, at the same time, as a covenant of works, and as a rule of duty to believers in the covenant of grace.

In the Sinaitic transaction, then, the eternal Son of God is to be considered as the Monarch or King of the Israelites (1 Samuel 12:12), and they are to be viewed as a nation or political community under a theocratic government. As their King, He enacted and proclaimed laws, exacted tribute, disposed of offices in the state, made war and peace, defended His people from their enemies, and punished with death those of His subjects who refused allegiance to Him. He gave the moral law to them as the primary rule of the obedience which He required in this covenant (Deuteronomy 4:13). He gave them also the ceremonial and judicial laws as appendages to it; and these were reducible to one or another of its precepts. The ceremonial institutions which in the sacred history are frequently called "statutes" were, for the most part, reducible to precepts of the first table; and the judicial laws which, in the same history, are often called "judgments" were mostly reducible to precepts of the second table. Some of the judicial institutions, however, were appendages to precepts of the first table.

Now, as the moral law required Israel to perform obedience both to the ceremonial and the judicial precepts, so, while the ceremonial institutions were to regulate them in their ecclesiastical capacity, the judicial precepts were to direct them in their civil capacity as a nation under the immediate government of God as their King. The laws, then, which Jehovah prescribed to the Israelites, by which He was to govern them as His subjects, were chiefly the judicial laws. And seeing these are all reducible to precepts of the moral law, they required internal as well as external obedience—the obedience of the heart as well as of the life. They directed and bound every Israelite in the inward man as much as in the outward. The sum of the duty required in the moral law is love. "Thou shalt love the Lord thy God with all thine heart, with all thy soul, and with all thy might" (Deuteronomy 6:5). "Thou shalt love thy neighbour as thyself" (Leviticus 19:18). These words of Moses to Israel are remarkable: "Know, therefore, that the Lord thy God, He is God, the faithful God, which keepeth covenant and mercy with them

that love Him, and keep His commandments, to a
thousand generations; and repayeth them that hate
Him to their face, to destroy them. He will not be slack
to him that hateth Him, He will repay him to his face"
(Deuteronomy 7:9–10). One of the precepts of the
second table of the moral law to which the judicial
precepts were reducible is: "Thou shalt not covet"
(Exodus 20:17). Seeing God was a Spirit under the old
as well as He is under the new dispensation, He, as the
king of Israel, required more from them than mere external obedience to His commands. Loyalty even to a
mere earthly prince comprises inward respect as well as
outward adherence to him and his laws.

The conditions, then, of that national covenant
which God made with the Israelites at Sinai were the
obedience both of the heart and of the life to all His
commands, and, more immediately, to those of His judicial law. "And it shall come to pass, if ye shall hearken diligently unto My commandments, which I command you this day, to love the Lord your God, and to
serve Him with all your heart, and with all your soul;
that I will give you the rain of your land in His due
season" (Deuteronomy 11:13–14).

The promises of that national covenant were
promises of temporal good things to the Israelites,
both as a body politic and as individuals, and of these
in subservience to their enjoyment of religious privileges. The inheritance of the earthly Canaan as typical
of the eternal inheritance was given to Abraham by
promise, by an absolute promise. "For if the inheritance be of the law," says the apostle, "it is no more of
promise; but God gave it to Abraham by promise"
(Galatians 3:18).

God promised freely the land of Canaan to Abraham and his seed as an inheritance; and therefore the promise of it was not a conditional promise, but an absolute promise. Accordingly it is called "the land of promise" (Hebrews 11:8–9). The typical inheritance of Canaan, then, was not of the law; that is, it was not given to Abraham and his seed on condition of their obedience, as if that had founded their title to it; but it was given to them by an absolute promise. In the Sinai transaction, Jehovah promised to Israel as a nation, in reference to Canaan, that they should easily subdue the nations of Canaan; that their land should abound with milk and honey, corn and wine, and everything else conducive to their external prosperity; that under the divine protection they should enjoy a long and peaceable possession of that country; that God would multiply them as the sands of the sea and as the stars of heaven; that He would render them valiant in battle and victorious over their enemies; that He would save them from famine, pestilence, and the other plagues which He had inflicted on the Egyptians; and that He would favor them with the symbols of His peculiar presence. These were the leading promises of the Sinaitic covenant considered as a national covenant; and they were all exhibited to the Israelites in a conditional form. This will appear evident if the following passages are considered: Exodus 23:22–31; Leviticus 26:3–13; Deuteronomy 7:12–24, 11:13–17, and 28:1–13. But conditions are of two sorts: antecedent or consequent—antecedent, when the condition is the cause of the thing promised, or is that which gives a contractual title to it; consequent, when the condition is annexed to the promise as an adjunct to the thing promised, or as a qualification in the party to whom the promise is made (see John Ball on *The Covenant of Grace*).

Now in the latter sense, the obedience of the Israelites to the precepts, especially of their judicial law, was a condition of those promises. It was not a cause why the good things promised were bestowed on them, but it was a qualification in them, or an adjuct, that was required to attend the blessings promised and freely conferred. Accordingly, Moses said to Israel, "The Lord hath avouched thee this day to be His peculiar people, as He hath promised thee, and that thou shouldst keep all His commandments" (Deuteronomy 26:18). Had the good things promised to the Israelites been suspended on their obedience as the cause of them, or that which was to give a contractual title to them, such promises would have been inconsistent with the absolute promise given them in Abraham, their illustrious progenitor. As the Israelites, even in their civil capacity, were a typical people, and their obedience a typical obedience, so their obedience was to be so connected with their temporal privileges as to resemble the obedience of God's spiritual Israel in its connection with their spiritual privileges under the gospel.

True believers among the children of Israel were the only persons who performed sincere obedience to the law of that covenant. The unbelievers yielded only an external and hypocritical obedience, and that merely to the letter of the law. So long, however, as they continued to yield even an external obedience, the promises of temporal good things were fulfilled to them; for the Lord "loved them for the fathers' sakes" (Romans 11:28). And therefore He favored them with many external benefits. He also conferred favors on them for the sakes of those among them who were the objects of His everlasting love (Isaiah 6:13; 2 Corinthians 4:15). And so great was His love of true holiness that He rewarded that external obedience which was only the shadow of it, with those external benefits which were shadows of good things to come.

The penal sanctions of that national covenant were, for the most part, temporal punishments. These were denounced to the Israelites not only as a nation, but as individuals. The punishments which the Lord threatened against the violations of that covenant by Israel as a community were chiefly these: famine, pestilence, and various other diseases, want of success in war, a smiting of their land with barrenness, a casting of them out of that promised land, and a dispersing of them among the heathen (Deuteronomy 4:25–28; 11:17; 28:15–68; and 29:22–28). The punishments which He threatened to inflict on the individual who would disobey the law of that covenant were such as these: that He "would set His face against that man, and cut him off from among His people," and that He "would blot him out of His book," or out of the register of the living (Leviticus 17:10; 20:2–6 and 23:29–30; Exodus 32:33).

Thus the law of God was promulgated from Mount Sinai in its threefold character: as a rule of life to believers, as a covenant of works, and as the matter of a national covenant between God and the Israelites.

What has been advanced in this, and the two preceding sections, may assist in guiding us to the meaning of what the apostle says in Hebrews 8:6–10, concerning the old and new covenants. The design in this

epistle to the Hebrew Christians was to show them the
preference of the new dispensation of the covenant of
grace, which has taken place since the death of Christ,
to that old dispensation of it, which had been established at Sinai, and had continued until His death.
This the writer illustrates not by stating the difference
between the covenant of works and the covenant of
grace, but by showing the difference between the old
dispensation, or former manner of administration, of
the covenant of grace and the new dispensation of the
same covenant. The former of these dispensations he
calls the "first or old testament," and the latter "the
new." The covenant of grace, according to the old dispensation of it, was published from Mount Sinai, and,
at the same time, the law was given to the Israelites as
the substance of a national or political covenant between God and them.

Now the apostle, in stating the difference between
the old and new dispensations of the covenant of
grace, affirms that the new dispensation or testament is
better than the old, and that the promises of the new
are better than those of the old. They are compara-
tively better than the spiritual promises of the old dispensation or testament since in them the grace of God
is held forth in more fullness, evidence, and spiritual
efficacy to all nations (*Westminster Confession of Faith*
VII:6) than in those of the old; and they are absolutely
better than the temporal promises of that national
covenant which the Lord made with Israel as a political
body. Since the land of Canaan had been given to the
posterity of Abraham by promise, or as an inheritance,
the apostle might, with strict propriety, call even the
national covenant that had been made with that peo-

ple a testament, and might show the preference of the new testament to it as well as to the old testament, or old dispensation of the covenant of grace. He seems in Hebrews 8:9 especially to have stated the contrast between the new testament and that national covenant. From the 6th verse to the end of the chapter, the original word which we render "covenant" the Geneva translators render "testament"; which seems to me more suitable to the apostle's argument, as well as to the analogy of faith, than to translate it "covenant." For one and the same covenant of grace was made with believers at Sinai, and is made with believers now, though under different dispensations, each of which is called a testament. That gracious covenant as published to Israel from Mount Sinai, was a testament; for it consisted of absolute grants and promises. Hence our apostle expressly calls it a testament, and "the first testament" (Hebrews 9:18–20). The promises of it were turned into a testament, for the spiritual blessings promised were, as they now are, gifts of sovereign grace.

From what has been said, we may learn also the meaning of these words above cited: "The law was given by Moses, but grace and truth by Jesus Christ" (John 1:17). The law which was given from Mount Sinai by the ministry of Moses, considered as the matter of the covenant of works, was a ministry of rigor and of terror in opposition to the gospel dispensation, which is called "grace"; it was a ministration of condemnation and of death. Considered as a rule of duty in the covenant of grace, and in the hand of Moses the typical mediator, it was a ministration of shadows as opposed to truth. The gospel, or New Testament dispensation of the covenant of grace, is called "grace and truth." It is grace, for it is a clear and efficacious exhibition of the covenant of grace to sinners of mankind. It is truth, as opposed not only to falsehood, but to shadows. While Jesus Christ has brought to His Church the clearest discoveries of redeeming grace, He Himself is the substance of all the Jewish types, and the accomplishment of all their predictions and promises. Moses was the minister of the law; Christ is the Author of grace and truth. All the promises and blessings of salvation flow from His grace, and are performed by His truth.

Must all the obedience required in the law as a rule of life be performed to the Lord as our God and Redeemer? Then, in order to perform spiritual and acceptable obedience to the Ten Commandments, a man must trust in the Lord Jesus for all his salvation, and trust that God in Christ is His redeeming God, or that Christ is his Redeemer, and God in Christ is his covenant God. No obedience to those commands is acceptable but that which flows in the channel of the covenant of grace, and is performed to God in Christ as our covenant God. The only way to yield evangelical and spiritual obedience is, first, to accept cordially the offer of Christ to trust that God in Christ is our God, and then to attempt universal obedience to Him as such. We cannot otherwise fear this glorious and fearful name, "The Lord our God" (Deuteronomy 28:58). We are not to do in order to believe, but to believe in order to do. We are to trust in Christ and in the promise in order to be strengthened for obedience to the precept; for acceptable obedience can never be performed but in the strength of our almighty Redeemer. "Without faith" in Him as the principle of obedience, "it is impossible to please God" (Hebrews 11:6).

To serve the Lord by keeping diligently His holy commandments is a most reasonable service. Instead of requiring obedience from us by His mere will, without assigning any other reason, He condescends to enforce His commands by the most engaging and endearing motives. He exhibits Himself to us as JEHOVAH, the infinite, eternal, and unchangeable One who has His being of Himself, and from whom all being is derived; who is supereminent in every adorable perfection, and at the same time is our Creator, Preserver, and Governor. Our obedience, therefore, is not only due to Him, but is infinitely reasonable. Besides, He makes a grant of Himself to us as our God, our God in covenant; related to us by an everlasting covenant, which is exhibited in the gospel to us so that we may so take hold of it as to take possession of Him as our God and portion. He also presents Himself to us as our redeeming God who, in the person of the Son, redeems us from all our iniquity; who delivers us from our spiritual thraldom, and purifies us to Himself a peculiar people zealous of good works (Titus 2:14). How delightful to reflect that He incites us to obedience not merely by His sovereignty over us, but by the attracting consideration that He is our God, our redeeming God who has obtained eternal redemption for us! When the believer considers what the great Redeemer is to him, and what He has done and is doing for him, should not his heart overflow with adoring gratitude, and should not he express his gratitude by a voluntary and cheerful obedience to all His commands? Can anything be more reasonable?

The children of fallen Adam are so bent upon
working for life that they will on no account cease from
it till the Holy Spirit so convinces them of their sin and
misery as to show them that Mount Sinai is wholly on
fire around them, and that they cannot with safety remain a moment longer within the limits of it. Strange
indeed it is that sinners, already condemned by the law
of works, should, nevertheless imagine a probability,
yea, a certainty of obtaining eternal life by their own
works according to that very law. The depraved sons of
Adam think, like Samson, to rouse themselves and
walk, as in former times, as if their strength were yet in
them; and multitudes never perceive that is gone till
after they have been seized in virtue of that violated
law and bound with chains of eternal darkness. And,
oh, what addition to the anguish of damned souls will
it be to reflect that they dreamed of attaining life by a
law which, to a sinner, is and cannot but be a
"ministration of death"; and that by supposing in themselves an ability still to answer the demands of the law
they have rendered it so much the more able to
condemn them! One reason, therefore, why the Lord
displayed the law as a covenant of works on Sinai was
that self-righteous Israelites, and all pharisaic professors to the end of time might see that as they have
sinned, and so have not performed perfect obedience,
it is absolutely impossible for them to attain justification and eternal life on the footing of their own works
(Romans 3:20). The law was there displayed in its
covenant form in order to discover sin and condemn
for it; and so to stir up secure sinners to inquire after
the perfect fulfilment of it by the second Adam

(Deuteronomy 27:26), for until self-righteousness is overthrown, a man will never submit to the righteousness of Jesus Christ.

We may hence learn the great difference between performing duties in the way of the covenant of works and in that of the covenant of grace. According to the first covenant, sinners perform duties in order that these may entitle them to life; but, according to the second, saints perform them because they already have a title to life. According to the former, unregenerate men do them in their own strength; but, according to the latter, regenerate persons perform them in the strength of grace derived from the second Adam. The motives of obedience, under the covenant of works, are the slavish fear of hell and the servile hope of heaven; whereas the motives of duty in the covenant of grace are love and gratitude to God not only as the Creator and Preserver of His people, but as the God and Redeemer of His people (2 Corinthians 5:14–15).

Chapter 3

The Properties of the Moral Law

The peculiar and distinguishing qualities of the moral law are these:

1. It is universal. It extends to all men, in every age, place, and condition, and to all their inclinations, thoughts, words, and actions. "Now we know," says the Apostle Paul, "that what things soever the law saith, it saith to them who are under the law; that every mouth may be stopped, and all the world may become guilty before God. Therefore, by the deeds of the law, there shall no flesh be justified in His sight" (Romans 3:19–20). While it binds all the human race, at all times and in all places and conditions, it reaches to all the dispositions, thoughts, and purposes of the heart as well as to all the words and actions of the life. It extends to every motion and affection of the soul, and to every part and circumstance of human conduct. The divine law is a rule for the heart as well as for the life of every descendant of Adam. "Thy commandment," says David, "is exceeding broad" (Psalm 119:96). No finite understanding can reach the boundary of it or find out how comprehensive it is. It extends to countless multitudes of things, in every moment and in every possible circumstance. The moral law, indeed, is summed up in the Ten Commandments; but it extends itself, notwithstanding, through the whole Word of God. So extensive are those commandments that everything

76

which He requires may be reduced to one or another
of them.

2. It is perfect. "The law of the Lord," says David, "is
perfect, converting the soul" (Psalm 19:7). So perfect is
it that it binds everyone to full conformity in the whole
man unto the righteousness of it, and to entire obedience forever—so as to require the utmost perfection of
every duty and to forbid the least degree of every sin
(Larger Catechism, Question 99; Matthew 5:21–48;
James 2:10). It requires all the duty which a man owes
to God, to himself, and to his neighbor; and it demands perfection of obedience. No partial or defective
obedience can be sustained. The smallest degree of
imperfection renders a person vulnerable to the curse;
so that salvation by the law is absolutely unattainable
because no man since the fall can perform the perfect
obedience which it demands. The perfection of every
grace, and of every act of obedience, is required in it.
Nothing must be taken from it or corrected in it, and
nothing is to be added to it (Deuteronomy 4:2). The
Lord Jesus explained the law, but He did not in the
smallest degree either correct or enlarge it. He and His
apostles taught nothing but what Moses and the
prophets had previously indicated (Matthew 7:12; Acts
26:22). He said, indeed, to His disciples, "A new commandment I give unto you, that ye love one another"
(John 13:34). This command, however, is not new as to
the substance of it, for it is a summary of the second
table of the law; and therefore it is called "an old
commandment which we had from the beginning"
(1 John 2:7); but it is called new because it is enforced
by the new motive and example of the immense love of
Christ in dying for us. This is evident from His words

which immediately follow; "As I have loved you, that ye also love one another." Christ also commands us to deny ourselves, and to take up our cross and follow Him; but these duties are comprised in that of loving God supremely. The prayer, likewise, which our Lord taught His disciples contains no petitions but what the saints under the Old Testament were taught to present to Jehovah (Isaiah 63:16; Psalm 57:11 and 143:10–12; Proverbs 30:8; Psalm 25:11 and 16:1). Indeed, such is the perfection of the divine law that it cannot require or sustain anything short of obedience which is absolutely perfect. It requires not only that there be no direct violation of any of its precepts, but that there be no appearance of transgressing any of them—no consent of the heart, no inclination or affection to the smallest violation of any, no secret delight in evil or desire that it were lawful—but, on the contrary, that there be a supreme delight in the purity and perfection of every one of its commands. This law is despised and dishonored if it is not acknowledged to be so perfect that nothing can be accepted by it but that which is in all respects perfect. It demands perfection in the principles, in the parts, in the degrees, and in the perpetuity of obedience. In a word, such is the perfection of it that it was sufficient to be the rule even of the consummate righteousness of Jesus Christ Himself.

3. This law is also spiritual. The Lawgiver is a Spirit, the God of the spirits of all flesh; and He beholds all the inclinations and affections of the soul as well as all the deeds of the body. His law therefore is spiritual (Romans 7:14), requiring internal as well as external obedience. It reaches the understanding, will, and affections, with all the other faculties of the soul, as well

as all the gestures, words, and actions of the body. It extends not only to external appearances, words, and works, but to the dispositions, thoughts, principles, motives, and designs of the heart, and requires the spiritual performance of both internal and external obedience (Hebrews 4:12; Matthew 22:37–39; Leviticus 19:17). It requires that every duty proceed from spiritual principles such as union with Christ, faith, love, and every right habit of the soul, so that it is performed in a spiritual manner, that is, according to a spiritual rule and in the exercise of the graces of the Spirit, and that it is directed to spiritual ends, the glory of God in Christ and the eternal enjoyment of Him. Every man is commanded by it thus "to mind the things of the Spirit," and so to "live and walk in the Spirit" (Romans 8:5; Galatians 5:16).

4. It is a holy law. "The law," says the Apostle Paul, "is holy, and the commandment holy" (Romans 7:12). The moral law is a fair transcript of the infinite holiness of God's nature, and an authoritative declaration of His will; it binds all the children of Adam to perfect holiness of heart and of life. It enjoins everything that is holy, everything which is conformable to those moral attributes and actions of God which are patterns for our imitation. Since it is intrinsically pure and holy, it gives no just occasion to the least motion of sin in the heart; but, on the contrary, it discovers, forbids, and condemns every inordinate affection, every unholy desire. It is the immutable and eternal standard of all true holiness, whether of the heart or of the life; and while it is both the rule and the reason of holiness, its direct tendency is to encourage and advance it in every regenerate soul. All the precepts of it are perfectly

holy, every way becoming an infinitely holy God to
publish, and rational creatures to obey. The divine law
is so holy that it calls for spotless obedience not only in
the words and actions of the life, but in all the inclinations, thoughts, and motions of the heart. It reaches
not only to the streams of actual transgression, but to
the fountain of original sin, and calls for perfect holiness of nature as well as of life. Hence the Apostle
Paul, as soon as he discerned the holiness of it, considered the first motions of irregular desire, even before
the will actually consented to them, as sinful, and bitterly bewailed them as well as firmly resisted them
(Romans 7:7).

5. Moreover, it is perfectly just and equal (Romans
7:12). This righteous law is exactly suited to our frame
as reasonable creatures, and to our condition in this
world. It requires nothing from us but what we owe to
God, to ourselves, and to our neighbor, and what we,
in the first Adam, had sufficient ability to perform.
Accordingly the holy Psalmist says, "The statutes of the
Lord are right, rejoicing the heart" (Psalm 19:8). "I will
praise Thee with uprightness of heart, when I shall
have learned Thy righteous judgments " (Psalm 119:7).
The law of God is just and right. Its demands are infinitely equitable. And therefore, to fret against any
command of it, or to wish that it were in the smallest
degree relaxed, is unjust, and is a breach of the whole
law. Seeing it requires nothing but what we already
owe to God, and nothing but what we are under infinite and immutable obligations to pay to Him. Our
obedience to it, supposing that obedience were perfect, could never merit the smallest blessing from Him.
Were we, indeed, to perform but a single act of obedi-

ence more than we owed to God, we would thereby merit some recompense from Him. But this is impossible for us ever to do. It is not the obedience even of a true believer that merits the blessings of salvation for him, but only the meritorious righteousness of Christ imputed to him.

6. The law is good, as well as holy and just (Romans 7:12). The commandments of it are so good that they require nothing but what is good in itself, and good for the observers of them. "In keeping of them there is great reward" (Psalm 19:11). They enjoin nothing but what is conducive to the happiness of both the souls and the bodies of men. "Great peace," says the Psalmist, "have they which love Thy law; and nothing shall offend them" (Psalm 119:165). The Apostle Paul also says, "Glory, honor, and peace to every man that worketh good; to the Jew first, and also to the Gentile" (Romans 2:10). And again, "We know that the law is good, if a man use it lawfully" (1 Timothy 1:8). The chief ingredient in the happiness of Adam in innocence was his having this law inscribed on his heart. And no man since the fall begins to be either good or happy till this promise begins to be fulfilled to him: "I will put My laws into their minds, and write them in their hearts" (Hebrews 8:10). It is this that makes a man a good man, and capable of performing good works. The law, then, is good, desirable, and excellent. But it is most unreasonable, as well as sinful, not to love it, and not to delight in performing universal obedience to it.

7. Last, this law is of perpetual obligation. The precepts of it are indispensable and perpetual (Psalm 119:89). They continue to direct and oblige all men to

perfect obedience not only through all time, but
through all eternity. "It is easier for heaven and earth
to pass than one tittle of the law to fail" (Luke 16:17).
"Till heaven and earth pass, one jot or one tittle shall
in no wise pass from the law till all be fulfilled"
(Matthew 5:18). The law as a covenant of works will
continue not only through time, but through eternity,
to bind all who live and die under that covenant; and
the law as a rule of life will continue binding on the
spiritual seed of the second Adam through time and
eternity. It is an immutable and an eternal law. "Every
one of Thy righteous judgments," says David, "en-
dureth forever" (Psalm 119:160).

Is the law of the Lord perfect, and does it require
that our obedience be perfect in its principles, parts,
degrees, and continuance? It is impossible, then, that
sincere obedience can entitle a sinner to eternal life. A
man's faith may be sincere, but if it is not perfect it
cannot be a proper condition of life; it cannot procure
for him a right to eternal life. His repentance also may
be deep and sincere; but if it is not absolutely perfect it
cannot afford him the smallest title, either to the
progress or the consummation of life eternal. This is
not to be understood as implying that the law, either as
a covenant or as a rule, requires either perfect or imperfect faith and repentance as the proper condition
of eternal life; but only that no instance of personal
obedience, however sincere that obedience may be,
can ever entitle a sinner to life eternal. His obedience,
in general, may be sincere; yet if it is not absolutely
perfect it cannot give him the smallest degree of title
to eternal salvation. These cannot entitle him in the
smallest degree to life, either according to the law as a

covenant of works or as a rule of life. They are necessary as parts of salvation, and as means of attaining
complete salvation, but they cannot be the grounds of
a man's title to salvation. Nothing can be the ground
of a believer's title to salvation but the perfect righteousness of Jesus Christ, received by faith and imputed to him for justification.

Is the moral law of perpetual obligation? Then it
follows that, as a covenant of works, it retains, and will
continue throughout eternity to retain, its whole authority and obligation over every sinner of mankind
who lives and dies under it. In its covenant form it
stands in full force and can never be repealed. It will
continue throughout all eternity to hold the finally
impenitent under both its commanding and its condemning power. They shall remain forever under an
infinite obligation, both to yield perfect obedience to
its righteous precepts and to give infinite satisfaction
for their disobedience of them. There is no possible
way in which a sinner can be freed from the perpetual
obligation of the law as a covenant but by presenting,
in the hand of faith to it, the infinitely perfect and
meritorious righteousness of the second Adam as a full
answer to all its high demands. When this glorious
righteousness is received by faith, and graciously imputed to a man, the law in its covenant form is fully satisfied with respect to him; and in that form it has nothing more to demand from him. He now passes from
the obligation of the covenant of works, and comes
under the perpetual obligation of the law as a rule of
duty in the covenant of grace—and he will remain under its infinite obligation, through all eternity. Even
the angels in heaven are under a law as their eternal

rule of duty (Psalm 103:20). And if the holy angels are not without law to God, surely glorified saints will be under the law to Christ as the eternal rule of their obedience. And so ardent will their love of this holy and righteous law be that they will account it their highest honor and their greatest happiness to continue eternally under the obligation of yielding perfect obedience to it. No man sincerely loves it, even in an imperfect degree, but the man who hopes to be under the eternal obligation of it.

Chapter 4

*Rules for Rightly Understanding
the Ten Commandments*

Understanding rightly the perfection, spirituality, and great extent of the divine law is necessary to qualify believers for delighting in it after the inward man, and for performing acceptable obedience to all its precepts. The holy Psalmist, therefore, prayed thus: "Give me understanding, and I shall keep Thy law; yea, I shall observe it with my whole heart" (Psalm 119:34). "I am a stranger in the earth; hide not Thy commandments from me" (Psalm 119:19).

The Ten Commandments contain very much in a few words, which cannot but render it more difficult to apprehend their full meaning. Therefore, the rules to be carefully observed for understanding them rightly are chiefly the following:

RULE 1. Where a duty is required, the contrary sin is forbidden (Isaiah 58:13); and where a sin is forbidden the contrary duty is required (Ephesians 4:28). Every command forbids the sin which is opposite to, or inconsistent with, the duty which it requires. The duties required in the law cannot be performed without abstaining from the sins forbidden in it; and the sins forbidden cannot be avoided unless the contrary duties are performed. We must not only cease to do what the commands forbid, but do what they require; otherwise we do not obey them sincerely. A negative holiness is far from being acceptable to God. Every affirmative precept includes a negative one, and every negative command contains an affirmative. Every precept, whether affirmative or negative, has two parts: it requires obedience and forbids disobedience. The fourth commandment, for instance, while it requires us to "remember the Sabbath day, to keep it holy," forbids us to profane that holy day. The Lord Jesus, accordingly, comprehends all the negative as well as affirmative precepts in these two great affirmative commandments: to love God and our neighbor. It is also remarkable that where a promise is annexed to a precept the contrary threatening is included (Exodus 20:12; Proverbs 30:17), and that where a threatening is annexed to a prohibition the contrary promise is implied (Jeremiah 18:7–8; Psalm 24:4–5).

RULE 2. Where a duty is required, every duty of the same kind is also required; and where a sin is forbidden, every sin of the same sort is prohibited. Under one duty, all of the same kind are commanded; and under one sin, all of the same sort are forbidden. When the Lord commands us to have no other gods before Him, He requires us to know and acknowledge Him to be the only true God, and our God, and to love, worship, and glorify Him accordingly. When He commands us to "remember the Sabbath day to keep it holy," He requires us to engage in prayer, praise, hearing the Word, receiving the Sacraments, and all the other duties of that holy day. Where a duty is commanded, the avowing of that duty is likewise required. Believing in Christ, and a profession of faith in Him, are enjoined in the same commandment (Romans

10:10). Where the duties of children to parents are commanded, not only are all the duties of inferiors to superiors in every other relation required, but also all the duties of superiors to inferiors. On the other hand, when the Lord forbids us to kill, He forbids us also to strike or wound our neighbor, or to harbor malice and revenge against him (Matthew 5:21–22). When He forbids us to commit adultery, He at the same time prohibits fornication, incest, and all impure imaginations, affections, and purposes (Matthew 5:27–28). Where great sins are expressly forbidden, all the lesser sins of that sort are forbidden; and they are prohibited under the names of the grosser sins in order to render them more detestable and horrible in our view, and also to show us how abominable even the very least of them is in the sight of an infinitely holy and righteous God. Instead of attempting an explanation of each of the Ten Commandments, which would increase the size of this volume to much, I refer the devout reader to Thomas Boston's excellent exposition of them in his sermons on our *Shorter Catechism.*

RULE 3. That which is forbidden is at no time to be done; but that which is required is to be done only when the Lord affords opportunity. What God forbids is sin, and is never to be done (Romans 3:8); what He requires is always our duty (Deuteronomy 4:8–9), and yet every particular duty is not to be performed at all times (Matthew 12:7). That which is forbidden is at all times sinful, and therefore ought never, on any pretense whatsoever, to be done (Genesis 39:9). That which is required, as it is always our duty, so it is to be performed as often as opportunity is afforded, and as it does not interfere with the performance of our other

duties. We are commanded, for instance, to honor our
parents; but unless they are alive or present with us, we
do not have the opportunity of performing this duty.
In the third commandment, we are required to use, in
a holy and reverent manner, the names and ordinances of God, especially in all our acts of worship; but
we cannot, and should not, be every moment employed in acts of immediate worship; for we are commanded to abound in the performance of other duties
equally necessary. Although the affirmative part of every precept is of as high authority and binding force as
the negative part, yet it does not bind us to the performance of every particular duty at all times. It obliges
us to be always in a suitable frame for our present duty,
but not to be always in the actual performance of every
duty. It binds us to the performance of a particular
duty every time that we are called to perform that duty;
every time in which the performance of it can glorify
God and the omission of it dishonors Him. There is,
however, one affirmative precept which binds us to
perform the duty required at all times, namely the
commandment to love the Lord our God with all our
heart, with all our soul, with all our strength, and with
all our mind (Matthew 22:37–39). There is no state,
nor time, nor place in which we can be exempted from
the duty of loving God supremely.

RULE 4. Whatever we ourselves are commanded to
be, do, or forbear, we are obliged to do all that it is
possible for us to do, according to our places and stations in society, to make others around us to be, do, or
forbear the same. We are strictly bound, according to
our different stations, to endeavor that every duty is
performed, and every sin is forborne, by all to whom

our influence can extend (Genesis 18:19; Deuteronomy 6:6–7; Leviticus 19:17). Accordingly, in the fourth commandment, are these words: "The seventh day is the Sabbath of the Lord thy God: in it, thou shalt not do any work, thou, nor thy son, nor thy daughter, thy man-servant, nor thy maid-servant, nor thy cattle, nor thy stranger that is within thy gates" (Exodus 20:10). Here, the duty of both the servant and the stranger is required of the master.

Whatever sin is forbidden to us also forbids us to partake with others in it, either by example, advice, connivance, or by giving them occasion to commit it. "Be not partaker of other men's sins; keep thyself pure" (1 Timothy 5:22). However free of personal transgressions we may pretend to be, yet we are transgressors of the law so far as, by connivance or otherwise, we are partakers of the sins of others (Ephesians 5:11) Whatever duty others around us are commanded to perform, we are required, by advice, encouragement, prayer, and other helps, to assist them in performing it (2 Corinthians 1:24). How much iniquity, alas, do many even of the saints themselves commit by not attending more than they usually do to this rule!

RULE 5. The same duty is required and the same sin is forbidden, in different respects, in several and even in all the divine commands. The transgression of one precept is virtually a breach of all. They are so intimately connected together that if the divine authority is disregarded in any one of them it is slighted in all (Colossians 3:5; 1 Timothy 6:10; James 2:10; 1 John 4:20). The first commandment, for example, is so closely connected with all the other precepts that it is obeyed in all our obedience or disobeyed in all our

disobedience to any one of them. Obedience or disobedience to it is virtually obedience or disobedience
to the whole law.

RULE 6. Where a duty is required, the use of all the
means of performing it aright, is required; and where a
sin is forbidden, every cause, and even every occasion
of it, are prohibited. When chastity in heart, speech,
and behavior is required, temperance and diligence in
our lawful employments, as means of preserving it, are,
at the same time enjoined. On the other hand, when
the Lord forbids the profanation of the Sabbath, at the
same time He forbids all the employments and recre-
ations by which men profane that holy day. When He
forbids uncleanness, at the same time He prohibits
drunkenness, gluttony, idleness, or whatever else may
be an incitement to that sin. Where He forbids murder, He also prohibits the wrath, malice, and revenge
which prompt men to commit that crime (Matthew
5:21–22; 1 John 3:15). When children are commanded
to honor their parents, parents are, in the same command, enjoined to regard their children with parental
affection, and to bring them up in the nurture and
admonition of the Lord (Ephesians 6:4).

RULE 7. No sin is at any time to be committed in
order to avoid or prevent a greater sin. We must not
"do evil that good may come" (Romans 3:8) The very
least sin ought not, on any account whatever, to be
committed. None of the dispensations of adorable
Providence lays a man under a necessity of sinning.
"Let no man then say when he is tempted, 'I am
tempted of God,' for God cannot be tempted with
evil, neither tempteth He any man" (James 1:13). As
no man is allowed by the law, so none is necessitated by

the providence of an infinitely holy and righteous God, to commit one sin in order to prevent another. We are commanded in the law, not only to abstain from all evil, but even "from all appearance of evil" (1 Thessalonians 5:22). But while no sin must be committed in order to prevent a greater sin, some duties required should, as was observed above, give place to other duties.

RULE 8. The commandments of the second table of the law must give place to those of the first when they cannot both be observed together. Our love of our neighbor, for instance, ought to be subjected to our love of God; and we are enjoined to hate, that is, to love in a less degree, father and mother for Christ, when our love of them comes at any time in competition with our love for Him (Luke 14:26). When our love for our nearest relations and dearest friends becomes inconsistent with our love for Christ, the former must yield to the latter. We must prefer Christ, and God in Christ, to all the other objects of our esteem and affection (Matthew 10:37). When the commands of our superiors among men are at any time contrary to the commandments of the Lord, then we are to obey God rather than men (Acts 4:19). But although our natural duties to men, required in the second table of the law, must give place to our natural duties to God required in the first (Acts 5:29), yet the positive duties enjoined in the first table must yield to the natural duties required in the second when they cannot both be performed at the same time (Hosea 6:6).

RULE 9. In our obedience, we should have a special and constant respect to the scope and final end at which the Lord aims by all the commandments in gen-

eral, or by any one of them in particular. The great
end at which God aims in general, in subordination to
His own manifested glory, is perfect holiness of heart
and life in His people, even as He Himself is holy
(2 Corinthians 7:1; 1 Peter 1:15). Whatever obedience,
therefore, He enjoins, He requires that it be absolutely
perfect; and whatever obedience we perform, we are
bound to aim at perfection in it (Philippians 3:13), and
to assure ourselves that in proportion as we fall short of
perfection, we sin and come short of His glory. This
rule, in the hand of the Spirit of truth, is of special use
to teach both sinners and saints the true meaning of
every divine precept. The aim of God in each of His
commandments is perfection of holiness, of conformity "to the image of His Son, that He may be the
firstborn among many brethren" (Romans 8:29). And
the perfection in obedience which He requires is, as
has been hinted above, a perfection of principle that
our obedience proceed from "a pure heart, from a
good conscience, and from faith unfeigned" (1 Timothy 1:5; Matthew 5:48); a perfection of the parts of it,
so that it is universal in respect of all the commands, or
of all things written in the book of the law; a perfection
of degrees, that every part of it be raised to the very
highest degree of conformity to the holy law; and a
perfection in respect of duration, that from the beginning to the end of our life we continue "in all things
which are written in the book of the law, to do them."
    RULE 10. The beginning and the end, as well as
the sum, of all the commandments is love. "Love is the
fulfilling of the law" (Romans 13:10). "The end of the
commandment is love" (1 Timothy 1:5). As all the
blessings of God to His people flow from, and are

comprised in, His love to them, so all the duties of man to God are comprehended in love to Him. The love of God to man is the sum of the gospel; the love of man to God is the sum of the law. Love to God as our God is the sum of what is required in the first table of the law; love to our neighbor is the whole of what is enjoined in the second. The former is called "the first and great commandment," and the latter is "like unto it." These two commandments are so closely connected together that obedience to the one cannot be performed without obedience to the other. We cannot love God supremely unless we love our neighbor as ourselves; nor can we love our neighbor, who was made in the image of God, as ourselves unless we love God, who created him in His own image, with supreme affection (1 John 4:20). All the duties required in the first table of the law are but the native expressions of supreme love to the Lord our God; and all the duties enjoined in the second are only the genuine expressions of sincere love to our neighbor.

Now is it so that our love of our neighbor is to be subjected or subordinated to our love of God? We may hence learn how we ought to love God, and how to love our neighbor. We must love God more than we love ourselves, and love our neighbor as ourselves. We are bound to love the Lord our God supremely, or with all the powers of our souls, and to love our neighbor co-ordinately, or as ourselves. To love the Lord our God, according to the commandment, with all our heart is to love Him with a perfect degree of sincerity (Romans 12:9). To love Him with all our soul is to love Him spiritually and affectionately, and that in a perfect degree; and to express our ardent affection to Him by

every instance of obedience in which any faculty of our
souls can be exercised. To love Him with all our
strength is to love no other amiable object as much as
Him, and none but in Him and for Him, or in subordination to Him (Luke 14:26). And to do it with all our
mind is to regard Him with an intelligent love or a su-
perlative esteem, and to love Him principally for His
own infinite amiableness, as manifested especially in
the person and work of our adorable Redeemer (Song
of Solomon 1:3; Philippians 3:8).

The highest degree of love, then, of which man,
even in his state of innocence, was capable is due to
our God; but a lesser degree of it is due to ourselves
and our neighbor. To love our neighbor as ourselves is
to love Him in the same manner as we ought to do
ourselves. A lawful and regular love of ourselves is here
implied; for it is made the pattern according to which
we ought to love others. This regular self-love is a habitual desire and endeavor always to aim at the happiness of our souls and bodies in subordination to the
glory of God. To love, then, our neighbor as ourselves
is to love Him as constantly, as sincerely, as tenderly, as
ardently, as actively, and as inviolably as we love ourselves (Ephesians 5:29). This love of our neighbor
should be expressed by our doing to Him all that we
would from a well informed judgment, and have Him
to do to us in the same relations and circumstances.
We are required to love all men with a love of benevolence and beneficence, but the saints not only with a
love of benevolence, but with a love of complacence
and delight (Psalm 16:3). This love of God and of our
neighbor must flow "from a pure heart, from a good
conscience, and from faith unfeigned" (1 Timothy

1:5). And when it proceeds from these principles, it is "the fulfilling of the law," the essence of true holiness, and "the bond of perfectness." Reader, trust in the Lord Jesus with all your heart for all His salvation to yourself in particular, and especially for purity of heart and peace of conscience; and then your faith will work by love.

It is evident from what has been said that we were all born into the world utterly destitute of conformity to the holiness of God's law. We were "born in iniquity and conceived in sin" (Psalm 51:5). We came in to the world entirely destitute of the moral image of God, and wholly under the dominion of natural depravity (Job 11:12). The holy law commands us to love God supremely, but by nature we love ourselves supremely. It enjoins us to love our neighbor as ourselves; but we, on the contrary, hate our neighbor, especially in relation to the momentous concerns of his immortal soul. The law requires us to delight supremely in the Lord our God; but instead of this we delight only in sin, or at least in that which is not God. We are commanded in the law to do all to the glory of God, but we are naturally disposed to do all to our own glory. These corrupt propensities are native in the heart of every descendant of Adam, and are directly contrary to the holy nature and law of God (Psalm 53:1–3). So great is the contrariety between the holy nature of God as expressed in His law and the nature of a sinner, that God is said to hate sinners (Psalm 5:5), and sinners to hate Him (Romans 8:7). And no man has attained a true conviction of his sin but he whom the Holy Spirit has made to see and feel that by nature he is a hater of God and of the whole revealed character of God.

Hence it is manifest also that the very best actions of unconverted persons are sinful in the sight of God. Such persons, indeed, do many things that are materially good, but nothing that is formally good; nothing from a good principle, in a good manner, or to a good end. All that they do is done, either directly or indirectly, in opposition to the holy commandments of the Lord; and so it is sinful and hateful to Him (Proverbs 15:8; Romans 8:8; Hebrews 11:6). How then can such performances atone for their past transgressions, and entitle them to the favor of God and eternal life? Ah, how deep the infatuation, how great the folly of relying on our own righteousness for a title to our eternal salvation!

From what has been said, it is evident that it is a righteous thing with God to require of unregenerate sinners what they cannot perform. He commands them to love Him with all their hearts, and so to perform perfect and perpetual obedience to His righteous law; but in their state of unregeneracy they have no moral ability to perform a single duty according to the commandment (Romans 5:6). It is infinitely just, however, that the Lord should require of sinners what they are unwilling—and so unable—to perform; and that He should condemn them to death, in all its latitude and extent, for not performing it. For nothing can be more just and reasonable than that they should yield perfect obedience to His righteous law. He gave them, in the first Adam, sufficient ability to perform perfect obedience, and they chose to deprive themselves of it by their transgression in Him as their federal representative (Ecclesiastes 7:29; Romans 5:12, 19). Besides, they have no inability but what is voluntary. They love the depravity of their hearts, and choose to commit iniquity. Indeed, if the Lord could not justly require of sinners what they cannot perform, it would inevitably follow that they could have no need either that the Son of God should fulfil all righteousness for them, or that His Holy Spirit should implant holiness in them. To say, then, that God cannot justly require sinners to perform that obedience to Him which of themselves they are unable to perform tends to undermine, at once, both the law and the gospel.

To conclude, we may hence see that no influences of the Holy Spirit but such as are irresistible will suffice to convert a sinner to God, and to the love and practice of sincere obedience to His law. So strong and inveterate is the corruption which is in the hearts of unregenerate sinners that elect sinners resist the saving operation of the Spirit as much and as long as they can; and were it not that the adorable Spirit is infinitely efficacious in His operation, they would all so resist Him as to hinder Him from converting them. An infinitely powerful operation of the Holy Spirit, such as will be sufficient to conquer all the resistance made to it by sinners, is necessary to change their natures and make them willing to believe in Jesus Christ, and return through Him to God as their God. Accordingly, the Holy Spirit, in converting sinners, is in Scripture represented as putting His laws into their minds, and writing them on their hearts, as creating them in Christ Jesus unto good works, as quickening and raising them up from the dead, and as opening their eyes and calling them out of darkness into His marvelous light. Hence they are said to be born of the Spirit, to be new creatures, and to walk in newness of life. This great and wonderful change is indispensably necessary to true conversion. Happy, inexpressibly happy are you, reader, if you are a subject of it! No sooner do you begin to experience this happy change than you begin so to believe the gospel as to have communion with the second Adam in His righteousness and salvation, and so to obey the law as to walk worthy of the Lord to all pleasing.

Chapter 5

The Gospel of Christ

The word "gospel" signifies "good news" or "glad tidings" of salvation to lost sinners of mankind through that "Savior who is Christ the Lord" (Luke 2:10–11). The term in Scripture is used in a twofold sense. It is taken in a lax and general meaning, and also in a strict and proper acceptance.

First, it is employed in a lax and general acceptance. The gospel, in its lax, large, or general meaning is the doctrine of Christ and His apostles which, strictly speaking, is a mixture both of law and gospel. It is used sometimes to denote the history of the birth, life, death, resurrection, and ascension of Christ (Mark 1:1); sometimes the New Testament dispensation of the covenant of grace (2 Timothy 1:10); sometimes the preaching of the Word of Christ, particularly of the doctrines and offers of salvation through Him (1 Corinthians 9:14); and more frequently the whole system of revealed truth (Mark 1:14). The whole of divine truth, comprising both the law and the gospel strictly taken, is in Scripture called "the gospel"; for in publishing it the law must be preached in subservience to the gospel in its strict acceptance. The law as a covenant of works must be preached to unregenerate sinners in order to convince them of their sin and misery, and to impel them to accept the compassionate Savior offered to them in the gospel. The law as a rule of life must be preached to believers in order to excite them to trust at all times in Christ, for new supplies of sanctifying grace, and to advance in holy conformity to Him. Since the law in its covenant form is of special use in the dispensation of the gospel; since the law as a rule of duty stands in the covenant of grace, and is to the spiritual seed of Christ the only rule of acceptable obedience; and since the gospel, strictly taken, is the centre in which all the lines of revelation meet, the whole of divine revelation is denominated "the gospel." The law, so far as I know, is never in Scripture contrasted with the gospel in this large acceptation of the word, but is rather comprised in it.

Some have thought that whatever is in the Old Testament is law and that whatever is in the New is gospel. But this is such a mistake as reveals great ignorance of the sacred Oracles. The law and the gospel, in their strict and proper sense, are intermingled with each other both in the Old Testament and in the New. Moses and the Prophets often published the gospel as well as the law. Christ and His apostles, on the other hand, frequently preached the law together with the gospel. As Moses wrote of Messiah (and so published the gospel, though he principally promulgated the law to the Israelites), so the Lord Jesus and His apostles explained and urged the law, though they chiefly employed themselves in preaching the gospel. If by the gospel we mean the whole of that doctrine which was delivered by our Lord and His apostles, it is manifest that the duties of the law are more clearly explained and more strongly enforced in the gospel than ever they were by Moses and the Prophets. And therefore this part of the gospel may well be called "the commandment of the apostles of the Lord and Savior," and "the perfect law of liberty." An apostle informs us that the new covenant or testament was established or brought into the form of a law on better promises (Hebrews 8:6). The gospel, in its large acceptance, contains the purest and fullest system of morals that has ever been presented to the world. It reveals the infinitely glorious perfections of God, for "He who is in the bosom of the Father hath declared Him." It affords, at the same time, plain and affecting discoveries of a future state. "Our Savior Jesus Christ," says the Apostle Paul, "hath abolished death, and hath brought life and immortality to light through the gospel" (2 Timothy 1:10).

The gospel, in this point of view, contains precepts, all the precepts that the Lord ever gave to the children of men, and all the precepts that are to be found in the whole compass of divine revelation and summed up in the Ten Commandments. It comprehends not only the commands to believe, to repent, and to perform new obedience, but all the other commandments of God to men; so that every precept in the Word of God is a precept of the gospel in its lax and general meaning. Accordingly, the Apostle Paul informs us that "the Lord Jesus shall be revealed from heaven with His mighty angels in flaming fire, taking vengeance on them that know not God, and that obey not the gospel of our Lord Jesus Christ" (2 Thessalonians 1:7–8). He also says of those who heard the gospel from himself and the other apostles that "they have not all obeyed the gospel" (Romans 10:16). And the Apostle Peter wrote, "If judgment first begin at us, what shall the end be of them who obey not the gospel of God?" (1 Peter

4:17). By the gospel in these passages is meant the
whole Word of God, comprehending both the law and
the gospel strictly so called. If, therefore, we exhort
one another to obey the precepts of the gospel, we certainly should, in order to prevent error, inform each
other at the same time that we do not mean the gospel
in its strict sense, which contains no precepts, but the
gospel in its lax and general acceptance, which comprises all the precepts which the Lord has given to the
sons of men.

Second, the term in Scripture is also used in its
strict and proper meaning. The gospel strictly taken
signifies "good news, glad tidings, or a joyful message."
It is the joyful tidings of a free salvation through Jesus
Christ to sinners of mankind (Matthew 11:5; Luke 2:
10–11; Romans 10:15), or it is a revelation and exhibition of the covenant of grace to men. The gospel reveals to us what the Father, the Son, and the Holy
Spirit have done for us, what inestimable blessings they
have provided for us and are willing to impart to us,
how fully and freely these are offered to us, and how
they are to be received and enjoyed as gifts of infinitely
free and sovereign grace. Now the gospel, in this point
of view, comprises the following particulars:

1. It contains the doctrines of grace, or the doctrinal declarations of God concerning the redemption of
lost sinners; concerning His counsel of peace, and also
His covenant of grace in the source, the parties, the
making, the conditions, the promises, and the administration of it; concerning the Lord Jesus, the only
Mediator of it, in His person, offices, relations, and es-
tates; concerning the Holy Spirit as the Quickener,
Enlightener, Sanctifier, and Comforter of elect sinners

according to it; and concerning the inestimable blessings promised in it. This is the sum of all the doctrinal
declarations of the glorious gospel. It is a declaration
or publication of the free grace of God to sinners of
mankind, manifested in His redemption of them by
Jesus Christ; and it is the best tidings that ever have
reached their ears. It is by His gospel that the great
Redeemer "saith to the prisoners, 'Go forth'; and to
them that are in darkness, 'Show yourselves' " (Isaiah
49:9). By enabling convinced and disquieted sinners to
believe with application to themselves the doctrines of
the gospel, "He gives them beauty for ashes, the oil of
joy for mourning, and the garment of praise for the
spirit of heaviness" (Isaiah 61:3). That joyful message
which Christ was anointed to preach, angels brought to
the shepherds, and the apostles, evangelists, and ministers of Christ published to the world.

The gospel, then, is glad tidings of good things. No
tidings were ever so joyful as those which are an-
nounced in the gospel; and no benefits were ever so
good as those which are exhibited in it. At the same
time, no man will ever love or so much as understand
rightly a single doctrine of the gospel unless he sees
and feels that as a sinner he is utterly undone. It is to
men as sinners that the word of this salvation is sent.
No doctrine deserves to be called gospel but that
which makes the adorable Redeemer "all in all," the
"Alpha and Omega" in the redemption of a sinner. Of
such high importance is the doctrine of our
Redeemer's divine Sonship that the evangelist Mark
begins his account of the gospel (Mark 1:1) and the
Apostle Paul began his ministry of it with that grand article (Acts 9:20). And so fundamental is the doctrine of

Christ's consummate righteousness for the justification of believers that the same apostle says of the gospel that "it is the power of God unto salvation to every one that believeth; for therein is the righteousness of God revealed from faith to faith" (Romans 1:16–17). The word of the gospel which the Apostle Peter spoke to the Gentiles that they might believe was the doctrine of peace by Jesus Christ, with remission of sins through His name, to be received by faith (Acts 10:36 and 15:7). The gospel, in this point of view, differs so much from the law as a covenant as to be the very reverse.

2. The gospel strictly taken comprises also all the promises of the covenant of grace as included in the great and comprehensive promise of eternal life. Every promise of that gracious covenant belongs to the gospel. The gospel, in the proper acceptation of it, consists of free and absolute promises of grace and glory; or it includes a free and gracious promise of justification and eternal life through our Lord Jesus Christ. It contains the promises of faith and repentance, and, indeed, of all the other blessings of the everlasting covenant. The gospel after the Fall was revealed in the form of a free and absolute promise of a Savior, with salvation in Him to lost sinners of mankind. It was then promised that the seed of the woman would bruise the head of the serpent (Genesis 3:15). The gospel was preached to Abraham also under the form of an absolutely free promise: "In thee and in thy seed shall all the nations of the earth be blessed" (Genesis 12:3 and 22:18; Galatians 3:8). In the gospel, salvation from sin, from the curse of the law, and the wrath of God, as well as restoration to fellowship with God, conformity to Him, and the eternal enjoyment of

Him is graciously promised in Christ to a..
dially believe in Him. The Lord promises in His gosp
that He will give His Holy Spirit to elect sinners to
quicken their dead souls, to enlighten their dark
minds, to enable them to believe in Jesus, to repent of
their sins after a godly sort, to love, obey and enjoy
Him now, and to attain the perfect fruition of Him
forevermore. In the gospel, as preached under the Old
Testament, were promises of the coming of Messiah in
human nature; and in the same gospel, as preached
under the New, are promises of the coming of the
Spirit, or of Christ's coming in a greater measure of
spiritual influences. These promises in the gospel are
presented or offered to sinners in common, and are
made and performed to such sinners as believe.

The gospel, in this its strict and proper sense, seeing it is the form of Christ's testament which consists of
absolute and free promises of salvation by Him, contains no precepts. It commands nothing. It does not
enjoin us even to believe and repent; but it declares to
us what God in Christ as a God of grace has done, and
what He promises still to do for us and in us and by us.
Every requirement of duty, all precepts, those to believe and repent not excepted, belong to the moral law
which binds the new duty upon us the moment that
the gospel exhibits the new object. Indeed, if but a single instance of duty owed by the reasonable creature to
God were not, either expressly or by consequence, or
commanded in the moral law, that divine law would be
so far defective; it would not be a perfect law. But in
the oracles or truth we read that "the law of the Lord is
perfect" (Psalm 19:7), and that "His commandment is
exceeding broad" (Psalm 119:96). The divine law then,

being perfect, cannot but reach to every condition of the creature, and require of him every duty. When therefore God in the gospel graciously promises to give elect sinners faith, repentance, and eternal life, the law which commands every duty obliges them, in common with all other sinners who hear the gospel, to believe and trust and plead those promises. It binds them to trust those promises especially, and to receive the fulfilment of them, in the order in which the gospel exhibits them; to exercise faith in order to the exercise of true repentance, and to exercise faith and repentance daily in order to be prepared for the consummation of eternal life. While every divine promise, then, belongs to the gospel of God, and none of them to His law, every divine precept is contained in His law, and none of them in His gospel strictly taken.

3. The gospel, in its proper acceptation, contains likewise God's gracious offers of Christ in His person, righteousness, fullness, offices, and relations, and of Himself in Christ to sinners of mankind in common (Isaiah 42:6–7 and 55:4; John 3:16 and 6:32). It comprehends also His offer of all His promises in and with Christ to sinners indefinitely (2 Corinthians 1:20; Acts 2:39; Hebrews 4:1). Hence we commonly call these offers "gospel offers" because they form a main and special part of the gospel. "This is the record," says the Apostle John, "that God hath given to us eternal life; and this life is in His Son" (1 John 5:11). That God has given to us an offer of eternal life in and with His Son is the record which He has given of His Son. It is the sum, or at least a leading part, of the testimony of God concerning His Son. As the gospel, then, cannot be published faithfully unless the unlimited offer is de-

clared to all who hear it, so, it cannot be cordially believed unless the gracious offer, and all that is offered, is accepted and received as a gift of infinitely free grace. While all duties are commanded in the law, all privileges and blessings are offered in the gospel. While the former are required of all, the latter are presented to all. Christ, and all the blessings of His great salvation are in the gospel offered freely, fully, presently, and particularly, and that to sinners of mankind in common; and as they are offered, so must they be received by sinners. The ministers of the gospel are authorized by the Lord Jesus to "preach the gospel to every creature" (Mark 16:15), that is, to publish the full and free offer of Himself, and of His righteousness and salvation, to every rational creature, every son and daughter of Adam, to whom they may have access to speak. And it is, indeed, good tidings of great joy which shall be to all people that to us sinners of the human race this Child is born, this Son is given (Isaiah 9:6). The receiving of Christ by faith supposes a previous offering or giving of Him to hearers of the gospel in order to afford them a warrant to receive Him. As the raining of the manna about the camp of Israel in the wilderness is called a giving of it prior to their eating of it, so the gospel offer of Christ is called a giving of Him previous to a sinner's reception of Him by faith (John 6:31–32). Indeed, it is as necessary a part of the glorious plan of salvation by Jesus Christ that He be given as an offering before believing as that He be given in possession in and after believing.

4. Last, the gospel strictly taken includes God's infinitely gracious and tender invitations to sinners of mankind in general to accept His offers of a Savior,

and of salvation by Him. In the gospel He graciously calls, and with inexpressible earnestness entreats men to come as sinners and receive all that He has offered to them on the warrant of His authentic offer of it. He earnestly invites and urges them to believe that the Lord Jesus Christ, with His righteousness and salvation, is graciously offered to them, and so to trust in Him for all their salvation (Proverbs 8:4 and 9:4–5; Isaiah 55: 1–3; Matthew 11:28–30; Revelation 3:17–20 and 22:17). Those invitations, when considered as calls to perform the duties of believing and repenting, belong to the law; but when viewed as expressions of the readiness or willingness of God to bestow salvation on sinners, and as affording them an additional warrant to trust in the compassionate Savior for it, they form a part of the gospel. No man believes the gospel cordially until, convinced of his sinfulness and misery, he believes with application to himself those invitations, and, upon the warrant of them, trusts in the Lord Jesus for all salvation to himself in particular. For the gracious invitations of the gospel, equally as the direct offers of it, are addressed to every sinner of mankind who hears the joyful sound of it. As for the commands to believe and repent, they, as I hinted above, belong entirely to the law. These commands, when given to unregenerate sinners, belong to the law as a covenant of works; and when given to believers, to persevere in believing and repenting, they belong to the law as a rule of life.

The gospel in its proper acceptation (as comprising the doctrines, promises, and offers of a free salvation, with invitations to accept these offers) is in Scripture called "the gospel of God." He devised and appointed it in all its parts. It contains the declarations and promises of His redeeming mercy and the gracious offers of Himself in Christ to sinners of mankind to be their God and Father; it affords the most illustrious displays of all His perfections, especially of His glorious grace in the salvation of such as believe (Romans 1:1). It is also called "the gospel of Christ." He is the glorious Author, the principal Messenger and Preacher, the blessed subject and end of it, in whom all its doctrines and promises are "yea and amen, to the glory of God" (Romans 1:16). It is called "the gospel of the grace of God" (Acts 20:24), for it proceeds from His free favor and good will to men. It manifests the exceeding riches of His grace and the kindness of His love; and it is the means by which He graciously communicates the undeserved blessings of salvation to sinful men. "The gospel of peace" is another of its names (Ephesians 6:15). It flows from God with Christ as its Mediator, to reconcile sinners to Himself. By means of it, the peace of God is published to men; and it is the means of reconciling their hearts to Him as the God of peace, and to one another as friends and children and heirs of Him. It is also called "the gospel of salvation" (Ephesians 1:13), for it reveals, promises, and offers salvation. And in the hand of the adorable Spirit it is the instrument of applying the great salvation of Jesus Christ to the souls of lost sinners. It is called, likewise, "the gospel of the kingdom" (Matthew 4:23), for it is issued from the royal authority of Christ the King of Zion, is proclaimed in His church, and is the means of bringing rebels and enemies, first, into His kingdom of grace, and afterwards into His kingdom of glory. Another of its qualities is that it is a "glorious gospel"

(1 Timothy 1:11). It affords the most illustrious displays of the infinitely glorious perfections, purposes, favors, mercies, and truths of God in Christ; the brightest discoveries of the glory of Him who is the brightness of the Father's glory and the express image of His person; and it is the means of His bringing many sons and daughters to glory. In a word, it is called "the everlasting gospel" (Revelation 14:6). It continues to be preached, heard, and believed from the beginning to the end of time; and the inestimable blessings exhibited in it will continue to be enjoyed by the saints through all eternity.

From what has here been advanced, it will be obvious to the attentive reader that there is a great difference between the gospel in itself and in its dispensation by Jesus Christ. If the gospel is considered in its large acceptation, or as dispensed by the Lord Jesus, the Messenger of the covenant, legal precepts and threatenings are comprised and dispensed in it. A dreadful sanction is contained in it in order that none may presume to turn the grace of it into licentiousness. On the other hand, if it is viewed in itself, or in its strict and proper meaning, it has neither precepts nor threatenings, but, as was observed above, it is an exhibition of the covenant of grace to sinners of mankind, or good tidings of great joy to all people.

Such expressions as the following are gospel in the strict sense of the word:

Christ "was delivered for our offenses, and was raised again for our justification."

"Unto you is born this day, in the city of David, a Savior which is Christ the Lord."

"My Father giveth you the true bread from heaven."

"This is the promise that He hath promised us, even eternal life."

But on the other hand, such expressions as these are gospel considered in its dispensation to the sons of men:

"Believe on the Lord Jesus Christ, and thou shalt be saved."

"He that believeth, shall be saved; but he that believeth not, shall be damned."

"He that believeth on the Son hath everlasting life; and he that believeth not the Son shall not see life; but the wrath of God abideth on him."

In these and similar passages, the command to believe on the Lord Jesus, and the denunciation of divine wrath against all who believe not, do not belong to the gospel in itself, or strictly taken; but they belong to the external dispensation of it to sinners. In the dispensation of the gospel, the law and the gospel are dispensed together. The law is promulgated in subservience to the gospel, and therefore it is included in the dispensation of the gospel. The gospel strictly taken is one thing; and the precept and threatening in the dispensation of it is another.

Do we read in Scripture that unbelievers do not obey the gospel? We are not from this to suppose that the gospel in its proper meaning is a law, but in all such passages it is to be understood not in its strict, but in its large acceptation as comprising both law and gospel.

Does the gospel in its large or extended sense include the law, the same law that was given to man at the beginning? Hence it is manifest that Christ as

Mediator gives no new law, either to saints or sinners, under the gospel. He indeed said to His disciples, "A new commandment I give unto you, that ye love one another; as I have loved you, that ye also love one another" (John 13:34). But this is not the command of a new law, and on that account called "new," for "it is an old commandment which we had from the beginning" (1 John 2:7 and 2 John 5). But it is called new because it is a most excellent one; because it is more clearly and fully explained than before; because it is to be kept in a new manner, or "in newness of spirit, and not in the oldness of the letter"; and because it is enforced by a new motive and pattern. For Christ says, "As I have loved you, that ye also love one another." He does not here say to His disciples, "Ye shall love your neighbor merely as yourselves," but "as I have loved you." The Lord Jesus, then, has not purchased or published a new law of grace to sinners in which faith, repentance, and sincere obedience to it are made the conditions of justification and eternal life. There is a deep silence throughout the Oracles of Truth with regard to any new law of easier terms, or any new conditions of justification and salvation. We read, indeed, that Christ, the last Adam, fulfilled all righteousness for His spiritual seed, and that "by His obedience shall many be made righteous." But nowhere in the Word of God do we read that He purchased a new law of grace for them, according to which they might fulfill a justifying righteousness for themselves, and according to which sincerity might be accepted instead of perfection of obedience.

Hence it is also manifest that if any good quality or work of ours were made the condition of our justification or title to eternal life, this would turn the covenant of grace exhibited in the gospel into a covenant of works. The covenant of grace revealed and offered to sinners in the gospel is the only covenant according to which a sinner can be justified and entitled to life eternal. It is absolutely impossible that he can be justified according to the broken covenant of works. But were any graces, acts, or works of his the proper conditions of his justification, the covenant of grace would be as much a covenant of works as ever the covenant made with Adam was. The condition of Adam's covenant was perfect obedience; and, according to this imaginary law of easier terms, the conditions of the covenant of grace are sincere faith and sincere obedience. But it was far easier for Adam in his state of innocence to perform the condition of perfect obedience than it is for an impotent sinner, or even for the holiest saint, to perform that of sincere faith and obedience. The terms of the new covenant, according to that scheme, would, instead of being more mild, be more rigorous and difficult than those of the old. The condition of the one covenant would be works as well as that of the other; for works are still works whether they are perfect or sincere. All indeed who, according to the covenant of grace, attain justification are justified by faith; but it is one thing to be justified by faith as merely the instrument of justification and another to be justified for faith as an act or work affording a title to justification. It is one thing for faith as an act of obedience, and as being seminally all sincere obedience, to give a title to justification; and it is a very different thing for faith as a means or instrument to receive a title to it. Faith, according to the gospel, gives

no manner of title to the smallest blessing of the everlasting covenant; but it receives the surety-righteousness of the second Adam, which gives a full title to every one of them (Romans 5:18). It gives possession of
nothing in that gracious covenant, but it takes possession of everything.

From what has been said, we may see when a man's
obedience to the law is evangelical. His obedience is
spiritually good and acceptable to God, or, in other
words, is evangelical when he performs it from faith
and love, from union with Christ, and justification for
His righteousness as the principles of it; when he performs it not to the law as a covenant of works, but to
the law in the hand of Christ as a rule of duty; when he
yields it not for life, but from life; not in the strength
of nature nor of grace already received, but in the
strength of "the grace that is in Christ Jesus," trusting
that Christ, according to the promise, affords him continual supplies of grace; and when he performs it
chiefly for the glory of Christ, and of God in Christ. It
is evangelical obedience when a man performs it not to
recommend him to the favor of God, but in the faith
of God's favor; not that it may be his justifying righteousness, but that it may be a continued expression of
adoring gratitude for the gift of his Redeemer's righteousness; not that it may dispose the Lord to become
his God, but because He is already his God and Father.
Only such obedience as that is agreeable to the gospel
of Christ.

Is the whole of Christ's salvation offered in the
gospel to sinners? Then salvation from the law as a
covenant of works is tendered to them. In the declarations and offers of the blessed gospel, the consummate

righteousness of Jesus Christ, which has not only answered all the demands of the law as a covenant, but
has magnified the law and made it honorable, is presented to them. In the gospel they are also invited to
receive the gift of that glorious righteousness, against
which the utmost rigor of the violated law can offer no
objection, because it is the righteousness of Him who is
God as well as man. When they are enabled to accept
the gift of it, and to rely with humble confidence on it
for all their title to justification and eternal life, it is
imputed to them; and they are so justified in the sight
of God as to be set free from all the demands of the
law in its covenant form. And when by means of the
gospel they are thus delivered from the dominion of
the law as a covenant, they are, in consequence, saved
from the dominion of sin. Well may the glorious
gospel, then, be called "the gospel of our salvation"
(Ephesians 1:13), for by being in the hand of the Holy
Spirit, the means of delivering us from the law in its
covenant form, which is "the strength of sin," it becomes the means of our salvation from the power of
sin.

Are the offers and invitations of the gospel addressed to all in general who are the hearers of it?
Then no man believes the gospel with his heart unto
righteousness unless he believes the declarations, offers, and invitations of it with application to himself. So
long as a sinner refuses to believe these with application, or to believe that they are addressed to him in
particular, he continues to reject the compassionate
Savior and make God a liar (1 John 5:10–11).
Whatever his profession of religion may be, he remains
under the dominion of unbelief, and under condem-

nation to eternal punishment. The gospel is the doctrine of free and sovereign grace; and it is to be preached to every creature descended from Adam. The righteousness and salvation revealed and offered in it, then, are free to every human creature to whom it is preached; and it is the first or principal duty of every sinner of the human race to accept the gracious offer, and to rely on the righteousness of the divine Redeemer for all his title to eternal life. It is only they, therefore, who receive Christ Jesus and trust in His name, who shall have life through His name; and it is only they who receive abundance of grace, and of the gift of righteousness, who shall reign in life by one Jesus Christ.

To conclude, is the reader desirous to know whether he is experimentally acquainted with the grace of the gospel or not? Let him pray that the Lord may examine and prove him, and then let him put such questions as these to himself: "Do I know spiritually, and believe cordially, the doctrines of this glorious gospel? Do I spiritually discern the excellence and suitableness of the plan of redemption exhibited in the gospel; and do I heartily approve, so far as I know them, all the parts of that wonderful scheme? Do I heartily comply with the invitations, and accept the offers of the gospel? Do I frequently endeavor to embrace and trust the promises of it, and do I place the confidence of my heart in the Lord Jesus for all the salvation which is offered and promised in it? Do I so love the gospel as to delight in reading, hearing, and meditating on it? Do I love and admire the gospel because it is the doctrine, the only doctrine 'which is according to godliness,' or because it is the only mirror in which believers so contemplate the glory of God in the face of Jesus Christ as to be 'changed into the same image from glory to glory, by the Spirit of the Lord?' And do I find that under the transforming and consoling influence of the gospel I, in some measure, delight in the law of God after the inward man, and run in the way of all His commandments?"

If the reader can answer these questions in the affirmative, he may warrantably conclude that he has attained, in some happy measure, that supernatural and experimental knowledge of the glorious gospel which is the beginning of eternal life in the soul, and is inseparably connected with evangelical holiness in all manner of conversation. His duty is, in the faith of the promise, to grow daily in grace, and in the knowledge of our Lord and Savior Jesus Christ, and never to be moved away from the hope of the gospel.

But if he cannot answer so much as one of them in the affirmative, he ought to conclude that he is yet a stranger to the grace of the gospel; and instead of yielding to despair he should, without delay, come as a sinner to the Lord Jesus, who is given for a light to the Gentiles that He may be God's salvation unto the end of the earth. And upon the warrant of the unlimited grant, he should trust in Him for all the salvation promised in the gospel.

Chapter 6

*The Uses of the Gospel and the Law
in Subservience to the Gospel*

The gospel, in its strict and proper sense, is of great
and manifold use to both sinners and to saints.

Section 1. The Principal Uses of the Gospel ·

The gospel in its strict acceptation is, in the hand of
the Holy Spirit, of special use:

1. To reveal Christ and God in Him as reconciled,
and as reconciling sinners of mankind to Himself. The
great use of the gospel is to make Christ known to lost
sinners as the only and the all-sufficient Savior; to reveal Him to them in His infinitely glorious person as
God-man and Mediator; in His surety-righteousness for
their justification before God; in His immeasurable
fullness of the Spirit for their sanctification and consolation, and in His saving offices and endearing relations to all who believe in Him. It serves to represent to
them how Jesus has loved them, what He has done and
suffered for them, and what blessings of salvation He
has purchased for them and is ready to dispense to
them (1 Corinthians 1:24 and 2:2; 1 Timothy 3:16). It
is of use also to reveal to them God as reconciled in the
Son, and as reconciling elect sinners to Himself
(2 Corinthians 4:3–6 and 5:18–20). Hence the mani-

fold doctrines, offers, and promises of the gospel are in Scripture called "the manifold wisdom of God" (Ephesians 3:10). They clearly show that God has devised the scheme of our redemption with such astonishing wisdom; that our salvation is all of grace and all of merit, all of mercy and all of justice; that our iniquities are forgiven, and yet the punishment due for them is inflicted; that the ungodly who believe are justified and yet ungodliness is condemned; and that salvation is freely bestowed and, after all, the demands of law and justice are fully answered.

2. It is the gospel which also discloses to sinners the covenant of grace into which the Father, and the Son as last Adam, with the infinite approbation of the Holy Spirit, have entered for the salvation of such sinners as believe. Sinful men cannot be otherwise saved than by being enabled to take hold of that everlasting covenant by faith as to come into the bond of it. This, however, they cannot do unless they are made so to know it as to discern spiritually the reality, glory, and suitableness of it to their miserable condition as lost sinners. But it is the gospel only, coming to them "in demonstration of the Spirit and of power," that reveals this gracious covenant to them, and that shows them how they may be so instated in it as to possess and enjoy the blessings of salvation. They could never, according to the plan established in the counsel of peace, have known that eternal contract but by the revelation of it in the everlasting gospel. It is by the gospel, accompanied with the illuminating influences of His Holy Spirit, that the Lord Jesus, the Messenger of the covenant, shows elect sinners His covenant (Psalm 25:14).

3. It serves, likewise, the highly important purpose

of revealing to sinners their warrant to trust in Christ Jesus for complete salvation. In the blessed gospel, Christ, and God in Christ, are freely offered to sinful men, and men are graciously invited as sinners to receive the offer and to entrust the whole affair of their salvation to Christ, and to God in Him (John 6:32; Isaiah 55:1–4). By the gospel, they are informed that the Lord Jesus offers Himself with all the inestimable blessings of the everlasting covenant to them, and that He graciously invites and urges them as sinners to accept Him as their all-sufficient Savior, and to place the confidence of their hearts in Him for salvation from sin and wrath. Were they to not know that a divine warrant is thereby afforded them to receive and trust in the Savior for their salvation, it would be as great presumption in any of them as it would be in a fallen angel to attempt trusting that He would save him. But by the declarations, offers, calls, and promises of the word of grace, an ample warrant is afforded them as sinners of mankind to trust in the divine Savior, and so to take possession of His great salvation. And it is by the gospel, accompanied by the illuminating grace of the Holy Spirit, that their warrant is revealed, that their full right of access to the compassionate Savior is disclosed to them, and that He manifests Himself to be so near them as to be within their reach (Romans 10:6–8). Oh, how great is the importance and utility of the gracious offers and invitations of the blessed gospel to convinced and despondent sinners! By these, under the illuminating influences of the adorable Spirit, they see that it is lawful and warrantable for them to come as sinners, and to entrust, with humble and strong confidence, the eternal salvation of their souls to the

Lord Jesus.

4. The gospel is the means which the Holy Spirit employs for communicating the grace of Christ to elect sinners, in order to produce that change of their state and of their nature to which they have been chosen. It is by means of the gospel that, in the moment of regeneration, the Spirit of Christ and His grace enter and take possession of the hearts of God's elect. Sinners who are born again "are born not of corruptible seed, but of incorruptible, by the Word of God, which liveth and abideth forever" (1 Peter 1:23). Hence the Psalmist, directing his speech to the Messiah, says, "The Lord shall send the rod of thy strength out of Zion; rule Thou in the midst of Thine enemies. Thy people shall be willing in the day of Thy power" (Psalm 110:2–3). The gospel, accordingly, is called "the spirit which giveth life" (2 Corinthians 3:6), "the grace of God that bringeth salvation" (Titus 2:11), and "the power of God unto salvation" (Romans 1:16). By the gospel, God exerts the exceeding greatness of His power in quickening and converting sinners to Himself. It is by means of it that He enlightens their minds, renews their wills, rectifies and sanctifies their affections, and so makes them partakers of a new and holy nature. Hence the Apostle Paul calls it "the law of the Spirit of life in Christ Jesus," which made him "free from the law of sin and death" (Romans 8:2).

5. The gospel is also the instrument by which the Holy Spirit implants the principle and habit of true faith in the hearts of elect sinners. "Faith cometh by hearing, and hearing by the Word of God" (Romans 10:17). The Spirit renders the reading and, especially, the hearing of the gospel effectual means of working

faith in the hearts of sinners, by which they believe
with application the gracious offers of Christ, and of
His righteousness and fullness, and trust in Him for
salvation to themselves in particular. It is by means of
the gospel, which the Apostle Paul calls "the word of
faith" (Romans 10:8), that the Spirit of Christ implants
and increases precious faith in the souls of His elect
(John 20:31). Is it then the believer's desire that he
may make swift progress in the habit and exercise of
that living faith by which he gives glory to God and receives grace and glory from Him? Let him, in humble
reliance on the promise, and on the Spirit of faith,
read, hear, and meditate frequently on the glorious
gospel.

    6. It is by means of the gospel that the Holy Spirit
continues to apply Christ, with His righteousness and
fullness, to the hearts of believers for increasing their
sanctification and consolation. They are said in Scripture to be "sanctified through the truth" (John 17:
17–19), to be clean through the word which Christ has
spoken to them (John 15:3), and to have their hearts
purified by faith (Acts 15:9). The Apostle Paul presented this prayer for the saints at Ephesus: "That
Christ may dwell in your hearts by faith, that ye may be
filled with all the fullness of God" (Ephesians 3:17–19).
And he informed them that they were "built upon the
foundation of the apostles and prophets" (Ephesians
2:20–22). It is in proportion, then, as the saints are enabled to believe with application to themselves the offers and promises of the gospel, and to trust in Jesus
Christ for salvation, that they advance in holiness and
comfort. And it is in the unity of the faith, and of the
knowledge of the Son of God, that they all come unto

a perfect man, unto the measure of the stature of the fullness of Christ (Ephesians 4:13).

7. The gospel is a means of increasing the knowledge, of restraining the depravity, and of reforming the external conduct of many unregenerate sinners; and so of qualifying them for being, in various respects, serviceable to the people of God around them. It is often a means, under the restraining influence of the Holy Spirit, of rendering many unregenerate men less hurtful and more useful to the saints of God than otherwise they would be. As the gospel is a special means of the renewing influences of the Spirit in holy men, so is it of His restraining influence on hypocrites and wicked men (Matthew 13:20–22; 2 Peter 2:20; Hebrews 6:4–5). Now this restraining or providential influence is of inexpressible importance to the saints. For as no saint could continue to live in communion with Christ and with other saints without sanctifying grace, and that daily communicated to him, so neither could he live among sinners unless restraining influences were afforded to them. He ought, therefore, in a very high degree, to esteem and love the gospel not only because it is the means of special grace to himself, but because it is the vehicle of common influence to the unregenerate around him.

8. Last, it is by means of the gospel that the glory of Christ, and of God in Him, is manifested to men and angels. It is in and by the gospel that the brightest displays "of the glory of God in the face of Jesus Christ" are graciously afforded (2 Corinthians 4:4–7). In the gospel, as in a mirror, the glory of the Lord Jesus, and of all the divine perfections, as harmonizing and mingling their refulgent beams in the redemption of sin-

ners by Him, is seen, contemplated, and adored
(2 Corinthians 3:18). It is the gospel strictly taken that,
under the illuminating influences of the blessed Spirit,
serves to discover to the eye of faith "the glory of the
only begotten of the Father, the brightness of His
glory, and the express image of His person." There the
glory of the great Redeemer's person and work shines
forth in the view of holy angels and redeemed men
with the most resplendent luster. Hence the gospel is
called "the glorious gospel of Christ, who is the image
of God" (2 Corinthians 4:4), and "the glorious gospel
of the blessed God" (1 Timothy 1:11). While the Lord
affords far more illustrious displays of His infinite glory
in redemption than in any other of His works, all the
transcendant displays of it in redemption which He
makes are in and by the gospel.

Section 2. The Uses of the Moral Law in its Subservience to the Gospel

The law, both as a covenant of works and as a rule
of life, is, in the hand of the Holy Spirit, of special use,
and that both to sinners and to saints. Though righteousness and eternal life cannot, since the Fall, be obtained by a man's own obedience to the moral law, because "by the works of the law shall no flesh be justified" (Galatians 2:16), yet it is of manifold use to men.
"The law is good," says the Apostle Paul, "if a man use
it lawfully" (1 Timothy 1:8), that is, if he uses it suitably, to the design for which it is given him, and to the
state in which he is, either as an unbeliever or as a believer—or, in other words, if he improves it as a

covenant for urging him to receive Jesus Christ, and improve it as a rule for directing him how to walk in Christ.

The law is of use to men in general:

1. To reveal to them the holy nature and will of God, or to show them the infinite holiness and rectitude of His nature and will. Jehovah said to the Israelites in the wilderness, "I am the Lord your God; ye shall therefore sanctify yourselves, and ye shall be holy; for I am holy" (Leviticus 11:44). "The law is holy," says the Apostle Paul, "and the commandment holy, and just, and good" (Romans 7:12).

2. It serves to inform them of their duty to God, to themselves, and to others around them; and to oblige them, by His sovereign authority, to perform it. "He hath showed thee, O man, what is good; and what doth the Lord require of thee, but to do justly, and to love mercy, and to walk humbly with thy God" (Micah 6:8)?

3. It is of use, likewise, to restrain men from much sin. By its peremptory commands and awful threatenings, it serves in some measure to keep them in awe, and to frighten them from committing many external acts of sin in which they otherwise would freely indulge themselves. It is of use, by its terrible denunciations, to curb those who, destitute of every good principle, would rush forward to all manner of sin, and to deter them, through fear of punishment, from many gross enormities. In this view, it serves as a curb to hold sinners within the limits of external decency, and to prevent the world from becoming a scene of robbery and blood. Accordingly our apostle says, that the law is not made for a righteous man, but for the lawless and disobedient, for the ungodly and for sinners, for unholy

and profane, for murderers of fathers, and murderers
of mothers (1 Timothy 1:9–10).

4. The law conduces also to excite and encourage
sinners to the practice of virtue, from the consideration that even the external resemblance of true virtue
will often be rewarded with exemption from many
outward calamities, and with the possession of many
outward advantages (Isaiah 1:19). Nay, it tends to impel sinners to virtuous actions, even from the consideration that, in the event of their performance of them,
and afterward of their dying in an unregenerate state,
their punishment in hell will be more tolerable than if
they had not performed them. Although sinners cannot, by their obedience to the law, procure for themselves a title to heaven; yea, and though they should
never be driven by the law from themselves to Christ
for righteousness and salvation, but should die under
condemnation; yet the more external obedience they
yield to the law, the lighter will their punishment be
(Luke 12:47–48). They cannot, by their obedience to
the law, merit even the lowest place in heaven; but they
can by it obtain for themselves an exemption from the
lowest place in hell.

5. Moreover, it is of special use to convince sinners
of their sinfulness and misery, and also of their utter
inability by any righteousness and strength of their
own, to recover themselves from their state of sin and
misery. "What things soever the law saith, it saith to
them who are under the law; that every mouth may be
stopped, and all the world may become guilty before
God. Therefore by the works of the law, there shall no
flesh be justified in His sight; for by the law is the
knowledge of sin" (Romans 3:19–20). And again, "But

sin, that it might appear sin, working death in me by that which is good; that sin by the commandment, might become exceeding sinful" (Romans 7:13). The precepts of the law serve to convince men of their sins of omission, and the prohibitions of it to convince them of their sins of commission. There are various evils which men would never have known to be sins unless the holy law of God had revealed the sinfulness of them. Accordingly our apostle says, "I had not known sin but by the law: for I had not known lust except the law had said, 'Thou shalt not covet' " (Romans 7:7). While the precepts of the law are of use to convince sinners of the reality and sinfulness of their sins, the threatenings of it are employed to discover to them the tremendous wrath and curse of God due to them for their transgressions (Galatians 3:10). And by disclosing to them the deep depravity of their nature, the precepts and threatenings of the law serve, in the hand of the Spirit, to convince them of their utter inability to recover themselves, and so to humble them under a painful sense of their sinfulness and misery (Romans 3:9).

6. Last, the law serves to show them their extreme need of Christ, and of His righteousness and salvation. "Wherefore then serveth the law?" asks our apostle, "It was added because of transgressions, till the seed should come to whom the promise was made" (Galatians 3:19). It awakens their consciences to a conviction of their guilt, and to a dread of everlasting punishment, and so discovers to them their absolute need of Christ and His perfect righteousness for their justification in the sight of God (Galatians 3:24; Romans 10:4). Thus the moral law is of use to men in general.

7. It is of special use to unregenerate sinners.
Under the awakening influences of the Holy Spirit, it
serves as a covenant of works to convince them of sin,
and to show them that as they are sinners, and so cannot perform perfect obedience to entitle them to life,
it is absolutely impossible for them ever to attain to justification and salvation by their own performances. "By
the deeds of the law," says the Apostle Paul, "there
shall no flesh be justified in His sight; for by the law is
the knowledge of sin" (Romans 3:20). "I was alive
without the law once; but when the commandment
came, sin revived, and I died" (Romans 7:9).

It reveals the wrath of God against them for their
innumerable transgressions of it, and so impresses
them with fear of eternal punishment. "The law worketh wrath" (Romans 4:15). It condemns every sinner
who is under it to death in all its direful extent, and so
it awakens his conscience to expect infinite and insup-
portable wrath as the just recompense of disobedience
to its righteous precepts. Hence the law, in this point
of view, is called "the ministration of condemnation"
(2 Corinthians 3:7). Thus, as a scourge, it troubles and
torments the consciences of impenitent sinners, and
renders them uneasy in a course of sin.

The law is of use, likewise, to urge or drive them to
Jesus Christ, the only Savior of lost sinners. Seeing it is
the means of convincing sinners of their sinfulness,
misery, and utter inability to recover themselves, it
drives them from confidence in themselves to the Lord
Jesus for righteousness and strength. And thus it is
their "schoolmaster to bring them unto Christ, that
they may be justified by faith" (Galatians 3:24). By demanding perfect holiness of nature, perfect obedience

of life, and complete satisfaction for sin, which none of the children of Adam is able to afford, the law shuts them up to see their need of Christ, who has fully answered all these demands for those who believe in Him (Romans 10:4). It serves as a looking glass in which they may contemplate the exceeding sinfulness, and demerit of their sins in order that, despairing of life by their own works, they may be necessitated to flee speedily to Jesus Christ, who has fulfilled a perfect righteousness for their justification.

It serves, at the same time, to convince them that they have those characters of sinfulness and misery under which the offers and invitations of the gospel are addressed to men. The offers and calls of the gospel are addressed to men as unjust, ungodly, as sinners, enemies, and persons without strength; as lost, dead in trespasses and sins, simple ones, scorners, fools, stout-hearted and far from righteousness; as backsliders and prisoners, as laboring and heavy laden, thirsting for happiness of any kind, spending their money for that which is not bread, and their labor for that which satisfies not, disobedient, gainsaying, and rebellious. Now the law, under the illuminating influences of the Holy Spirit, is of use to show sinners that these are their very characters, and therefore that they are the very persons to whom the Savior is offered, and whom are invited and commanded to receive Him with His righteousness and salvation. In this view, it is eminently subservient to the gospel.

Last, the law serves to render those of them inexcusable who, turning a deaf ear to its dictates respecting their sinfulness and misery, refuse to accept the offer of a Savior, and of salvation by Him (Romans 1:20

with 2:15). And it not only leaves all who reject the divine Redeemer without excuse and under its dreadful curse, but it dooms them to greater, to redoubled condemnation. "He that believeth on the Son hath everlasting life; and he that believeth not the Son shall not see life; but the wrath of God abideth on him" (John 3:36). "He that despised Moses' law died without mercy under two or three witnesses; of how much sorer punishment, suppose ye, shall he be thought worthy who hath trodden under foot the Son of God, and hath counted the blood of the covenant, wherewith he was sanctified, an unholy thing, and hath done despite unto the Spirit of grace? For we know Him that hath said, 'Vengeance belongeth unto Me. I will recompense,' saith the Lord" (Hebrews 10:28–30).

8. The law is of special use, likewise, to regenerate persons or true believers, and that both as a covenant of works and as a rule of duty.

In its covenant form, it serves to show them what Christ, the second Adam, did and suffered in their stead. By requiring from all who are under it perfect holiness of nature and perfect obedience of life, with complete satisfaction for sin, as the conditions of eternal life, it teaches believers what the Lord Jesus, in the greatness of His astonishing love, condescended to become, to do, and to suffer for them. They may see in it as in a glass that He did infinitely more for them than any mere man or angel could ever have done (Romans 8:3–4; Philippians 2:8; Galatians 3:13–14). Thus the law, in subservience to the gospel, teaches believers indirectly what the gospel teaches them in direct terms. It is of use also to show them under what infinite obligations they lie to the Lord Jesus for having fulfilled all the righteousness of it in their stead, Though they are not under the law in its covenant form to be either justified or condemned by it, yet it is of special use to them how much they are bound to love and serve Christ who, by obeying the precepts, and enduring the penalties of it in their stead, has brought in everlasting righteousness for their justification. And so it is a means of exciting their gratitude to Christ, and also to God, who so loved them as to send Him to answer all its demands for them (2 Corinthians 9:15; Colossians 1:12–14).

The law as a rule of life is also of great use to believers. For although, as I already observed, they are not under it as a covenant of works, either to be justified by it for their obedience or to be condemned by it for their disobedience, yet they are under it as the rule of their new obedience, and they count it their exalted privilege and pleasure to be so (1 Corinthians 9:21). Now in this point of view, it serves, under the illuminating influences of the Holy Spirit:

(1) To show them how far they are from perfection of holiness. In order to render them more humble and contrite, to cause them to renounce, in a higher degree, all confidence in their own wisdom, righteousness, and strength, and to trust constantly and only in the Lord Jesus for all their salvation, the law discovers to them the sin that dwells in them, and that cleaves to all their thoughts, words, and actions. It is of great use to teach them the need that they have to be more humble, penitent, and holy. And so it serves, in a high degree, to promote their sanctification, and their desire to attain perfection of holiness (Philippians 3:10–14; Romans 7:22–24). As it requires them to be holy in

a perfect degree (Matthew 5:48), it shows them that their want of perfect conformity to it is, every moment, their sin, and that they ought continually to press on toward perfection, and long for heaven, where their holiness and happiness will be perfect (2 Corinthians 5:2–4; Philippians 1:23).

(2) It serves, under the witnessing of the Spirit, to evidence to their consciences the reality of their sanctification. The holy law serves as a touchstone by which believers may try, and so discover, their begun conformity to the image of the Son of God, the first-born among many brethren. Comparing their hearts and lives with that standard, they sometimes perceive that, though they are far from having a perfection of the degrees, yet they have a perfection of the parts of sanctification; and so the law as a rule conduces, in the hand of the Holy Spirit, to promote their comfort as well as their holiness. "Our rejoicing is this," says an apostle, "the testimony of our conscience, that in simplicity and godly sincerity, not with fleshly wisdom, but by the grace of God, we have had our conversation in the world" (2 Corinthians 1:12). As a covenant of works, the law is the instrument of the Spirit, as a spirit of bondage, for convincing and alarming secure sinners; but as a rule of life in the hand of the blessed Mediator, it is a means employed by the Spirit, as a Spirit of adoption, for comforting and encouraging true saints. Their habitual desire and endeavor from faith and love, and for the glory of God, to keep all the commandments of it are a good evidence to them that they are the children of God, and are conformed to the image of His Son.

(3) It is of great use to show believers what duty

they owe to their God and Redeemer, and to direct them how to perform it. Christ, whom the Father has given for a leader and commander to the people, gives to believers that law to be the rule of their obedience, to inform them what grateful service, what holy obedience, they owe to Him, and to God in Him, and to direct them in the course of their obedience. Accordingly, the holy Psalmist says, "Through Thy precepts I get understanding: therefore I hate every false way. Thy word is a lamp unto my feet, and a light unto my path" (Psalm 119:104–105). The law as a rule directs them how to express their gratitude to the Lord Jesus for fulfilling it for them in its covenant form (Romans 8:3–5). It enjoins them to show their love and thankfulness to Him by a growing conformity of heart and life to it as the rule of their obedience (John 14:15; 1 Timothy 1:5; Romans 12:1–2). While it shows them what is good and what is evil, what they ought to do and what they ought to forbear, it guides them in the exercise of their graces and in the performance of their duties. No sooner does the law as a covenant urge men to Christ for deliverance from the dominion of it in that form than Christ leads them back to the law as a rule for the regulation of their heart and conduct, in order that they may express their gratitude to Him for His perfect obedience to it as a covenant in their stead, by their stead, by their sincere obedience to it as a rule (John 14:15).

(4) Finally, it serves the highly important purpose of binding or obliging the saints to all their various duties. The law as a rule of life to believers comes invested with infinite authority, and therefore lays them under infinite obligations, even to perfect obedi-

ence. Seeing they do not cease to be creatures by becoming new creatures, they are, and ever will be,
obliged to yield personal obedience to the moral law as
a rule of life, and that by the sovereign authority of the
Father, the Son, and the Holy Spirit, their Creator. But
this divine authority, as was hinted above, issues to
them from the Lord Jesus, the great Mediator, who has
created as well as redeemed them, and who has "all the
fullness of the Godhead, dwelling in Him bodily." They
therefore receive the law at His mouth. And surely the
law can lose nothing of its original authority by being
conveyed to them in such a glorious channel as the
hand of Christ: for not only is He Himself God over all,
but all the sovereignty and authority of the infinitely
glorious Godhead are in Him as Mediator (Exodus
23:21). The Lord Jesus, therefore, instead of dissolving
or in the smallest degree weakening the moral law,
greatly strengthens the original obligation of it
(*Confession of Faith* XIX:V). Indeed, it is only to God as
in Christ, only according to the law as in the hand of
Christ, and only by a real believer in Christ that the
smallest acceptable obedience can be performed. The
law as a rule in the hand of Christ, then, is of special
utility to believers inasmuch as it shows them how high
their obligations are to the love and practice of holiness. And thus it eminently subserves the gospel, that
"doctrine which is according to godliness."

From the foregoing detail it will be obvious to the
devout reader that the law as a covenant is of standing
use in the effectual vocation of sinners to Christ. The
Holy Spirit makes the offers and calls of the gospel effectual to no sinner without setting home the law as a
covenant of works to their minds and consciences.

Sinners may be drawn to the Savior by a discovery of His redeeming love (Hosea 11:4), and so may be effectually called without legal terrors; but no man is persuaded and enabled to come to Him without a true conviction of sin and of the want of righteousness. But it is by the law in its covenant form that sinners are convinced of sin, and of their need of a perfect righteousness to free them from eternal death. Thus the law is of standing use to them to show them their extreme need of the compassionate Savior, and of His perfect righteousness, and so to "break up the fallow ground" of their hearts. In this way, the fiery law continues, by the almighty agency of the Spirit, to subserve the merciful design of the blessed gospel.

Hence we may also learn how much conviction of sin and of righteousness by the law is requisite to true conversion. Such a measure of it in adult persons is necessary as will suffice to make them sensible that they are sinners in heart and in life; that they are already undone, and that their misery under the curse of the law is inexpressible; that they have no righteousness to answer the just demands of the broken law; and that they are so dead in sin as to be totally unable to save themselves, or so much as to prepare themselves for salvation. Such a measure as this is requisite because, without it, they would not see their absolute need of the Lord Jesus to save them either from their sin or their misery, nor would they desire above all things a personal interest in Him and His great salvation. Not that it is requisite as a federal condition of their being graciously received by Christ, but only as an excitement to urge them to flee speedily for refuge to Him.

From what has been said, we may also infer that a minister of the gospel may often preach the law to his hearers and yet not deserve to be called a legal preacher. He cannot preach the gospel faithfully and successfully unless he preaches the law in subservience to it. If he is a faithful and able minister of the New Testament, he will preach the law as a covenant of works, and will press it upon the consciences of secure sinners and self-righteous formalists. He will denounce the tremendous curse of it on those who continue under it, and who rely securely on their own works for a title to eternal life in order to tear away every pillow of carnal security on which they repose themselves, and to show them the vanity of every lying refuge. In proportion also as he is faithful, satisfaction for sin as well as perfect obedience? Or does it demand from every unregenerate sinner perfection of suffering as well as of doing? Then, though a descendant of fallen Adam could say that he never had, in his own person, transgressed the law, and that he would to the end of his life "continue in all things which are written in it, to do them," yet even this perfect obedience of his would not suffice to fulfil the law, and so to entitle him to eternal life according to the covenant of works. For the law as a covenant would still demand from him full satisfaction for the sin that he committed in the first Adam: and satisfaction for sin cannot be given by obeying the precept, but by suffering the penalty of the law in that form. Ever since the fall, the law and the justice of God demand not only full payment of the original debt of perfect obedience, but complete payment, likewise, of the debt of infinite satisfaction for the offense given by sin to the infinite Majesty of heaven (Genesis 2:17).

Nay, in the order of law and justice, the debt of full satisfaction ought to be discharged previous to that of perfect obedience. The infinitely righteous Jehovah will first be pacified by a complete satisfaction to His justice for the infinite insult offered to His glorious Majesty by transgression before He can consistently, with the honor of His character and government, be pleased with any degree of obedience from the sinner. If a sinner, then, hopes for eternal life on the ground of his own righteousness, he must first give infinite satisfaction for all his innumerable crimes, and then begin and complete a course of perfect obedience as the condition of life. He must first of all make complete satisfaction to the penalty of the righteous law before his obedience to the precept can be acceptable to God.

But is this possible? Is it possible for one who is to continue through all eternity to be a sinner as well as a sufferer? Is it possible for a sinner, first, to endure the whole of infinite punishment or eternal wrath, and after endless torments shall have been completely endured to return, and, under the dominion of sin, to perform perfect obedience as the condition of eternal life? Oh, that self-righteous and secure sinners would consider before it is too late how impossible it will be for them ever to obtain eternal life by their own righteousness; and that they would, by faith, submit themselves to the righteousness of Jesus Christ by which He has magnified the law and made it honorable!

Moreover, it appears from what has been said that when our apostle asserts, in his epistles to the Romans and Galatians, that no man can be justified before God by the works of the law, he does not mean the law merely as promulgated from Sinai, or the law of Moses

as such; for those churches consisted chiefly of Gentile
converts who had no concern with the law of Moses
merely as such. Before their conversion they were heathens; they were under the law not as delivered from
Sinai, but as the law of nature and as a covenant of
works made with Adam, and with them in him. As
therefore no Jews can be justified by the works of the
moral law as a covenant displayed on Mount Sinai, so
no Gentiles can be justified by the works of the moral
law as a covenant made with Adam. They among the
Gentiles who have been redeemed are said to have
been redeemed from the curse of the law (Galatians
3:13), that is, of the moral law in its covenant form as
given to Adam.

Once more, is it by the law as a covenant that sinners are convinced of misery as well as of sin? Then
how great is the misery, and how intolerable will the
punishment be, especially of those under the gospel
who obstinately continue in their unbelief and impenitence! While the violated law continues in all its binding force against them, their condemnation will be inconceivably more dreadful than if they had never
heard the gracious offers of the gospel. "This is the
condemnation, that light is come into the world, and
men loved darkness rather than light because their
deeds were evil" (John 3:19). "Whosoever shall fall
upon that stone shall be broken; but on whomsoever it
shall fall, it will grind him to powder" (Luke 20:18).
Impenitent sinners under the gospel shall be punished
not only for their innumerable transgressions of the
law, but for hating and stifling their convictions of sin
and misery by it; and their punishment for condemning and rejecting the great Redeemer offered to them

in the gospel will be far more tremendous and intolerable than if they had never heard of His name.

No punishment of sinners will be as dreadful as that of those who hear of an only Savior and yet refuse to believe in Him. Suppose that He is offered, and that sinners reject the gracious offer a thousand times; they are a thousand times greater sinners than they were when He began to be offered to them—and according to the greatness of their sin will their punishment be. Oh, that the secure sinner under the gospel would now begin to consider the heinousness of his sin, and the horrible depth of the misery which awaits him in the place of torment! You are under the law as a broken covenant, and obnoxious to its dreadful curse. You believe not on the Son of God for His salvation, and therefore the wrath of God abides on you.

Can you imagine that the omniscient and righteous Judge of all the earth will take no notice of you; or that He who is of purer eyes than to behold evil, and who cannot look on iniquity but with infinite abhorrence will suffer you to sin against Him with impugnity? Oh, how inexpressibly dreadful will your condition be if you remain asleep in your sinfulness and misery till everlasting fire, prepared for the devil and his angels, awakens you! Alarmed by the terrors of the fiery law, let your heart be won to the compassionate Savior by the mild accents of the blessed gospel. In the glorious gospel, Jesus, with His meritorious righteousness and His great salvation, is freely, wholly, and particularly offered to you as a lost sinner of mankind; and the unlimited and authentic offer affords you a right to receive and trust in Him for complete salvation. Oh, do not any longer despise this unspeakable, this ines-

timably precious gift! Come to the Lord Jesus, and He
will in no wise cast you out. Believe in the dear
Redeemer and you shall never perish, but have eternal
life.

Chapter 7

The Difference Between the Law and the Gospel

By "the law" here is meant the moral law as a covenant of works, and by "the gospel" is meant the gospel in its strict and proper sense. To know the difference so as to be able to distinguish aright between the law and the gospel is of the utmost importance to the faith, holiness, and comfort of every true Christian. It will be impossible otherwise for a man so to believe as to "be filled with joy and peace in believing." If he does not know the difference between the law and the gospel he will be apt, especially in the affair of justification, to confound the one with the other. The consequence will be that in his painful experience, bondage will be mixed with liberty of spirit, fear with hope, sorrow with joy, and death with life. If he cannot so distinguish the gospel from the law as to expect all his salvation from the grace of the gospel, and nothing of it from the works of the law; he will easily be induced to connect his own works with the righteousness of Jesus Christ in the affair of his justification. This was the great error of the Judaizing teachers in the churches of Galatia. They mingled the law with the gospel in the business of justification, and thereby they so corrupted the gospel as to alter the very nature of it and make it another gospel. They taught that unless men were circumcised and kept the law of Moses, they could not be justified or saved (Acts 15:1–5). They informed the

people that while the righteousness of Christ received
by faith was necessary, their own works of obedience
were also requisite in connection with it to entitle
them to justification before God. This is a fundamental
error, and such a one that if even an angel from
heaven would publish it he should be accursed.
Accordingly, the apostle boldly affirmed to the Galatians, and he deliberately and earnestly repeated his
declaration, that though he himself, or even an angel
from heaven, were to preach any other gospel to them
than that which he had preached unto them, he
should be accursed (Galatians 1:8–9). To mingle, then,
the law with the gospel, or to teach men to join the
works of the law to the perfect righteousness of Jesus
Christ as the ground of a sinner's title to justification
in the sight of God, is, according to our apostle, to
preach another gospel.

As this is a great error, so it is a very dangerous error. If a man attempts to add any works of his own to
the consummate righteousness of Jesus Christ as the
ground of his justification before God, Christ profits
him nothing. The obedience and death of Christ have
become of no effect to him. "Behold, I Paul say unto
you, that if ye be circumcised, Christ shall profit you
nothing. For I testify again to every man that is circumcised, that he is a debtor to do the whole law. Christ is
become of no effect unto you, whosoever of you are
justified by the law; ye are fallen from grace" (Galatians
5:2–4). If a man tries to connect his own performances
with the righteousness of Jesus Christ for the pardon of
his sins and the acceptance of his person as righteous
in the sight of God, he deprives himself of all benefit
from that perfect righteousness. If he relies on his own

works of obedience for even the smallest part of his title to eternal life, he is a debtor to the whole law in its covenant form, and he fixes himself under the dreadful curse of it. Christ will profit him nothing unless he relies on His infinitely glorious righteousness only for all his title to justification and eternal life. A sinner depends on the righteousness of Christ for justification to no good purpose if he does not rely on it only, and neither in whole nor in part on his own obedience.

If an exercised and disquieted Christian does not distinctly know the difference between the law and the gospel, he cannot attain to solid tranquility or established comfort of soul. He will always be in danger of building his hope and comfort partly—if not wholly—upon his own graces and performances, instead of grounding them wholly on the surety-righteousness of Jesus Christ; and so he shall be perpetually disquieted by anxious and desponding fear. For since the law knows nothing of pardon of sin, the transgressions which he is daily committing will be greater grounds of fear to him than his graces and performances can be of hope. The spirit of a depressed Christian cannot be raised to solid consolation but by being able so to distinguish between the law and the gospel as to rely only, and with settled confidence, on the spotless righteousness of the second Adam, presented to him in the gospel, for all his title to the justification of life.

Ignorance of the difference between the law and the gospel promotes also, in a great degree, the strength and influence of a self-righteous temper. When a man is driven to acts of obedience by the dread of God's wrath revealed in the law, and not drawn to them by the belief of His love revealed in the

gospel; when he fears God because of His power and
justice, and not because of His goodness; when he regards God more as an avenging Judge than as a compassionate Friend and Father; and when he contem-
plates God rather as terrible in majesty than as infinite
in grace and mercy, he shows that he is under the dominion, or at least under the prevalence, of a legal
spirit. If he builds his faith of the pardon of sin, of the
favor of God, and of eternal life upon any graces which
he supposes are implanted in him, or upon any duties
which are performed by him, he is evidently under the
power of a self-righteous temper. He shows that he is
under the influence of this hateful temper by grounding his hope and his comfort upon conditions performed by himself and not upon the gracious and absolute promises of the gospel. In a word, when his
hope of divine mercy is raised by the liveliness of his
frame in duties, and not by discoveries of the freeness
and riches of redeeming grace offered to him in the
gospel; or when he expects eternal life not as the gift
of God through Jesus Christ, but as a recompense from
God for his own obedience and suffering, he plainly
shows, that he is under the power of a legal spirit. Now,
if he is ignorant of the leading distinctions between the
law and the gospel, this ignorance will strengthen his
legal propensity and confirm him in his resolution to
seek justification partly, if not wholly, by the works of
the law.

If awakened sinners are ignorant of the leading
points of difference between the law and the gospel,
this will discourage them much from attempting to
come to Christ for salvation. If they cannot distinguish
aright between the law and the gospel, they will mingle

the works of the one with the grace of the other; and the consequence will be that they will form confused, false, and discouraging notions of the compassionate Savior. And so, instead of being drawn to Him, they will be deterred from trusting in Him for salvation. They will allow themselves to apprehend that they must have something to bring with them to the Savior in order to recommend them to Him; some good qualifications to entitle them to His favor. Although it is declared in the gospel that all things are already given to Christ by the Father, yet when the thoughts of convinced sinners about the law and the gospel are indistinct, they imagine that they must still have something of their own to bring and present to Him. They conceive that they must, in some measure, have that which is commanded in the law before they can have a right to receive that which is offered in the gospel; or that they must have those holy dispositions to bring to Christ which He only can bestow, and for which they ought as sinners to come to Him. Thus, having the righteousness required of them in the law, and not the infinitely perfect righteousness freely offered to them in the gospel, before their eyes, their consciences are brought into trouble and perplexity; and instead of coming as sinners to Christ for righteousness and strength, they are ready to harden themselves in despair of His mercy, and in aversion from Him.

As a man's ignorance of the difference between the law and the gospel is inexpressibly hurtful to him, so his being able to distinguish aright between them must be of unspeakable advantage to him. It is an attainment in which the present and future welfare of his soul is deeply concerned. If a good man understands well the leading points of distinction between them, it will, under the illuminating influence of the Holy Spirit, enable him to understand the Scriptures clearly, and to reconcile all such passages as seem to contradict one another. It will also help him to determine rightly in difficult cases of conscience, and so to try all doctrines by the touchstone of the Word as easily to distinguish truth from error. And if he is at any time in distress of mind, it will, in the hand of the Holy Comforter, be a special mean of recovering for him that peace of conscience and joy of faith which will enable him to serve the Lord with gladness (Psalm 100:2). In few words, it will enable him to show such regard to the gospel as to receive, by the daily exercise of faith, the person, righteousness, and fullness of Christ therein offered to him; and such respect to the law in its covenant form as to present in the hand of faith to it the consummate righteousness of Jesus Christ as the only ground of his right to justification and eternal life. It will also qualify him for honoring the law as a rule of duty by advancing in the love and practice of that universal holiness which it requires.

As it is, then, of unspeakable importance both to sinners and to saints to distinguish aright between the law and the gospel, especially in the affair of justification, I shall, in dependence on the Spirit of truth, endeavor to point out the difference between them.

The law, especially in its covenant form, and the gospel, in its strict and proper sense, may be distinguished from each other in the following respects:

1. The law, in all that is essential to it, proceeds necessarily from the very nature of God; but the gospel, in all its doctrines, offers, and promises, flows

from His love, grace, and mercy, or from His good will to men. The manifestation of God's love, grace, and mercy in redeeming sinners to Himself was no more necessary than the display of His wisdom, power, and goodness in creating them (Leviticus 19:2; Ephesians 1:4–7 and 2:4–8).

2. The law is known partly by the light of nature (Romans 2:14–15), but the gospel is known only by a revelation from heaven (Matthew 11:27). Man, though he is a fallen creature, has in some degree a natural knowledge of the law; but he has no natural knowledge of the gospel. The gospel was wrapped up in profound secrecy till it was revealed from heaven by the Son of God immediately after the Fall; and therefore it is called "a mystery," and "the mystery of Christ" (Romans 16:25; Ephesians 3:4). Hence, unregenerate sinners are commonly not so averse from hearing the doctrine of the law as they are from hearing that of the gospel. Legal doctrine they can naturally understand, for it has a testimony in their consciences; but evangelical doctrine is a strange, unaccountable, and incredible doctrine to them (1 Corinthians 1:23).

3. The law regards us as creatures originally formed with sufficient ability to yield perfect obedience to it; and accordingly it requires us to retain and exert that ability in performing perfectly all the duties which we owe to God, ourselves, and our neighbors. The gospel considers us as sinners, condemned to death in all its extent, and totally destitute of strength to perform the smallest degree even of sincere obedience; and it declares to us what God, as a God of infinite grace and mercy, has done, and what He offers and promises still to be and do for us (Isaiah 42:6–7; Matthew 18:11;

Romans 5:6–10). It declares that in the Lord Jesus believing sinners have righteousness and strength, and
that in Him they are justified and have life eternal.
Accordingly, the doctrines, offers, and promises of it
continue to be dispensed to them so long as sin remains in them, but no longer.

4. The law shows us what manner of persons we
ought to be in all holy conversation and godliness, but
it does not inform us by what means we may become
such (Luke 10:27–28). The gospel teaches us how we
may be made such, namely by union and communion
with Christ in His righteousness and fullness, or by the
imputation of His righteousness to us and the sanctification of His Spirit in us (Acts 16:31; 1 Corinthians
1:30; 2 Corinthians 5:21; Galatians 2:16).

5. The law in its commanding power differs much
from the gospel. The law says, "Do and you shall live;
you shall, by performing personal and perfect obedience, entitle yourselves to eternal life" (Matthew
19:17). The gospel says, "Live, for all is already done;
all the righteousness, meritoriousness of eternal life for
believers, is already fulfilled by the second Adam, their
adorable Surety. First, live in union and communion
with Him, and then do—not for, but *from* life already
received." The law proceeds upon the supposition that
we still have all that we originally had, and requires
perfect obedience; the gospel supposes that we have
nothing, and furnishes us with all that the law demands. The former requires perfection from us, but
offers us no supply of strength to attain to it; whereas
the latter teaches us that we have it in Christ, and offers it to us as an inestimable gift of grace (Romans
5:17). When, therefore, the law as a covenant of works

comes to us with its requirements of perfect obedience as the condition of life, and of complete satisfaction for sin, we ought to refer it to our divine Surety for an answer to both its demands. The law requires obedience on pain of death; the gospel attracts and encourages to obedience by the promise of life, as "the gift of God through Jesus Christ our Lord." The former exhibits the charge of paying what we owe for a title to life; the latter, the discharge in consequence of its having been already paid by the Surety in our stead. The law commands faith and repentance; the gospel strictly taken does not command them, but it teaches them: it teaches every duty, but commands none. The former accepts no obedience but that which is perfect and perpetual; the grace of the latter accepts, though not in a justifying righteousness, sincere obedience from persons already justified, though it is far from being perfect.

In a word, the law says, "Do this and you shall live"; but the gospel, in the dispensation of it, says, "Believe this, and you shall be saved." The law is God in a command; but the gospel is God in Christ, God in a promise. The law gives man more to do for eternal life than they are able to do; the gospel gives them less to do than they are willing to do. The law gives man all the work: the gospel gives grace all the work and all the glory.

6. The law, as it has a promise of life, is very unlike the gospel. The former promises eternal life to a man on condition of his own perfect obedience, and of the obedience of no other; whereas the latter promises it on condition of the perfect obedience of Christ received by faith, and of that of no other. The promise of

the law as a covenant is the promise of God as an absolute God; but the promise of the gospel is the promise of God as a God of grace in Christ. The promise of the former was to have been performed after obedience, whereas the promise of the latter begins to be performed to the true believer before, and in order to, his obedience. In the law of works the promise of privilege is grounded on the performance of duty; but in the gospel the performance of duty is founded on the promise, and even on the enjoyment, of privilege. The promise of the law is strictly conditional, but the leading promises of the gospel are, to us, entirely absolute.

7. In its condemning power, the law is very different from the gospel. The law condemns, and cannot justify a sinner: the gospel justifies, and cannot condemn the sinner who believes in Jesus. In the law, God appears in terrible threatenings of eternal death; in the gospel, He manifests Himself in gracious promises of life eternal. In the former, He curses as on Mount Ebal; in the latter, He blesses as on Mount Gerizzim. In the one, He speaks in thunder and with terrible majesty; in the other, with soft whispers or a still small voice (1 Kings 19:12). By the trumpet of the law, He proclaims war with sinners; by the jubilee-trumpet of the gospel, He publishes peace, "peace on earth and good will toward men" (Luke 2:14). The law is a sound of terror to convinced sinners; the gospel is a joyful sound, "good tidings of great joy." The former represents God as a God of wrath and vengeance; the latter as a God of love, grace, and mercy. The one presents Him to sinners as "a consuming fire"; the other exhibits the precious blood of the Lamb which quenches the fire of His righteous indignation so that it may not

consume such sinners as believe. That presents to the view of the sinner a throne of judgment, this a throne of grace. Every sentence of condemnation in Scripture belongs to the law; every sentence of justification forms a part of the gospel. The law condemns a sinner for his first offense, but the gospel offers him the forgiveness of all his offenses.

8. The law, as it convinces sinners of sin and misery, is to be distinguished from the gospel. While the law, in the hand of the Holy Spirit, serves to convince the sinner of his sin, and of his want of righteousness, the gospel presents him with a perfect righteousness for his justification before God. The law wounds and terrifies the guilty sinner; the gospel heals and comforts the guilty sinner who believes in Jesus. The one shows him that his debt is infinitely great, and that he has nothing to clear it; the other informs him that, by the obedience and death of Jesus, his divine Surety, it is paid to the utmost farthing. The spirit of the law is a spirit of bondage to fear, but the spirit of the gospel is an ingenuous, free Spirit. The law is a house of bondage; "it gendereth to bondage," whereas the gospel proclaims the opening of the prison to those who are bound. By the law is the knowledge of sin; by the gospel is the knowledge of a Savior and remission of sin, as well as of salvation from the love, power, and practice of sin. The law says to every man, "You are a sinner." The gospel says, "The blood of Jesus Christ cleanses from all sin." The law shows the sinner his disease; the gospel presents him with healing balm, the balm in Gilead, and the Physician there. The former presents grounds of fear; the latter a foundation of hope. That reveals God as displeased; this shows that His wrath has

been endured and appeased. In the law Christ is concealed; in the gospel He, with His righteousness and salvation, is revealed and presented to sinners. The law is a killing letter, a ministration of death; the gospel is the ministration of the Spirit as a Spirit of life (2 Corinthians 3:8). The former is the law of sin and death, the law which connects sin and death together; the latter is "the law of the Spirit of life in Christ Jesus" (Romans 8:2), the doctrine which is according to godliness. The one is the ministration of condemnation; the other is "the ministration of righteousness" (2 Corinthians 3:9).

9. When the law is viewed in its irritating power, it differs much from the gospel. The law as a covenant, by forbidding all manner of sin, and that under the most dreadful penalty, irritates the reigning depravity of the sinner; and so it is the innocent occasion of his hardening his heart the more in committing sin (Romans 4:15), whereas the gospel and the grace revealed in it renew and melt the obdurate heart. The law, by affording sin in the depraved heart an occasion of exerting itself the more, "is the strength of sin" (1 Corinthians 15:56); the grace of the gospel, on the contrary, subdues the iniquity, slays the enmity, and, in the hand of the Holy Spirit, sanctifies the heart of the believing sinner. When the love of God revealed in the gospel is known and believed with application, it melts down the obdurate heart into penitential sorrow for sin; whereas the terrors of the law increase the power of indwelling sin and harden the heart against godly sorrow.

10. Last, the law, as it admits of boasting, is very different from the gospel. "Where is boasting then?" asks

the Apostle Paul. "It is excluded. By what law? Of works? Nay, but by the law of faith" (Romans 3:27). By the law of faith here is meant the doctrine of faith: the doctrine of a sinner's justification only on the ground of the righteousness of Jesus Christ received by faith alone. This doctrine of faith leaves the sinner no room to boast, as if he had, by his own good qualities or works, entitled himself, either in whole or in part, to justification before God. But the law or covenant of works does not exclude, but when obedience is performed, admits of boasting in the creature. The gospel or doctrine of faith, on the other hand, admits of no boasting of one's own obedience. "He that glorieth, let him glory in the Lord" (1 Corinthians 1:31). "My soul," says the Psalmist, "shall make her boast in the Lord" (Psalm 34:2). The Apostle Paul says to the saints at Ephesus, "By grace ye are saved through faith; and that not of yourselves; it is the gift of God, not of works, lest any man should boast" (Ephesians 2:8–9). The man who is under the dominion of the law of works hopes that they will, in a greater or lesser degree, procure justification and eternal life for him; whereas he who is under the sanctifying influence of the grace of the gospel boasts only of the righteousness of his incarnate Redeemer (Isaiah 45:25; Galatians 6:14). According to the law of works, justification can only be by works of perfect and personal obedience, which admit of boasting; whereas, according to the gospel, justification can only be by faith, the only instrument of receiving Christ and His righteousness, which excludes boasting.

It may be proper here to remark that, although the law and the gospel comprehend the whole doctrine of Scripture, yet they are not to be distinguished by the books of Scripture, or by the Old Testament and the New. All that is contained in the books of the Old Testament is not to be considered as the doctrine of the law; neither is all that is found in the books of the New Testament to be viewed as the doctrine of the gospel. The law and the gospel are declared in each of them. In the Old Testament we find much of the gospel, and in the New we find much of the law. In many places, Moses and the Prophets publish the gospel; so that Jerome questioned whether he should call Isaiah a prophet or an evangelist. In many passages Christ and His apostles promulgate the law. For instance, Christ says, "He that doeth the will of My Father which is in heaven shall enter into the kingdom of heaven" (Matthew 7:21). "He that denieth Me before men shall be denied before the angels of God" (Luke 12:9). "He that believeth not the Son shall not see life, but the wrath of God abideth on him" (John 3:36). His apostles also say, "The law is not of faith, but the man who doeth them shall live in them" (Galatians 3:12).

"Whosoever shall keep the whole law, and yet offend in one point, he is guilty of all" (James 2:18). "The wrath of God is revealed from heaven against all ungodliness and unrighteousness of men" (Romans 1:18). These, and many other passages in the New Testament similar to them, contain the doctrine of the law. When a man is commanded, either in the Old Testament or in the New, to perform any work in order to secure him from temporal or eternal punishment, or to entitle him to a temporal or eternal reward, it is to be accounted the doctrine of the law. On the other hand, where the blessings of salvation are declared, offered, and promised freely, without any work to be performed by sinners as the proper condition of them, all such passages, whether in the Old Testament or in the New, contain the doctrine of the gospel.

While we thus distinguish aright between the law as a covenant and the gospel strictly taken, we should always take heed that we do not apply to ourselves the gospel where the law should be applied, nor the law where the gospel ought to be applied. If we are impenitent and secure and need to be convinced of our guiltiness and misery, we ought, for this purpose, to apply the law immediately to our consciences, and not the gospel. If, on the contrary, we are truly convinced of our sinfulness and misery, and are deeply sensible that we have no righteousness nor strength of our own, we should, for our relief and comfort, apply the offers and promises of the gospel to our consciences, and not the curses of the law. In the former case, we ought to apply the law as a covenant to our consciences in order to apply the gospel; in the latter, we should apply the gospel in order to be enabled to keep the law as a rule. When any question or doubt arises respecting our justification before God, the law (and works of the law) must be excluded and stand at a distance in order that grace, reigning through the righteousness of Jesus Christ to eternal life, may appear sovereign and free, and that the offer and promise of the gospel, as well as the faith of the believer, may, in that momentous affair, stand alone. For although the believing sinner is not justified by a faith which is alone, yet he is justified by the instrumentality of faith alone, and that "without the works of the law" (Romans 3:28; Galatians 2:16). Faith justifies not as it is an act or work, for as such it is a work of the law, an act or work commanded in the law; but it justifies as it is the instrument or means of justification. In this instrumentality, no other grace of the Spirit, and no work of the law, are to be associated with it. Nor is it for its own intrinsic worth that a man is justified by the instrumentality of it; for he is nowhere said in Scripture to be justified *for* faith, but only to be justified *by* it.

From the preceding particulars, the following reflections will be obvious to the devout and intelligent reader:

Although the covenant of works revealed in the law and the covenant of grace exhibited in the gospel are different from one another, yet they are not contrary to each other. The one is not, strictly speaking, contrary to the other, but is only dissimilar to it or different from it. Whatever is required in the covenant of works as the condition of eternal life is, according to the covenant of grace, provided and given gratuitously to believing sinners. They who believe "receive abundance of grace and of the gift of righteousness, and so reign in life by one, Jesus Christ" (Romans 5:17). If by one man's disobedience many were made sinners according to the first covenant, "by the obedience of One shall many be made righteous," according to the second (Romans 5:19). In the former, eternal life is promised to a man on condition of a perfect righteousness to be fulfilled by himself; in the latter, it is promised to a believer on condition of the infinitely perfect righteousness of Jesus Christ, received by faith and imputed by God (Romans 8:3).

In the affair of justification, the law as a covenant of

works is not only to be distinguished, but to be separated from the gospel. When a true believer is at any time in doubt of his justification and title to eternal life, he ought to set the law as a covenant, and the works of that law, entirely aside, and to rely anew, for all his title to life eternal, on the spotless righteousness of the second Adam offered to him in the gospel. He ought in that case to contemplate only the free and super-abounding grace of the gospel, and to embrace, by the renewed exercise of an appropriating faith, the gracious offers and promises of it. He should exclude from his view the law and all legal righteousness, and, relying only on the righteousness of Christ revealed in the gospel, he should trust that this glorious, this consummate righteousness alone gives him a complete title to justification and eternal life. As it is not by the law, nor the works of the law, but by means of faith only, applying the righteousness brought near in the gospel, that a man is justified before God; so in the business of his justification he must set aside all works of the law and depend wholly on the righteousness and grace of the great Redeemer. While in the business of sanctification the law as a rule is to be connected with the gospel, in that of justification the law as a covenant is always to be separated from it.

None can successfully minister true consolation to a discouraged and disconsolate believer without teaching him to distinguish, in his own case, between the law and the gospel. If the exercised Christian cannot distinguish aright between them, the consequence will be that he will often hang in anxious suspense between hope and fear. The legal temper that remains in him, availing itself of his indistinct views, will frequently prompt him to ground his hope and comfort not on the righteousness of Christ and the promises of God only, but partly on these, and partly on his own endeavors to keep the law. Hence it cannot but follow that the sins of his nature and life will often afford him greater cause to fear than his attainments and duties will to hope. Every fresh discovery of the evils of his heart, and of the sin which cleaves to that obedience on which his hope and comfort, in a great measure, are founded will disquiet and perplex his soul. Thus, he will remain a stranger to settled comfort, and to habitual cheerfulness of spirit, in the performance of his duty. But if he is taught to distinguish aright between the law and the gospel, he will, on almost every occasion, flee from the law of works to the righteousness of Christ granted to him in the gospel, and make this the sole ground of all his hope. He will rely, with settled and strong confidence, on the Lord Jesus, for righteousness to justify and for grace to sanctify him.

Hence we may also be enabled to discern when we are self-righteous and servile in the performance of our duties. We evidently are so when, instead of being constrained to obedience by the astonishing love of Christ manifested in the gospel, we are either driven to it by the slavish fear of hell or dragged to it by the mercenary hope of heaven; when we obey God not with filial affection and fear of dishonoring Him, but with slavish dread of His vindictive justice and wrath; when we labor to obey in order that our obedience may afford us a right either to salvation itself or to the Savior, either to the favor of God or to the promises of the gospel. Our manner of performing our duties is legal when we ground our comfort on any thing wrought in us or done by us, and when our hope of salvation rises by the liveliness of our frame in performing duties, and not by the righteousness of Christ in the offers, or by the grace and faithfulness of God in the promises of the gospel.

What has been advanced may serve likewise to show us the exceeding sinfulness, the horrible malignity, of a self-righteous temper. It strives to thwart the infinitely great and gracious design of God in giving His only begotten Son for us. The grand design of God in the inestimable gift of His dear Son to obey and suffer for us is to display in our redemption the transcendant glory of all His perfections, and especially of the exceeding riches of His grace (Ephesians 2:4–9). Hence the glorious gospel is called "the word of His grace" (Acts 20:32). Now the legalist presumes to cross or counteract that glorious design of God as a God of grace. He would have the glory of self displayed, and not the glory of God, in the person and work of Jesus Christ; the honor of his own righteousness manifested instead of the glory of the divine Redeemer's righteousness; the luster of his own good qualities discovered in opposition to the glory of redeeming grace. The gracious intention of the Son of God in assuming the human nature was that He might fulfill all righteousness for the elect of God, in order that grace— free, sovereign, distinguishing grace—might reign through His righteousness unto eternal life for them (Romans 5:21). On the contrary, the intention of the legalist is to establish his own righteousness in the affair of justification, and so to frustrate the design of Christ; for "if righteousness comes by the law, then Christ is dead in vain" (Galatians 2:21). Thus the self-

righteous formalist resolutely sets himself in hostile
opposition to the glory of redeeming grace; and so he
attempts to rob the Most High of His transcendant
glory as a God of grace. No man exercises evangelical
repentance even in the smallest degree but he who re-
pents of this diabolical enmity and opposition of his
heart to "the glory of God in the face of Jesus Christ."
And none has ever begun to mortify the members of
the body of sin in his heart except he who is mortifying
this self-righteous temper. Unbelief and a legal spirit,
are the very soul or life of the body of sin. From
1 Corinthians 15:56, Mr. Ralph Erskine infers, "The
dangerous influences of legal doctrine tends to keep
sinners under the law; for thus they are under the
power of sin. The text says, 'The strength of sin is the
law.' The legal strain, under covert of zeal for the law,
has a native tendency to mar true holiness and all acceptable obedience to the law; insomuch that the
greatest legalist is the greatest antinomian, or enemy to
the law." Unless the mortification of sin, therefore, begins in them, it cannot penetrate the whole body of
sin.

Chapter 8

The Agreement Between the Law and the Gospel

As the law in its covenant form and the gospel in its proper and strict sense are not contrary to one another, but only different from each other, so while they differ in some respects they agree in others. As the infinitely glorious attributes of Jehovah harmonize and mingle their refulgent beams in the redemption of sinners by Jesus Christ, so His holy law and His glorious gospel agree and subserve the honor of each other in the accomplishment of that redemption.

By the harmony of the law and the gospel is meant their mutual subservience to one another, or their admirable fitness for securing and advancing the honor of each other in subordination to the glory of God, Father, Son, and Holy Spirit, as displayed in the person and work of the great Redeemer. They are admirably adapted to reflect mutual honor on one another, and so to afford the most illustrious displays of the glory of their divine Author. The law, as a covenant of works and a rule of life, demands nothing of sinners but what is offered and promised in the gospel; and in the gospel everything is freely promised and offered to them which the law, in any of its forms, requires of them. The gospel presents to them for their acceptance the consummate righteousness of Jesus Christ, the Surety of such sinners as believe, which fully answers every demand of the law in its covenant form, and so magnifies it in that form and makes it honorable. It also exhibits to them, in its offers and promises, the infinite fullness of Christ from which they may be regenerated and sanctified, and so be enabled to yield such obedience to the law as a rule of life as will in due time become perfect. While it reveals and offers righteousness to satisfy the law as a covenant, it promises and offers strength to obey the law as a rule. It promises all the supplies of grace and strength which are necessary for the acceptable performance of every duty that the law as a rule of life, requires of believers. The righteousness, too, which the law as a covenant demands, and which the gospel affords, being imputed to believers, merits for them that holiness of heart and life which the law as a rule requires, which the gospel promises, and which is perfect in parts here and will be perfect in degrees hereafter. Thus, in general, the law and the gospel agree together or mutually subserve each other.

But more particularly, the law as a covenant of works agrees with the gospel:

1. In its commanding power. Though it is altogether distinct from the gospel strictly taken, yet it is in concord with it. When a man cordially believes the gospel, he, in effect, presents perfect obedience to the commands of the law as a covenant. When he so believes as to receive the gift of righteousness, that perfect, that divinely excellent, righteousness of the last Adam, he presents it in the hand of faith as his only righteousness for justification to the law and the justice of God; and so he cannot believe with the heart without believing unto righteousness. He cannot cordially

believe the gospel without presenting, at the same time, perfect obedience to the law. Neither is it possible for him to yield perfect obedience to the law otherwise than by believing the gospel. Thus the law and the gospel unite in serving the interests of each other, although they are entirely distinct from each other. Although they are entirely distinct from each other, yet they have no separate, no interfering interest to serve. "Do we then make void the law through faith?" asks the Apostle Paul. "God forbid: yea, we establish the law" (Romans 3:31). The precepts of the law and the promises of the gospel harmoniously accord to reflect the highest honor on each other. "Is the law," asks our apostle, "against the promises of God? God forbid; for if there had been a law given which could have given life, verily righteousness should have been by the law" (Galatians 3:21). Does the law require from the sinner a perfect human righteousness (Romans 10:5)? The gospel affords this to it, yea, much more than this—a righteousness which is not only perfect, but divine (Romans 3:21). Are the commandments of the law "exceeding broad?" So is the righteousness of God our Savior revealed in the gospel. Whatever the law requires, the gospel, in the most abundant measure, supplies. Moreover, does the law command the sinner to believe in the great Redeemer (Exodus 20:3)? From the promise of the gospel he may be amply supplied with faith (Matthew 12:21). Does it enjoin him to repent of all his sins? The grace revealed and offered in the gospel can afford him not only an occasion and a powerful motive, but a disposition to "remember and turn to the Lord" (Psalm 22:27). While the law commands the tears of penitential sorrow to flow; the

gospel, and the astonishing grace promised and offered in it, *cause* them to flow (Zechariah 12:10). The
authority of the law reaches to every article of the glad
tidings of the gospel, and obliges the sinner to believe
these joyful tidings cordially and with application to
himself (1 John 3:23). The law seals all the grace offered in the gospel, and the gospel, in its turn, seals,
with the infinitely precious blood of Christ, all the requirements of the law. In a word, if the law requires
perfect and perpetual obedience as the condition of
eternal life, the gospel admits and asserts the necessity
of such obedience by affording it to the believing sinner (Daniel 9:24).

2. The law in its condemning power is also in concord with the gospel. The terrors of the violated law
serve, under the illuminating grace of the Holy Spirit,
to show a convinced sinner his extreme need of the
salvation which is presented to him in the gospel
(Galatians 3:10). The tremendous curses of the righteous law pursue him closely, whatever path he chooses
to take, until he begins to run upon gospel-ground,
and then they drop the pursuit. If the law as a covenant
is a fiery law, the blood of Jesus Christ presented in the
gospel, in one view, is fuel for that flame, and in another, it serves to extinguish it. The payment of the
sinner's debt of punishment by his divine Surety, offered to him in the gospel, is so complete as abundantly to answer the high demand made by the broken
law (Galatians 3:13). The law's demand of satisfaction
for sin is such that none but God Himself could, in a
limited time, answer it; and the infinite grace of the
gospel has provided that God Himself in human nature should satisfy it. " 'Awake, O sword, against my

Shepherd, and against the man that is my Fellow,' saith the Lord of hosts. Smite the Shepherd" (Zechariah 13:7). The law, on the one hand, condemns all who reject the gospel (John 3:18), and the gospel, on the other, disfavors all who finally transgress the law. The terrors of the law frighten and impel convinced sinners to Jesus Christ; and the redeeming love manifested in the gospel constrains and draws them to Him (Hosea 11:4). The former lay open the wound, and the latter applies a sovereign cure. Those plow up the fallow ground, and this sows the good seed in it.

3. The law, in its commanding and condemning power considered jointly, is in harmony with the gospel. The law leads the sinner indirectly to Christ, and the gospel conducts him directly to Him. While "the law is our schoolmaster unto Christ" to teach us our absolute need of Him, and if necessary to drive us as with a scourge to Him (Galatians 3:24), the gospel presents Christ as "the end of the law for righteousness to everyone who believeth" (Romans 10:4). The law in the hand of the Holy Spirit serves to make the awakened sinner long for and relish the grace of the gospel; and the gospel dignifies the law, and renders it illustrious in his view. The law magnifies the grace of the gospel by showing the sinner his need of justification and salvation by that grace; and the grace of the gospel establishes and magnifies the law (Isaiah 42:21). That the law is holy in its precepts, just in its threatenings, and good in its promises (Romans 7:12) the gospel not only declares, but seals with the blood of the incarnate Redeemer. While the precepts and penalties of the law serve as a guard to the gospel, the doctrines, promises, and offers of the gospel serve to support the authority

and honor of the law (Matthew 5:17). In Christ Jesus,
the precepts and threatenings of the law have, to everyone who believes, their end; and the promises of
the gospel, their establishment, in order to be completely performed (2 Corinthians 1:20). The truth or
faithfulness pledged in the threatenings of the law, and
the mercy revealed in the promises of the gospel, meet
together in Him. The righteousness manifested in the
law and the peace proclaimed in the gospel in Him
embrace each other (Psalm 85:10). The law in the
hand of the Spirit renders the grace of the gospel precious and desirable in the eyes of convinced sinners;
and this grace, when it is received, makes the law salu-
tary and pleasing to them (Romans 7:22). The law is an
awful commentary on the doctrines of the gospel, especially on these: the astonishing love of God manifested in our redemption, the infinite value of the ran-
som paid for us, the inexpressible felicity of them who
are redeemed from the curse of the law, and their infinite obligations to their God and Savior. And the
gospel is a delightful commentary on the high demands and sanctions of the law. While the law is an infallible witness that sinners of mankind have those dis-
graceful characters under which the offers and calls of
the gospel are addressed to them, the gospel exhibits
in the wonderful person and work of Christ the highest
proofs of the infinite authority and perpetual stability
of the law. In few words, though the law does not reveal a Savior and a justifying righteousness, yet these
having been revealed by the gospel, the law charges,
and that on pain of the greatest condemnation, every
hearer of the gospel to receive them (Mark 16:15–16).
To such an infinite degree is the consummate righ-

teousness of Jesus Christ the fulfilment of the law and the glory of the gospel; that sinners of mankind are peremptorily commanded in the law, and earnestly invited in the gospel, to accept the gift of it, and to present it in the hand of faith to the law in answer to its high demand of infinite satisfaction for sin, and of perfect obedience as the condition of eternal life. Thus the law, as it is the covenant of works, is in harmony with the gospel.

The law, likewise, as a rule of life to believers agrees with the gospel. When the law as a covenant presses a man forward, or shuts him up to the faith of the gospel; the gospel urges and draws him back to the law as a rule (Leviticus 11:44). The law is his schoolmaster to teach him his need of the grace of the gospel; and this grace will have his heart and his life regulated by no rule but the law (2 Peter 1:15–16). Nothing is gospel-obedience but obedience to the law in the hand of Christ as a rule of duty. The gospel is no sooner believed than obedience is yielded, both to the law as a covenant and to the law as a rule. The righteousness of Christ in the hand of faith is obedience to it in the former view, and personal holiness of heart and life to it in the latter. If the law commands believers, the grace of the gospel teaches them to love, and to practice universal holiness (Titus 2:11–12). What the law as a rule of life binds them to perform, the grace of the gospel constrains and enables them to do (Leviticus 20:8; 2 Corinthians 5:14–15). That which the precept of the law requires as a duty, the promise of the gospel affords and effects as a privilege (Ezekiel 18:31 and 36:26–27). Whatever holds the place of duty in the law occupies the place of privilege in the gospel. Duties required in the law are graces or exercises of grace in the language of the gospel. The commands of the law reprove believers for going wrong, and the promises of the gospel, so far as they are embraced, secure their walking in the right way (Jeremiah 32:40). The former show them the extreme folly of backsliding; the latter are means of healing their backslidings and restoring their souls (Psalm 23:3). The gospel, or word of Christ, dwells richly in none but in such as have the law of Christ put into their minds and written on their hearts. The law cannot be inscribed on the heart without the gospel, nor the gospel without the law. As they are found together in the same divine revelation, so they dwell together harmoniously in the same believing soul. So great is the harmony between them that they can reside nowhere separate from each other. While the precepts of the law show the redeemed how very grateful and thankful they should be for redeeming grace, the grace of Christ in the gospel produces and excites that adoring gratitude. The law enjoins and excites believers to receive daily by faith more and more of the grace of the gospel to qualify them for more spiritual and lively obedience to its precepts; and the gospel supplies them with every motive, preparative, assistance, and encouragement requisite for such obedience.

The law requires true holiness of heart and of life, and the gospel promises and conveys this holiness. The former shows the nature and the properties of it; the latter, the place of it in the covenant of grace. It is by the almighty influence of the gospel in the hand of the Holy Spirit that the law is inscribed on the hearts of believers; and it is in consequence of having the law written on their hearts that they desire, trust in Christ for, and relish, the blessings promised in the gospel. The law reveals to believers their duty, and the gospel reveals the object of duty. The law enjoins the habit and exercise of faith; the gospel presents Christ, the glorious object of faith. The law requires believers to love God with all their heart; but it is the gospel only that presents God in such a view as to become an object of love to a sinner, namely as He is in Christ reconciling the world unto Himself. The law enjoins mourning for sin; the gospel presents Christ as wounded for our transgressions. When believers view Christ with the eye of faith, they mourn for Him as for an only son, and are in bitterness for Him as for a first born. In a word, the law commands them to worship God as their God; the gospel discloses to them both the object and the way of acceptable worship.

Here it will be proper to remark that these words, "I am the Lord thy God, which have brought thee out of the land of Egypt, out of the house of bondage," are the preface to the Ten Commandments as a rule of life to the true Israel of God. According to these words, all the obedience of the redeemed of the Lord to the precepts of His law is founded upon His being Jehovah, their God and Redeemer. And it is remarkable that in the giving of the law at Sinai this offer or grant of Himself as Jehovah, our God and Redeemer, is five times repeated. But in these words of our redeeming God, it is the doctrine and offer of His gospel that are expressed and repeated, and that in order to enforce our obedience to every commandment of His law. The gospel, then, is that which enforces and also insures the sincere obedience of believers to the law as a rule

of life. It is because God is the Lord and their God and
Redeemer not only in offer, but in possession, that
they are enabled and constrained as well as bound to
keep all His commandments (Luke 1:74–75).

So much for the agreement between the law and
the gospel, or the mutual subservience of the one to
the other.

From the foregoing particulars, it may be inferred
that a man cannot be an enemy to the gospel without
being, at the same time, an enemy to the law. Every
enemy to the gospel is, in the same degree, an enemy
to the perfection, spirituality, and honor of the law.
The law and the gospel are in such harmony with each
other as to have no divided interests. The man, then,
who is destitute of unfeigned love to the doctrines, offers, and promises of the gospel, however strict his profession of religion may be, is really an antinomian, an
enemy to the honor of the holy law. He is an adversary
to the honor of the law as a covenant of works: for by
rejecting the spotless righteousness of Jesus Christ tendered to him in the gospel he refuses to present to the
law in that form the only righteousness by which it can
be magnified and made honorable. He is an enemy
likewise to the authority and honor of the law as a rule
of duty; for by his disbelief of the offers and promises
of the blessed gospel he refuses to receive from the
fullness of Christ that grace without which he cannot
honor the law with so much as a single act of acceptable obedience.

Hence also we may learn that, as the law is a transcript of all the moral perfections of God, so likewise is
the gospel. The law is the image of the holiness, justice, and goodness of Jehovah, and therefore it is holy

and just and good; but so also is the gospel. Accordingly, the gospel is called "the glorious gospel of the blessed God" (1 Timothy 1:11). The glory of the holiness, justice, and goodness of God, as well as of His wisdom and faithfulness, shines brightly in the law; but it is displayed still more illustriously, in the gospel. These glorious attributes are delineated in the law, but in the gospel they are painted in the most glowing colors. Much of God is to be seen in the law, but in the gospel His infinitely glorious image, is exhibited more to the life, and is more eminently conspicuous (2 Corinthians 3:18). The honor of His holy law, therefore, and also of His glorious gospel, is infinitely dear to Him. He takes infinite complacency in beholding His righteous law magnified and made honorable by the surety-righteousness of His dear Son, and in seeing a multitude which no man can number justified and sanctified according to His gospel. And all who are renewed after His image in knowledge, righteousness, and true holiness evidence this renovation of heart by delighting in His law and by loving and admiring His gospel; by rejoicing greatly in imputed righteousness by which the demands of His law as a covenant are all answered, and in salvation by sovereign grace in which the promises of His gospel are all performed.

If a man has attained a saving and experimental knowledge of the gospel, he will undoubtedly evidence it by obedience of heart and life to the law in the hand of Christ as a rule of duty. A man can never perform holy obedience to the law as long as he remains ignorant of the gospel; but when he begins spiritually to discern the truth, suitableness, and glory of the doctrine of redeeming grace, he will then begin to perform spiritual and sincere obedience to the law of Christ as a rule. "Christ died for all" who were given Him by the Father "that they which live should not henceforth live unto themselves, but unto Him which died for them, and rose again" (2 Corinthians 5:15). When a man spiritually discerns and sincerely loves the grace of the gospel, at the same time he sees and loves the holiness of the law. The consequence will be that he will sincerely and cheerfully obey the law. He will yield this obedience not only because the authority of God obliges him and the love of Christ constrains him, but because he discerns the beauty of the holiness that is in the law itself, and loves it. While the law as a covenant is the appointed means of convincing the secure sinner of his need of that justifying righteousness which is offered to him in the gospel, the gospel, bringing righteousness and salvation to him, is the instituted means of conciliating his affection to the law as a rule of duty. Everyone, then, who knows by experience the boundless grace of the gospel will perform sincere, cheerful, and constant obedience to the law as a rule.

Is everything that is required in the law provided and promised in the gospel? Then every duty is, at the same time, a privilege or advantage to a real Christian. "Godliness with contentment is great gain" (1 Timothy 6:6). Practical godliness is the most profitable, pleasant, satisfying, and permanent gain, both for this world and that which is to come. A true believer is, in proportion as he is sanctified, rich in faith and in good works. Although the exercise of graces and the performance of duties gain nothing at the hand of God for the believer, yet they themselves are unspeakably great gain to him. He accounts it a privilege and a pleasure to have duties to perform, and to have a disposition given him to perform them to the glory of his God and Savior. For as there can be no happiness without holiness, so the believer is comfortable and happy in proportion as he is holy. The more he believes the gospel with application, and trusts cordially in the Lord Jesus for salvation to himself in particular, and the more his faith works by love, so much the more communion with Christ and enjoyment of God as his infinite portion he attains. The legalist expects happiness for his duties, but the true believer enjoys it in them; and the less he expects for them, the more he enjoys in them.

Finally, do the law and the gospel harmoniously agree and subserve the honor of each other? Then let believers always take heed that they do not set them in opposition to one another. Beware, O believer, of ever setting the law in hostile opposition to the gospel, or the gospel in opposition to the law. Never, in your exercise of graces or performance of duties, set them at variance one against the other. Study to understand clearly, on the one hand, the difference, and on the other the agreement between them; that knowing distinctly in what respects they differ, and in what they agree, you may, in your exercise, make the one subservient to the honor of the other, and both subservient to the glory of God in your sanctification and consolation. Clear and just views, especially of the agreement between the law and the gospel, tend exceedingly, under the influences of the Spirit of truth, to promote an evangelical, holy, and cheerful frame of spirit. Under such views, you will be able to guard

more effectually against setting the law in opposition
to the gospel by relying on your own graces and duties
for a right to the favor and enjoyment of God, and
against setting the gospel at variance with the law by
taking the smallest encouragement from the gospel to
neglect the performance of any of the duties required
in the law.

Chapter 9

The Establishment of the Law by the Gospel

Although in the preceding chapter I have antici-
pated some of the thoughts which will be expressed
here, yet the subject of this chapter is of such inexpressible importance that I cannot forbear considering
it by itself. After the Apostle Paul had, in the third
chapter of his epistle to the Romans, asserted and
proved that all mankind are sinners, and that the justification of believing sinners in the sight of God is utterly unattainable by their own righteousness, and is
entirely founded on the surety-righteousness of Jesus
Christ, imputed by grace and received by faith; he has
in the following words obviated an objection which he
foresaw would be made to that fundamental doctrine:
"Do we then make void the law through faith? God
forbid; yea, we establish the law" (Romans 3:31). One
of the objections then made, and still urged, by the
enemies of the gospel against the doctrine of a sinner's
free justification for the righteousness of Christ received by faith is that it derogates from the honor and
obligation of the law, nay, that it annuls or abrogates
the law. "Do we then," says he, by asserting that a man
is justified by faith only, and not by the works of the
law, "make void," or nullify the obligation of the moral
law? With deep abhorrence of such an insinuation, he
replies, "God forbid"; far be it from us; on the contrary, we, by that doctrine, "do establish the law."

It is as if he had said, "We are so far from making
void or annulling the law through faith that we thereby
establish and make it stand in all its force." By the law
here, the apostle cannot mean the ceremonial law; for
by the word of faith as preached by the apostles of
Christ this was made void, but the moral law, and that
both as a covenant of works and as a rule of life. By
faith, in this place, the apostle seems to mean both the
doctrine of faith and the grace of faith. The doctrine
of faith is the gospel strictly taken as distinguished
from the law. The grace of faith is that grace of the
Holy Spirit in the hearts of regenerate persons by the
exercise of which they receive that doctrine, and the
righteousness and salvation exhibited in it.

It will be proper here, in order to prevent mistakes
concerning what is afterwards to be advanced, to remark that to make the law void is so to abrogate, abolish, or set it aside as to prevent it from being any
longer binding on the conscience. It is to annul the divine authority and obligation of its precepts and penalties. The moral law, as the law of the infinitely glorious
Jehovah, is enforced by all His sovereign and immutable authority. His infinite authority enforces every
precept of it, and lays every rational creature under the
firmest obligations possible to yield perfect obedience
to it. Now to make this law void is to set aside its high
authority and obligation, or to decline the authority
and dissolve the obligation of its righteous precepts.
Not that any man can do this effectually, but his attempting either directly or indirectly to do it is as criminal as if he could accomplish his design. To make it
void is also to attempt setting aside the perfection, spirituality, and great extent of it. A man may be said to

make void the law when he practically declares that the perfection, spirituality, and vast extent of it are not to be regarded, or when he puts it off as a covenant with imperfect and even with carnal, selfish, superficial, and partial obedience. Every sinner is guilty of this who goes about to establish his own righteousness in order to his justification; or endeavors to satisfy the law with imperfect instead of perfect obedience; with carnal instead of spiritual performances, and with partial instead of universal obedience.

To make the law void is likewise to invalidate the perpetuity of it. Not that any sinner has it in his power effectually to do this—for the moral law continues to be of immutable and eternal obligation upon all who are under it—but he attempts to abolish the perpetuity of it, with respect to himself, by persuading himself that although it originally obliged him to perform perfect obedience, yet now, in consequence of the mediation of Christ, it obliges him to yield such obedience no longer (Jude 4), and by presuming to satisfy the requirements of it as a covenant with sincere instead of perfect obedience, as if it ceased to require perfection of obedience any longer. Moreover, when sinners under the curse of it labor to persuade themselves that it cannot now exact from them perfect and perpetual obedience on pain of its tremendous curse, or when they stifle their convictions and try to keep their consciences easy under the condemning sentence of it, they do what they can to make it void. In few words, they may be said to make the law void when they deliberately set aside any of the uses of it. Though it cannot, since the entrance of sin into the world, justify sinners on the ground of their own obedience to it, yet, as was observed above, it is of standing use to sinners as well as to saints. Now if sinners set aside any of its uses, or refuse to "use it lawfully," they thereby treat it with contempt, as if it was useless and insignificant. It is in these ways especially that self-righteous men attempt to make void the law of God.

I shall now endeavor to show that all true believers, through faith, not only do not make void the moral law, but on the contrary establish it or make it stand in all its force. To establish the law is, as was hinted above, to make all the infinite authority and obligation of it stand firm, or to place them on their original and immovable basis, and instead of invalidating to confirm or strengthen them. Believers, then, by faith, that is, by the doctrine and the grace of faith, establish the law.

In the first place, by the doctrine of faith, they do not make the law void, but establish it, and that both as a covenant of works and as a rule of life.

1. By the doctrine of faith, or the gospel strictly taken, all true believers and faithful ministers of the Word, establish the law as it is a covenant of works. For, in the first place, it is the doctrine of faith that shows men how firm and irreversible the law as a covenant is, and how infinitely concerned the glorious Majesty of heaven is for the stability and honor of that holy law. According to that doctrine, He will save no transgressors of it but upon condition of His only begotten Son's being their Surety, and of His answering completely all the demands of it in their stead. He will not save them from the full execution of its righteous and awful penalty but upon Christ's enduring it for them, nor account them righteous and entitled to eternal life but upon His performing as their substitute the perfect

obedience which it requires as the condition of life. Thus, by the doctrine of faith, the sovereign authority of the law in its covenant form is acknowledged and declared; its infinite obligation on sinners of mankind is confirmed; and its honor is completely secured.

Second, according to the doctrines of grace in general, and to the doctrine of a sinner's justification by faith without the works of the law in particular, the law in that form is, as has been already said, of standing use to convince sinners of their sin and misery, to discover to them their need of a better righteousness than their own, and so to render Christ and His perfect righteousness precious to such as believe. A sinner must be convinced by the law that justification on the footing of his own obedience is absolutely impossible before he will listen to what the gospel says of Christ and His righteousness (Romans 7:9). Accordingly, the Spirit of God does not lead a man to Christ by the gospel without first convincing him of sin and of his want of righteousness by the law.

Third, by that doctrine we are informed that the law received a complete answer to all its high demands by the unsinning obedience and satisfactory death of the Lord Jesus, the Surety of elect sinners. We are thereby instructed that He came into the world "not to destroy, but to fulfil the law" (Matthew 5:17), and that He "is the end of the law for righteousness to everyone that believeth" (Romans 10:4). According to the doctrine of faith, the law as a covenant receives from our divine Surety all the obedience and satisfaction which it can demand. He, in the room, and as the representative of an elect world, fulfilled all the righteousness of it (Matthew 3:15). He yielded to it perfect holiness of human nature, perfect obedience of life, and complete satisfaction for sin; and from His divine nature, united to the human in His infinitely glorious person, His whole righteousness has derived such infinite value as to be strictly meritorious of eternal life for His spiritual seed. According to that doctrine, the law in its federal form is far more honored by the righteousness of the second Adam than it was dishonored by the disobedience of the first. It is represented as honored not only by a perfect righteousness, but by the righteousness of God, the righteousness of Him who is God as well as man. In proportion to the stupendous humiliation of the Son of God, who stooped so low as to become subject to a law which was adapted only to creatures who as such are infinitely beneath Him, is the honor done to the precept and penalty of that law by His obeying the one and His enduring the other. It required only a human righteousness, but it is infinitely honored with one which is divine (2 Corinthians 5:21; Isaiah 42:21). Now by this consummate, transcendently-glorious righteousness which is revealed in the gospel, the sovereign authority and high obligation of the law are most illustriously displayed and most firmly established.

2. By the doctrine of faith, the law is also established as rule of life to believers. According to this doctrine, it is established in the hand of the Son of God, the glorious Mediator, whom the eternal Father "hath given for a Commander to the people" (Isaiah 55:4), and has set as His King and Lawgiver "upon His holy hill of Zion" (Psalm 2:6). In the hand of the adorable Mediator, the sovereign authority of the law, as the instrument of government in his spiritual kingdom and as the rule of duty in His holy covenant, is confirmed;

and the high obligation of it is not only confirmed, but increased. Although believers are, in their justification, delivered from the law as a covenant of works (Romans 7:4–6), yet according to the gospel they are represented as "being not without law to God, but under the law to Christ" (1 Corinthians 9:21; Galatians 6:2). In the doctrine of faith, the eternal obligation of the law on them is declared; obedience to it is enforced by the strongest motives, and represented as performed under the best influences, from the best principles, and for the best ends. According to that doctrine, all believers are bound by infinite authority to obey; they are enabled sincerely to obey; they are constrained by redeeming love to obey; they resolve and delight in dependance on promised grace, to obey; and they cannot but obey the law as a rule of duty. The love of Christ, as revealed in the gospel, urges them; the blood of Christ redeems them; the Spirit of Christ enables them; and the exceeding great and precious promises of Christ encourage them to obey and yield spiritual and acceptable obedience. The holy law as a rule is written on their hearts, and therefore they consent unto it that it is good, and delight in it after the inward man. While they do not obey it for life, but from life, they account obedience to it not only their duty, but their privilege and their pleasure. Thus, according to the doctrine of faith, they present, in the hand of faith, perfect righteousness to the law as a covenant of works; and they perform, as the fruit of faith, sincere obedience to it as a rule of duty. And so effectually do they, by the doctrine of faith establish the law as a rule of duty that they never account their obedience to any of the precepts of it sincere and acceptable but in proportion as their performance of it flows from the unfeigned faith of that doctrine. In their view, nothing is obedience to it but what proceeds from evangelical principles, and is excited by evangelical motives.

In the last place, by the grace of faith also, believers establish the law, and that both as a covenant of works and as a rule of life.

1. By the grace of faith, they do not make void the law, but on the contrary they establish it as it is a covenant of works. Sinners who are destitute of the grace of faith have such mean, disparaging notions of the holy law as to offer to it, in answer to its demand of perfect obedience as the condition of life, with their own partial, superficial, and polluted works instead of the perfect righteousness of Jesus Christ. But true believers have such high and honorable sentiments of the authority and obligation, as well as of the perfection, spirituality, and vast extent, of the divine law in its federal form, as to receive and present, in the hand of faith, to it the consummate and glorious righteousness of their adorable Surety. Instead of making void the law, they, by the habit and exercise of their holy faith, consult in the most effectual manner the stability and honor of its precepts and penalties. Instead of presuming to put it off as a covenant with their own mean and imperfect performances, they, by the exercise of their faith, appropriate and present to it the infinitely perfect and meritorious righteousness of their divine Redeemer as the only ground of their security from eternal death, and of their title to eternal life. By faith they receive and exhibit to it Christ's holiness of human nature and obedience of life in answer to its demand of perfect obedience as the condition of life, and

His suffering of death in answer to its demand of infinite satisfaction for sin. Thus, by the habit and exercise of their faith, they recognize and assert the sovereign authority and high obligation of it as a covenant; and so they establish and make it honorable in that form. By presenting to it the only righteousness which can fully satisfy its just demands, they practically assert the divine and immutable authority of it as well as the equity and reasonableness of its demands. "Surely shall one say, 'In the Lord have I righteousness and strength; even to Him shall men come. In the Lord shall all the seed of Israel be justified, and shall glory' " (Isaiah 45:24–25). "I will make mention of Thy righteousness, even of Thine only" (Psalm 71:16). "Yea, doubtless, and I count all things but loss, for the excellency of the knowledge of Christ Jesus my Lord . . . that I may win Christ, and be found in Him, not having mine own righteousness, which is of the law, but that which is through the faith of Christ, the righteousness which is of God by faith" (Philippians 3:8–9). "The Lord is well pleased for His righteousness' sake; He will magnify the law and make it honorable" (Isaiah 42:21).

2. By the grace of faith, believers do not make void the law, but establish it likewise as a rule of life. Instead of setting it aside as the rule of duty, faith makes it stand in all its binding force. By the habit and exercise of their faith, the saints not only believe that the authority of the law in the hand of the glorious Mediator is infinite, immutable, and eternal, and that the obligation which it lays on them even to perfect obedience is firm and unalterable; but they derive from the fullness of Christ continual supplies of grace to enable them to perform sincere and increasing obedience to all the

commands of it. By the exercise of faith, they receive
from His fullness that conformity of heart to the holy
law, which is perfect in parts, and that conformity both
of heart and of life to it, which will afterwards be perfect in degrees. And when they shall attain perfect conformity, or ability to yield perfect obedience to it in the
mansions of glory, this they shall attain as the end of
their faith, as the completion of that eternal salvation
which they receive by faith. All acceptable obedience
to the law in the hand of Christ must be the obedience
of faith, obedience springing from vital union with
Him by faith as the principle of it, and performed in
consequence of grace derived by faith from His overflowing fullness. As it is believers, and they only, who
are under the law as a rule in the hand of the Mediator, so it is they, and they only, who are enabled to perform that sincere, holy obedience which flows from
faith working by love. That faith is neither a true nor a
living faith which is not accompanied with sincere and
universal obedience to the law of Christ; and that obedience is neither sincere, nor universal nor acceptable
to God which does not proceed from the habit and exercise of a living faith (Hebrews 11:6).

Till a man has saving faith implanted in his heart by
the omnipotent agency of the Holy Spirit, he can do
nothing but transgress the commandments of God's
holy law (Proverbs 21:4). He can trample upon the
authority and despise the obligation of it, but he
cannot, either in principle or in practice, establish it. It
is only they who are justified and sanctified by the
instrumentality of faith who begin and advance in such
holy obedience as honors and establishes the law as a
rule of duty. We may as soon suppose that a living man

can be without vital acts as that a man who is by faith vitally united to Christ can live without yielding such obedience to His law. When that living faith which works by love is implanted and increased in his heart, vital motions and acts of spiritual obedience cannot but follow. Such a man will not only account it a privilege and a pleasure to yield sincere obedience to the law as the rule of his duty in time, but will rejoice in the cheering prospect of being able to honor it with perfect obedience through eternity. He delights in it after the inward man, and therefore he rejoices in the hope that, by the grace of his adorable Redeemer, he shall be eternally bound *by* it and eternally conformed *to* it.

Thus it is evident that true believers and faithful ministers of the gospel do not, either by the doctrine or the grace of faith, make void the law of God; but on the contrary they establish it, and that both as a covenant of works and as a rule of life.

From what has been said, we may learn what reason we have highly to esteem the divine law. The establishment of this holy law, both by the doctrine and the grace of faith, has entered deeply, into the wonderful plan of our redemption by Jesus Christ. That amazing scheme has been so devised as to secure, in the most effectual and astonishing manner, the stability and honor of the law as well as the manifested glory of the sovereign Lawgiver. As the ultimate end which God has proposed to Himself in our redemption is the glory of His infinite perfections, so His chief subordinate end, as the righteous Governor of the universe, is the honor of His holy law. Such is the inestimable value that

Jehovah the Father sets upon His righteous law that, rather than suffer the honor of it to be in the least obscured, He would expose His only begotten, His infinitely dear Son, to the deepest abasement, the most direful anguish, and the most ignominious and tormenting death. He would have His only Son, in the human nature, to live a holy and righteous life, under the curse of His law—this was in order to answer its demand of perfect obedience as the condition of life— and to endure the infinite execution of that curse, due to His elect for sin, so as to be brought to the dust of death in order to answer its demand of infinite satisfaction for sin. The Lord Jesus, according to the everlasting covenant made with Him, must submit to all this humiliation, service, and suffering so that the honor of the divine law might be vindicated, and the sovereign authority of it established. Ought not we, then, to regard the law of God with the highest esteem and veneration, and to tremble at the most distant thought of ever disobeying any of its holy commands?

Is the law established by the gospel? Surely the gospel, then, cannot have the smallest tendency to licentiousness, either in principle or in practice. If it tends to establish the sovereign authority of the divine law it cannot, surely, at the same time, tend to weaken or set aside that authority. The gospel, when it is accompanied with the demonstration of the Spirit of God, and is received in the love of it, not only excites the believer to obey the law as a rule of duty, but it is the only doctrine that can excite and dispose him to yield to it voluntary and sincere obedience. It not only establishes the law, but it is the only doctrine that infinite wisdom employs to establish it, the only "doctrine, which is according to godliness." It is true that this heavenly doctrine which God has made the city of refuge for guilty sinners is, by many, alas, made a sanctuary for sin, and so is wickedly abused to licentiousness. But it is one thing to view the gospel in itself, and in its genuine tendency, and another to consider it as it is perversely abused by wicked men (Romans 3:8). The immediate principle of all acceptable obedience to the law as a rule of life is supreme love to God; but we cannot love God supremely unless we first know and believe His love to us as it is exhibited in the blessed gospel. "We love Him," says the Apostle John, "because He first loved us" (1 John 4:19). As the sun cannot be without light and heat, so the faith of Christ and of redeeming love as offered to us in the gospel, cannot be without that love to Christ and to God in Him which "is the fulfilling of the law" (Romans 13:10).

The second Adam's perfect holiness of human nature, and obedience of life to the precept of the law as a covenant, are as necessary to the justification of sinners as is His suffering of its penalty. The doctrine of justification by faith establishes the law, the whole law, the honor of the precept as well as that of the penal sanction. But this it could not do if it did not represent the righteousness of Jesus Christ as consisting in His active obedience as well as in His passive. Active obedience, strictly speaking, cannot be said to satisfy vindictive justice for sin. And, on the other hand, suffering for punishment gives right and title unto nothing, it only satisfies for something; nor does it deserve any reward, as John Owen mentions in his work on justification. Christ's satisfaction for sin could not render His perfect obedience to the precept unnecessary; nor could His perfect obedience make His satisfaction for sin by suffering the penalty unnecessary, because it was not of the same kind. The one is that which answers the law's demand of perfect obedience as the ground of title to eternal life; the other is that which answers its demand of complete satisfaction to divine justice for sin. The meritorious obedience of Christ to the precept could not satisfy the penal sanction; and the sufferings and death of Christ, could not satisfy the precept of the law. The commandment of the law as a covenant requires doing for life; the curse of that law demands dying as the punishment of sin. These, though they are never to be separated as grounds of justification, yet are carefully to be distinguished. The perfect obedience of Christ is as necessary to entitle believers to eternal life as His suffering of death is to secure them from eternal death. His satisfaction for sin, applied by faith, renders them innocent or guiltless of death; and His obedience makes them righteous or worthy of life (Romans 5:19). As the latter, then, is as necessary to complete their justification, according to the gospel, as the former, so it is as requisite as the former to establish the honor of the law.

It is evident also from the foregoing particulars that the righteousness of Christ which is revealed in the gospel, and which is presented in the hand of faith to the law as a covenant, is not only the meritorious cause, but the matter of our justification before God, and in the eye of the law. It is right, indeed, to call it the meritorious cause of justification; but this is not sufficient: it is also the matter of it. Many pharisaic professors of religion have admitted that the righteousness of Christ is the meritorious cause of justification; that is, as they understand the phrase, that Christ, by His righteousness, has merited that our own obedience should justify us. It is not enough, then, to say that His consummate righteousness is the meritorious cause, but also that it is the matter of our justification; the very righteousness for which, or on account of which, we are justified. The righteousness of our divine Surety, received by faith, and according to the doctrine of faith, imputed to us is that which justifies, that which is the immediate and the only ground of justification, and that only in which it can be safe, consistently with the authority and honor of the law, to stand before the dreadful tribunal of the omniscient and righteous Judge of the world.

The divine law is established and honored more in the salvation of one sinner than in the damnation of all the sons of men. In the justification and salvation of a believing sinner, both the precept and the penalty of the law are established and honored; but in the damnation of unbelievers it is the penal sanction only that is honored. The holy precept will never, in their case, be honored with obedience, far less with perfect obedience. The convinced and alarmed sinner who wishes to believe in the Lord Jesus may, for his encouragement, warrantably and successfully plead that at the throne of grace.

Is the holy law as a rule of life put into the reader's mind and written on his heart? Then it rejoices his heart. "The statues of the Lord are right, rejoicing the heart" (Psalm 19:8). The Apostle Paul accordingly says, "I delight in the law of God after the inward man" (Romans 7:22). When a man is justified and, as an evidence of that, is sanctified, he rejoices to think that the

law as a covenant is honored and established by the
righteousness which his faith receives for his justification, and that the law as a rule is established by the
grace which his faith derives from Christ for his sanctification. He rejoices to reflect that as the law is established forever, so it is holy, just, and good. Instead of
wishing that it were less extensive or spiritual or strict,
he rejoices that every command, and even every
threatening, are what they are. He meditates on the
holy commandments of God with delight, and takes
pleasure in hearing them explained to him and enforced upon him. Nothing, perhaps, is a surer symp-
tom of reigning hypocrisy in a man than to take pleasure in hearing the promises and blessings of the
gospel preached to him, but to disrelish all such dis-
courses as, even by evangelical motives, enforce the duties of the law upon him. It is only the man who is se-
cretly resolved not to perform all his duties who commonly is unwilling to hear of them.

What has been said may serve to suggest to us how
deep and inveterate the depravity of human nature is.
Unregenerate men either suspect that the law is made
void if it is asserted that a man is justified by faith without the works of it, or they suppose that good works
are unnecessary. The spirit which is in them is either
that of the pharisee or that of the libertine. They are
ready to conclude that, if they are not to be justified on
the ground of their own obedience to the law, the authority of the law is annulled (Galatians 3:19), or that,
if their works are to form no part of their righteousness
for justification, they need not perform good works at
all. They choose to be at liberty either to establish their
own righteousness in the affair of justification, or to

continue secure in the love and practice of sin; either to expect justification by the law as a covenant, or to trample upon the authority of the law as a rule. They either quarrel with the gospel, as if it made void the law, or dishonor the law, as if it was an enemy to the gospel. To leave the self-righteous man no works of his own to boast of is too humbling to be endured. It appears strange to him that he himself should do nothing to merit his justification. Whenever he reads or hears that justification is by faith only, without the deeds of the law, he is disposed to count it a licentious doctrine. He can see no necessity for his obedience but to merit divine favor and eternal life by it. And no sooner does a man, under the dominion of enmity to God and His law, pretend to be justified without his own works than he neglects good works, as if they were wholly unnecessary. Thus, unregenerate men reveal their inveterate enmity both against the law and the gospel of God.

Was it requisite that the Lord Jesus, in order to repair the honor of the law, should, as the Surety of elect sinners, endure the full execution of its condemning sentence due to them for sin? We may hence see what a malignant, detestable, and horrible thing sin is. How exceeding sinful, how infinitely displeasing to the Lord, and how injurious to the honor of His righteous law must it be, when even His own dear Son must suffer infinite punishment, and that without the smallest abatement, in order to satisfy His justice and vindicate the honor of His law! How inconceivably detestable must it be to the holy Lord God, seeing He chose rather that His only begotten Son should endure all the tremendous punishment of it than that it should pass unpunished! Should not we, then, learn to abhor, to repent of, and to forsake all manner of sin?

Is it by the doctrine and the grace of faith that we establish the law? Then it is plain that they who transform the gospel or doctrine of faith into a new law requiring faith, repentance, and sincere obedience as the proper conditions of salvation thereby make void the law. By substituting sincere faith and sincere obedience in place of perfect obedience as grounds of title to justification, they make void the law as a covenant; and by inventing what they call "gospel precepts," requiring sincerity only in place of those old and immutable precepts which require of believers perfect obedience, they invalidate the authority of the law as a rule. By asserting that Christ has satisfied for the breach of the old law of works, and has procured and given a new law, a remedial law, or a law of milder terms than the old, suited to our fallen state and accepting sincere obedience instead of that perfect obedience which the old law required; that Christ has, by His death, obtained that our sincere obedience to this remedial law should be accepted for a gospel righteousness, and that we are truly justified before God by gospel works. The act of faith as the principle of all sincere obedience is our righteousness, which entitles us to justification and eternal life. And the act of faith is our justifying righteousness not as it receives the righteousness of Jesus Christ, but as it is our obedience to that new law.

By these assertions, I say, they set aside the obligation of the moral law and so make it void. Though such men have usually been called "legalists," yet, perhaps, they may, with more propriety, be termed "antinomians," or "enemies to the authority and honor of the divine law (see Charles Simeon's *Helps to Composition*). They undermine, as was already hinted, the whole authority and honor of it, both as a covenant of works and as a rule of life. Reader, the moment you rely on your faith and obedience for a title to justification before God, you thereby rob the law as a covenant, both of its commanding and condemning power; and no sooner do you satisfy yourself with yielding merely sincere obedience, instead of pressing on to perfection, than you invalidate the high obligation of the law as a rule of duty.

Finally it may hence also be inferred that it is the first duty of every unregenerate sinner to come to Jesus Christ, and to trust cordially in Him for deliverance from the law as a covenant, and for ability to perform acceptable obedience to the law as a rule. Be assured, O secure sinner, that you cannot otherwise be delivered from the law as a covenant of works than by union with the second Adam, and communion with Him in His righteousness; and that without deliverance from the dominion of the law as a covenant you cannot be saved from the guilt and dominion of sin. "The strength of sin is the law" (1 Corinthians 15:56). Now it is absolutely impossible for you ever to attain union with Christ, and communion with Him in His righteousness, otherwise than by a true and living faith. "The righteousness of God," of Him who is God in our nature, "is by faith of Jesus Christ unto all and upon all them that believe" (Romans 3:22). Believe then in the Lord Jesus, that by means of faith you may be found in Him and be justified in Him. Trust in Him who is "Jehovah our Righteousness" for justification and

complete salvation. Receive the gift of His glorious
righteousness and, as a guilty sinner, rely upon it for all
your title to justification before God. Present it in the
hand of faith as your justifying righteousness, to the
law as a covenant of works in answer to its just demands of perfect obedience, and of complete satisfaction for sin. So shall you, by faith, establish the law as it
is a covenant of works.

Trust in Christ also for grace and strength to perform sincere obedience to the law as a rule of life. Rely
on His consummate righteousness for all your title to
sanctification and glorification; trust in Him with all
your heart for sufficient supplies of sanctifying and
comforting grace to enable you to yield acceptable
obedience to the law as a rule, and to press on toward
perfection of obedience. And by this obedience of
faith you will establish His law as a rule of duty. By well
doing, you will put to silence the ignorance of such
foolish men as presume to say that the doctrine and
faith of the gospel are unfriendly to the interests of
true morality.

This reminds me of what Theodorus long ago
replied to Philocles, who was often hinting that he
preached doctrines which tended to licentiousness because he enlarged diligently and frequently upon faith
in Jesus Christ: "I preach salvation by Jesus Christ," said
Theodorus; "and give me leave to ask, whether you
know what salvation by Christ means?" Philocles began
to blush, and would have declined an answer.

"No," said Theodorus, "you must permit me to in-
sist upon a reply. Because if it is a right one, it will justify me and my conduct; if it is a wrong one, it will
prove that you blame you know not what, and that you

have more reason to inform yourself than to censure others."

This disconcerted him still more, upon which Theodorus proceeded. "Salvation by Jesus Christ means not only a deliverance from the guilt, but also from the power of sin. 'He gave Himself for us, that He might redeem us from all iniquity and redeem us from our vain conversation,' as well as deliver us from the wrath to come. Go now, Philocles, and tell the world that, by teaching these doctrines, I promote the cause of licentiousness. And you will be just as rational, just as candid, just as true, as if you should affirm that the firemen, by running the engine and pouring in water, burnt your house to the ground, and laid your furniture in ashes."

Indeed, both the doctrine and the grace of faith, are evidently, yea, and designedly injurious to heathen morality as well as pharisaic righteousness. But with regard to true morality, which forms a necessary part of godliness or evangelical holiness, instead of being, in the smallest degree, injurious to this, they directly tend to it; yea, and they are the necessary, the fundamental principles of it. Sooner might fire be without heat, and a solid body be without weight, than a true faith of the gospel be without evangelical holiness.

Chapter 10

The Believer's Privilege of Being Dead to the Law
as a Covenant of Works, with a Highly
Important Consequence of It

The Apostle Paul, when speaking in his epistle to
the Romans of this important privilege, expresses himself thus: "Wherefore, my brethren, ye also are become
dead to the law by the body of Christ. . . But now we
are delivered from the law, that being dead wherein we
were held" (Romans 7:4, 6). By "the law," in these passages, our apostle evidently means not so much the
ceremonial as the moral law under the form of a
covenant of works. For it is the same law that says that a
man should not steal, and should not commit adultery
(Romans 2:21–22). It is also the law which "says to
them who are under it, what things soever it says; that
every mouth may be stopped, and all the world may
become guilty before God." It is also the law by which
"is the knowledge of sin," and which is not "made void
through faith," but on the contrary "is established"
(Romans 3:19–20, 31). It is the law, likewise, which
"entereth that the offence might abound" (Romans
5:20), and of which the apostle speaks thus: "When we
were in the flesh, the motions of sins, which were by
the law, did work in our members, to bring forth fruit
unto death. . . I had not known sin but by the law: for I
had not known lust except the law had said, 'Thou

shalt not covet.'. . . I was alive without the law once; but when the commandment came, sin revived, and I died. . . The commandment which was ordained to life, I found to be unto death. . . The law is holy, and the commandment holy, and just, and good. . . Sin by the commandment, became exceeding sinful. . . We know that the law is spiritual. . . I consent unto the law that it is good. . . I delight in the law of God after the inward man. . . With the mind, I myself serve the law of God" (Romans 7:5–25).

The law in question is that the law, the work of which "the Gentiles show to be written in their hearts" (Romans 2:15); that law by the transgression of which "Jews and Gentiles are all under sin" (Romans 3:9); that law against which "all have sinned and come short of the glory of God" (Romans 3:23); and that law without which "there is no transgression" (Romans 4:15). It is also the law to which, as their first husband, the believers in Rome were, in their unregenerate state, espoused, and by which "they were held" (Romans 7:4–6). But most, if not all, of those believers were Gentiles (Romans 1:13 and 11:13) who were never held by the ceremonial law of the Jews, and therefore could not be said to have been delivered from it. In a word, it is that law the righteousness of which was fulfilled in those believers (Romans 8:4).

Now, in most, if not all, of those passages the things asserted by our apostle are peculiar to the moral law. This, then, is the law which he had in view when he affirmed to those believers that they had become dead to, or were delivered from, the law, and that the law in which they had been held was dead to them. But lest they should imagine that it was the law of creation, and

the law as a rule of life, to which they were dead, he
compared the law of which he was speaking to the law
of a husband (Romans 7:2–3), which is a covenant or
contract between him and his spouse, and which establishes her relation to him as long as they both live. By
this comparison he plainly hinted to them that it was
the moral law not as a rule of life, but as a covenant of
works only to which they were dead. The believers at
Rome, then, were dead to the law in its covenant form,
or were delivered from it, and it was dead to them; so
that it could no longer hold them in subjection to its
precept of perfect obedience as the condition of life,
nor to its sentence of condemnation for sin (Romans
7:6).

As it was the privilege of the Christians in Rome, so
it is the privilege of all true Christians, in every place
and in every age, that they are dead to the law as a
covenant of works, and that the law in that form is
dead to them. They are dead to it, that is, they are delivered from the dominion or obligation of it in that
form, and also from a prevailing desire to be under it.
The righteousness of the second Adam, by which He
fully answered in their stead, all the requirements of it
as a covenant, is graciously imputed to them; and
therefore, in that form, it has nothing more to demand
from them. Its demands of perfect obedience as the
condition of eternal life and of complete satisfaction
for sin have, by their divine Surety, been fully answered
for them. His surety-righteousness, received by faith
and imputed by God to them, is their righteousness for
the justification of life—their complete answer to all
the demands of the law as a covenant of works. The
consequence is that though the law in that form is not,

with regard to them, abrogated, yet it is fulfilled and satisfied; and, being fully satisfied by them in their Surety and Representative, it will not, it cannot, oblige them in their own persons to answer the same demands a second time. The holy and just law of God will never exact from them a double payment of the same debt. Thus true believers are, in their justification, delivered from the dominion and obligation of the law, as it is a covenant of works. And, as they are delivered from it, or dead to it, in that form, so it is dead to them. For the apostle not only compares it to a dead husband, to whom the surviving spouse is, by the law of marriage, no longer bound, but he says plainly that is dead "in which ye were held" (Romans 7:2, 6). The law as a covenant is dead to believers inasmuch as it will not and cannot exercise any commanding or condemning power over them. It can neither justify them for their personal obedience nor condemn them for their disobedience (Romans 8:1–3). "True believers," as our excellent *Confession of Faith* expresses it (XIX: VI), are "not under the law as a covenant of works, to be thereby justified or condemned." On the ground of Christ's fulfilling it in their stead, they are delivered from all its demands of personal and perfect obedience, and of punishment for sin in order to justification before God.

In order to explain the meaning of what has now been said, as well as to pave the way for what is afterwards to be advanced, on this fundamental and important subject, it will be proper to remark that since Christ, the second Adam, performed perfectly all that, according to the covenant of works, was to have been done by man himself to entitle him to life, and that seeing all that He did and suffered is imputed to sinners who believe, believers therefore are justified in the sight of God. They are in the very same state, with respect to righteousness entitling them to life, in which they would have been had the first Adam fulfilled for himself and his posterity the condition of life in the covenant of works. Accordingly we read that the just, by faith, are entitled to the same life to which man, by his fulfilment of that condition, would have been entitled (Habakkuk 2:4; Romans 10:5). If Adam had continued to yield perfect obedience until the time appointed for his trial had elapsed, he, as the representative of his descendants, would have entered upon a state of confirmation in holiness and happiness or in the begun possession of eternal life; and the covenant of works, as a contract fulfilled on his part, would henceforth have continued to be an everlasting security to him for his own and his posterity's enjoyment of the eternal life promised him for himself and them. But in this state of confirmation, the law as a covenant could not have continued to be the rule of his obedience; because to subject him still to the law in its federal form, as the rule of his duty would have been to reduce him again to a state of trial, and to require him to work over again for that life to which he was already entitled by his having performed the condition of the covenant.

At the same time, as man could in no state whatever be released from his obligation to obey his Creator, he must have had a rule of obedience. And as the law as a covenant could not, for the reason now mentioned, have been a rule to him, it follows that in his state of confirmation the law of nature, divested of its covenant form, or of its promise of life and threatening of death, would have been the immutable rule of his obedience, both in time and in eternity. As the first Adam, then, upon his having fulfilled the condition of the covenant of works for himself and his posterity, would have been released from the obligation of the law in that form; so they to whom the righteousness of the second Adam is imputed for the justification of life are delivered from the law in its federal form, and, at the same time, they continue under it as the law of Christ and as divested of that form.

The Lord Jesus, as the Representative and Surety of elect sinners, condescended to subject Himself, in their stead, to the moral law as a covenant of works in order to redeem them from it in its covenant form. The Apostle Paul informs us that "God sent forth His Son, made of a woman, made under the law, to redeem them that were under the law" (Galatians 4:4–5). From this passage it is plain that Christ was made under the law in that form in which they whom He came to redeem were under it. Now as they were under it as a covenant of works, it was requisite that He also should be made under it as a covenant of works in order to answer for them all its demands in that form, and so to redeem them from the bondage of it. Were any man to suppose or affirm that Christ was made under the law not as a covenant, but merely as a rule, according to such a supposition the meaning of the passage cited above would be this: "God sent forth His Son, made under the law as a rule, to redeem them who were under the law as a rule from the authority and obligation of it, and consequently from all obedience to it." Now would not this be the very soul of antinomianism? Would it not be to make the holy One of God the minister of sin? Far be it from us to suppose it possible for the holy, inspired apostle to teach such doctrine as that!

As it is chiefly the moral law of which our apostle is there speaking, his meaning then must be that the Son of God became subject to that law not as a rule of life to believers, but only as a covenant of works in order to redeem sinners from it in its covenant form.

By the covenant of works, a twofold connection is established between sin and eternal death; one between a state of sin and eternal death, and another between thoughts, words, and acts of sin, and eternal death. The former is indissoluble and cannot but remain firm. A sinner cannot be in a state of unbelief and sin without being, at the same time, under the dominion of spiritual death, and bound over by the curse of the violated law to death eternal. Accordingly, such threatenings as "He that believeth not the Son shall not see life; but the wrath of God abideth on him." (John 3:36) and "if ye live after the flesh ye shall die" (Romans 8:13) bind over all unbelieving and impenitent sinners, continuing in their state of sin under the law as a covenant, to eternal death. The latter is dissolvable and, to all true believers, is actually dissolved. In the satisfaction given by Christ and imputed to believers, the penalty of eternal death with regard to them is already satisfied; and therefore the execution of it can never be renewed on them. Their debt of satisfaction for sin, being already discharged, cannot be charged a second time (John 5:24). The covenant form of the law, or "the law of sin and death," is so dissolved to believers that it can no longer promise eternal life to them for their personal obedience, nor threaten them with eternal death for their disobedience. And, indeed, how can it either threaten eternal death or promise eternal life to believers who, in their justification on the ground of the infinitely perfect righteousness of Jesus Christ, imputed to them, have already escaped eternal death, and have already not only a complete title to life eternal, but a begun possession of it (John 3:16; Acts 13:39; Romans 6:14). In the Oracles of Truth, we are informed that saints on earth are, upon their vital union with the second Adam, really possessed of eternal life as the saints in heaven are; and sinners, who have no such union with Him, are as really under the begun execution of the sentence of eternal death as the damned in hell are, though in a far lower degree (John 3:36 and 5:24).

Believers are dead to the law as a covenant, relatively and really. First, they are dead to it relatively, or with respect to their state before the Lord. This is the happy, inestimable privilege of all who are instated in the covenant of grace, and justified before God. As the relation between husband and spouse is dissolved by death (Romans 7:2), so the relation between the law as a covenant and believers is, in the moment of their justification, dissolved (Romans 7:4). The moment they become alive in the eye of the law, they become dead to the law. And as their justification is at once perfect, so is their deliverance from the law as a covenant. As the former admits of no higher and lower degrees, so neither does the latter. It is the peculiar privilege of those who are in a state of union with Christ, and of justification in Him, to be wholly delivered from the covenant of works. They are not under the law, but under grace (Romans 6:14), not under the law or covenant of works, but under the covenant of grace. Second, believers are also dead to the law as a covenant really, or in respect of their inclination and practice. Though a legal temper remains in them, yet the dominion of it is taken away; and therefore they no longer desire to be under the law as a covenant, or to go about as formerly, to establish their own righteousness in the affair of justification; but they rely only on the righteousness of God their Savior for all their title to life eternal.

At the same time, seeing that some degree of a legal spirit, or of an inclination of heart to the way of the covenant of works, still remains in them and often prevails against them, they sometimes find it extremely difficult to resist that inclination to rely on their own attainments and performances for some part of their title to the favor and enjoyment of God. If at any time they are uncommonly frequent and lively in their exercise of graces and performance of duties, they then especially find it inexpressibly difficult to refrain from flattering themselves that such exercises and duties entitle them, in some degree, either to the Savior Himself or to the joy of His salvation. Indeed, they find nothing in their spiritual exercise more difficult than so to mortify their legal temper as to die to all hope from the law as a covenant. This death to the law, then, admits of degrees in believers, and it will not be perfect in any of them so long as sin remains in them. They cannot, in their practice, become perfectly dead to the law till they are perfectly dead to sin. Their relative death to the law of works is perfect, but their real death to it is imperfect. The former is the dissolution of a relation; the latter is the gradual extinction of a disposition. The one refers to their justification; the other to their sanctification.

There are two errors respecting the deliverance of believers from the law which are equally contrary to the Oracles of Truth. The one is that of the legalist who maintains that believers are still under the moral law as a covenant of works; the other is that of the antinomian who affirms that believers are not under it even as a rule of life. These errors are as contrary to the Scriptures of truth as they are to each other; and they are equally subversive to that evangelical holiness which is a principal part of eternal life, and which is so requisite that without it no man shall see the Lord (Hebrews 12:14). The plain doctrine of Scripture is this: while true believers are dead to or delivered from the law as a law or covenant of works, they are under it, and account it their high privilege to be under the infinite obligation of it, as a rule of life. Indeed, to be freed from the law in its federal form is nothing more than to be delivered from the covenant of works, and from an inclination to cleave to that covenant; and our affirming according to the Scriptures that believers are delivered from the law as a covenant of works necessarily implies that they are under the law in some other respect. Accordingly, the Apostle Paul informs us that they "are not without law to God, but under the law to Christ" (1 Corinthians 9:21), that is, they are under the law of the Ten Commandments as the law of Christ, or as the law in the hand of Christ the Mediator. No man can live to God, in point of sanctification, till after he becomes dead to the law as a covenant in justification; neither can he otherwise live to God than by holy con-

formity of heart and life to the law as a rule of duty
(Galatians 2:19). The death of legal hope in him is
necessary to a life of evangelical obedience.

Having premised these observations in order to
prevent mistakes, and to enable the candid reader to
understand with more ease than which is to follow, I
shall now take a more particular view of the important
subject, and consider, first, what it is in the law as a
covenant of works to which believers are dead; second,
what is included in their being dead to the law under
that form; third, the means of their having become
dead to the law as a covenant; fourth, the consequence
of it; and, last, the necessity.

Section 1. What it is in the law as a Covenant of Works to which Believers are Dead

It is true that believers, and they only, have become
dead to the law as a covenant. All unbelievers are alive
to it: they are under the dominion of it; and indeed
they so cleave to it as to desire to be under its dominion. They resolutely persist in relying on their own
obedience to that law for a title to justification and
eternal life. On the contrary, all true believers, having
been convinced of their utter inability both to yield
perfect obedience to the precept as the condition of
life, and to suffer the dreadful penalty of it so as to give
full satisfaction to divine justice for their innumerable
transgressions, receive the perfect righteousness of
Jesus Christ, which not only satisfies, but magnifies the
law; and so they become dead to the law by the body of
Christ. Upon their union with the second Adam, and

communion with Him in his righteousness, they are delivered, as has been observed above, both from the obligation of the law in its federal form and from a reigning inclination of heart to be under it in that form. Being already justified and, in their justification, wholly delivered from condemnation (Romans 8:1), they are no longer under the law as a covenant of works to be thereby justified or condemned. They are set free from the dominion or power of it. There are four sorts of power belonging to the law as a covenant from which believers are delivered; namely the commanding power, the promising or justifying power, the condemning power, and the irritating power of it.

1. Believers are, in the act of justification, set free from the commanding power of the law as a covenant of works. This will be evident if we consider that, in case of transgression, the commanding and condemning power of the law as a covenant are inseparable. By the condemning sentence of the law of that covenant, every transgressor of its commands is bound over to eternal death. "Cursed is every one that continueth not in all things which are written in the book of the law to do them" (Galatians 3:10). "Now we know that what things soever the law saith, it saith to them who are under the law" (Romans 3:19). It is as if the apostle had said, "Whatever things the law says, especially in its condemning sentence, it says to those who are under the commanding power of it." If believers, then, are still under the commanding power of the law as a broken covenant of works, they must also be still under its condemning power, and so be, every moment, bound over to eternal death since every moment they come short of perfect obedience to its commands. But they

are not under the condemning power of the law as a
covenant of works (Galatians 3:13; Romans 8:1). And
therefore they are not under the commanding power
of the law in its covenant form.

Our apostle does not say to the believers in Rome,
"You have become dead to the curse of the law
merely," but, "Ye are become dead to the law. . . Ye are
delivered from the law" (Romans 7:4, 6), from the law
itself, from that which is most essential to the law in its
federal form. In another place he addresses them thus:
"Ye are not under the law, but under grace" (Romans
6:14). Neither does he say here, "You are not under
the condemning sentence or curse of the law," but, "Ye
are not under the law" (Galatians 4:4).

To believers in union with Christ he says, "Ye are
not under the law." This plainly shows that they are not
under it as a covenant, in the sense in which He was
under it. But He was under its commanding power as a
covenant as well as under its condemning power.
Considered as the Surety of elect sinners, He was as
much bound to perform perfect obedience to its precept as to suffer the full execution of its penalty
(Matthew 3:15; Hebrews 10:9). Therefore, believers are
not under the commanding power of it as a covenant
of works. Justified on the ground of that consummate
righteousness which Christ in their stead fulfilled in
answer to its demands of perfect obedience and full
satisfaction for sin, they are delivered as much from
the commanding as from the condemning, power of it.
He discharged their debt of perfect obedience to the
precept for eternal life as fully as He did their debt of
infinite satisfaction to the penalty of the law of works.

The precept requiring perfect obedience as the

condition of life is the principal part of the law or covenant of works. "Do this and thou shalt live." "If thou wilt enter into life, keep the commandments." It is to this precept requiring perfect and personal obedience as the condition of life, and requiring it on pain of eternal death for the smallest failure, that believers are dead. The reader, I hope, will not mistake me. I do not say that believers are delivered from the precepts of the law simply, but only that they are set free from them in their federal form. The precept to perform perfect obedience simply is not the command of the covenant of works. Man was bound to perfect obedience previous to the covenant of works, and would have been obliged to perform it though such a covenant had never been made with him; for it is essential to the divine law to be a rule of human obedience, but not to be a covenant of works.

The reader is here requested to observe that although the law and its commands as a covenant and a rule are formally different, yet they are materially the same. Though the true believer, therefore, is, in his justification, delivered from them in their federal form, or under the form of a covenant of works, yet he still is, and cannot but be, under the whole original authority and obligation of them as his rule of duty. He continues to be firmly bound, as will afterwards be explained, by the precepts of the law as a rule of life to personal and perfect obedience not only in time, but even to all eternity. His obligation to perfect and perpetual obedience, instead of being in the smallest degree relaxed by his having been delivered from them in their federal form, is thereby increased and confirmed.

But the command to perform perfect obedience as the condition of life is the form of that covenant. Now it is from the command only in this form that believers are set free. And the ground of their deliverance from the precept of the law in its federal form, or from the rigorous demand of perfect obedience as the condition of life, is the perfect obedience of their divine Surety to it in their stead. This is the proper condition of life to all His spiritual seed. "By the righteousness of One, the free gift came upon all men unto justification of life. By the obedience of One, shall many be made righteous" (Romans 5:18–19). The obligation to do, or to obey the law, is eternally binding on all believers; but, from the obligation to do and live, to do in order to procure a title to eternal life, they are delivered. They are under immutable and eternal obligations to yield perfect obedience to the law of the Ten Commandments as a rule of life; but they are delivered from the obligation and, in a great measure, from the desire, to yield in their own persons perfect obedience to it as a covenant of life. Eternal life is, by the perfect obedience of their adorable Surety, already merited for them; and therefore, though they are under every obligation to obey from life, they are under no obligation to obey for life. The famous Dr. Owen was not afraid to say that the whole power and sanction of the first covenant was conferred upon Christ, and in Him fulfilled and ended. Nay, to attempt obedience in order to procure a title to eternal life, especially after they have been already, by the consummate righteousness of Jesus Christ imputed to them, perfectly entitled to it, would, instead of being their duty, be their aggravated sin (Galatians 5:4).

2. Believers are also set free from the promising or justifying power of the law as a covenant of works. The promise of the covenant of works is a promise of eternal life on condition of personal and perfect obedience to the law in its covenant form. Now since believers are released from their obligation to yield perfect obedience for life, as required in that covenant, they are no more to expect eternal life as promised in it. They hold all their title to life eternal in the second Adam, their blessed Surety. In Him they have that perfect righteousness, to which eternal life is promised, and which is the only foundation of their sure title to it. Their own sincere obedience is not the legal ground of their title to life; and therefore it has not the legal promise of life. Their evangelical obedience is an evidence of their union with the last Adam, and communion with Him in His righteousness has, indeed, a promise of the covenant of grace connecting eternal life with it (Romans 2:7; 1 Timothy 4:8). But of the promise of eternal life in the covenant of works, which makes a man's own obedience the ground of his right to justification and eternal life, the law to believers is wholly divested. The law as a covenant makes no promise of life but to the man who performs personal and perfect obedience. But to believers, this rigor of the law in that form is relaxed; a responsible Surety is admitted and allowed to take their place in law, to whose perfect and meritorious righteousness imputed to them eternal life is promised. Believing, then, in the Lord Jesus, they have eternal life not according to the promise of the first covenant, but according to that of the second (Titus 1:2; Romans 5:21).

3. Believers are, in their justification, delivered

likewise from the condemning power of the law as a covenant. The law in its federal form condemns every sinner who is under it to death in all its dreadful extent. Spiritual, temporal, and eternal death is the awful penalty of the law in that form. "In the day that thou eatest thereof, thou shalt surely die" (Genesis 2:17). "The wages of sin is death" (Romans 6:23). But as the law is so divested of its promise of life to believers that it cannot justify them for their obedience, so it is denuded of its threatening of death to them, and it cannot condemn them for their disobedience. In consequence of communion with Christ in His righteousness, by which the law's demand of infinite satisfaction for sin is completely answered, they are dead to it as a covenant of works, and it is dead to them. It has no more power to frown upon them or condemn them than a dead husband has to frown on his deceased spouse.

Hence are these cheering passages of Scripture: "Christ hath redeemed us from the curse of the law, being made a curse for us" (Galatians 3:13). "He that heareth My Word, and believeth on Him that sent Me, hath everlasting life, and shall not come into condemnation" (John 5:24). "There is, therefore, now no condemnation to them which are in Christ Jesus, who walk not after the flesh, but after the Spirit" (Romans 8:1). When a man is justified in the sight of God, all his sins, past, present, and future, are together and at once pardoned. The guilt of eternal wrath for his past and present iniquities is actually and formally removed. The obligation under which he was lying to suffer eternal punishment for those transgressions is completely dissolved. And the guilt of eternal wrath for sins to come is, in the act of his justification, effectually prevented from recurring upon him. For, although this pardon of sins yet to come is not a formal remission of these sins, but merely a non-imputation of them, yet it effectually secures the believer from ever coming into or falling under condemnation (John 5:24). This distinction between the formal remission of sins past and present, and the not imputing of sins to come, is clearly marked in the Oracles of Truth (Psalm 32:1–2; Romans 4:7–8). Thus, in their justification, true believers are fully and forever set free from the condemning sentence or curse of the law as a broken covenant (*Confession of Faith* XX:I) For as in legal estimation they sinned and fell under the condemning sentence of the law as a covenant in the first Adam, so they endured the execution of that sentence, and thereby satisfied divine justice in the second Adam (Galatians 2:20; Ephesians 2:6).

4. Last, believers are, in consequence of their justification, set free from the irritating power of the law as a covenant. While the commanding, promising, and condemning power of the law in its federal form is essential to it in that form, the irritating power of it is only accidental. It is occasional or accidental merely in that motions of sin are by the law. When a man, under the covenant of works and the dominion of sin, obtains a transient view of the purity, spirituality, and strictness of the law, and at the same time of his innumerable and aggravated transgressions of it, with the tremendous wrath to which they have exposed him, this not only fills his mind with a disquieting dread of hell, but inflames the corruptions of his heart and makes them rage vehemently against the holy law. The evil passions

of his depraved nature, irritated by the purity of the
precepts, and the severity of the curses of the law as a
covenant, urge him more violently to the commission
of that which it prohibits. The law, strictly forbidding
all motions of sin in his heart, and that without affording him the smallest degree of strength to resist them,
irritates, provokes, and so renders them more fierce
and intractable.

Accordingly, the Apostle Paul says of himself, and
of the believers in Rome in their unregenerate state,
"When we were in the flesh, the motions of sins, which
were by the law, did work in our members to bring
forth fruit unto death" (Romans 7:5). And of himself
in particular he says, "Sin, taking occasion by the
commandment, wrought in me all manner of concu-
piscence" (Romans 7:8). This is not to be imputed as a
fault to the holy law, but is wholly to be charged to the
reigning depravity of the sinner's nature; for although
the law never gives the sinner any just occasion of
committing sin, yet the inveterate corruption of his nature takes occasion from the holy strictness of its precepts, and the awful severity of its threatenings, to rise
in violent opposition to it, and to work in him all manner of sinful desire to that which is forbidden in it, and
because it is forbidden. It is like a mighty torrent which
rises, rages, and overflows: the more that means are
employed to stop its current, the reigning depravity of
the heart, rising in rebellion against the holy commandment, bursts forth with the greater impetuosity,
and irresistibly employs all the faculties of the soul, and
all the members of the body, "as instruments of unrighteousness unto sin" (Romans 6:13). Now believers
are graciously delivered from this irritating power of

the law as a broken covenant. Trusting in the Lord Jesus for complete salvation, relying on His meritorious righteousness for all their title to life eternal, constrained by His redeeming love, and enabled by His sanctifying Spirit to mortify their depravity and perform spiritual obedience, they delight in the law as a rule of duty and serve God in newness of Spirit (Romans 7:6).

It is not here insinuated that believers are in this world perfectly set free from the irritating power of the law. As in their practice they are only dying to it as a covenant, so in proportion to the degree of the legal temper that remains in them, they may on many occasions be exposed to its irritating power.

Thus it is plain that true believers are dead to the commanding, promising, condemning, and irritating power of the law as a covenant of works.

Section 2. What the Believer's Being Dead to the Law as a Covenant Includes

It is the inestimable privilege, as well as the indispensable duty, of all who have believed through grace to be "dead to the law" as a covenant of works. To be dead to it relatively, or with respect to their state, is their exalted privilege; and to become dead to it really, in the disposition of their minds, is their bound duty. The latter is both a consequence and an evidence of the former. Now to be dead to the law in its federal form comprises especially the following particulars:

1. Their despairing of salvation by the works of the law. In death there is no hope, but "to him who is

joined to all the living, there is hope" (Ecclesiastes 9:4). They who are alive to the law as a covenant have hope from the law, and from their own works of obedience to the law. They presume to hope that God will justify and save them because they intend well and do well, because they are just in their dealings and diligent in their duties, or because they wrong no man and endeavor to perform as many good works as they can, consistent with human infirmity. Thus they go about to establish their own righteousness as the foundation of their hope; and "touching the righteousness which is in the law," they fancy that they are blameless (Philippians 3:6). And though they say that without Christ they cannot be saved, yet their hope of salvation is founded on their own obedience to the law. On the contrary, they who are justified by the faith of Christ, and are dead to the law, have no expectation from the law, no hope of justification or title to life by the works of the law. They see plainly that no righteousness can secure them from eternal death and entitle them to eternal life but one which is in all respects perfect.

2. Believers being dead to the law includes an entire dissolution of the relation between them and the law as a covenant. In death the relations between husband and wife, master and servant, are dissolved. "The servant is free from his master" (Job 3:19). In like manner, when they who are justified by faith are dead to the law, the former relation between them and it is dissolved. So long as they were alive to the law as a covenant, that relation stood firm; they were "debtors to do the whole law" (Galatians 5:3); they were bound to give infinite satisfaction for their sins, and to yield perfect and perpetual obedience as the condition of

life. But now that they have, in the hand of faith, presented to the law the perfect and infinitely meritorious righteousness of their divine Surety, which answers fully all its demands upon them, they are honorably as well as legally acquitted from their obligation to suffer for satisfaction to divine justice, and to yield perfect obedience for a right to eternal life. They are, indeed, obliged still to obey the holy law of God, but not to obey it as a covenant of works—not to obey it in order to procure a title to justification and eternal life. They are now divorced from the law as a covenant, their first husband, and are married to another, even to Him who is raised from the dead. They are dead to the law in that form, and the law is dead to them; so that their relation to it as a covenant is entirely dissolved. The redeemed of the Lord, therefore, should no more expect eternal life for their own works than a widow would hope for favors and comforts from a dead husband. They are no more exposed to the curses of the broken law than a widow is to the threats of a husband who is lying in the grave. For inasmuch as deliverance from a covenant is the dissolution of a relation which does not admit of degrees, they, in respect of their state before the Lord, are perfectly or wholly set free from the covenant of works.

3. The death of believers to the law comprises also their deliverance from anxious concern or care about the works of the law in the affair of justification. "There is no work," says Solomon, "nor device, nor knowledge, nor wisdom, in the grave whither thou goest" (Ecclesiastes 9:10). In death there is no concern nor solicitude about performing any work. A dead body in the grave is nowise careful to do any of the

works in which it was employed when alive. So they
who are dead to the law as a covenant of works, though
they are careful to maintain good works, yet have no
care about the works of the law in the affair of justification. They work, but they do not, as formerly, work for
life. While they were alive to the law, all their concern
was to establish their own righteousness and to rely on
it for the justification of life; but now that they are
dead to the law, they no longer have any allowed solicitude of that kind.

4. Last, in their becoming dead to the law as a
covenant, believers enter into rest. When a man dies,
he rests from his labors. There is no labor no wearisome toil in the grave. "There the weary are at rest"
(Job 3:17). They who are alive to the law "are wearied
in the greatness of their way" (Isaiah 57:10). The law as
a covenant, appoints them a wearisome task. It requires from them perfect and continual obedience as
the condition of life, and that without affording them
the smallest degree of strength to perform it; and it
loads them with direful and overwhelming curses if the
task is not performed. The consequence is that in going about to establish their own righteousness they are
weary and heavy laden. But when a sinner, in compliance with the call of the gospel, comes wearied and
heavy laden as he is, to the Lord Jesus, He gives him
rest (Matthew 11:28). Having thus become dead to the
law by the body of Christ, the weary is at rest. He attains rest to his conscience in the righteousness of
Christ, for "He is the end of the law for righteousness
to everyone that believeth" (Romans 10:4). He also obtains rest to his affections in the fullness of Christ, and
in God as his God and portion. In proportion as his le-

gal spirit is mortified, he rests from his legal and slavish fear of that wrath which is threatened in the law. He is at rest also from those legal cares and sorrows which attended his self-righteous and laborious efforts. He rests from his legal desires and delights. Formerly he desired to be under the law as a covenant; and he sought righteousness, as it were, by the works of the law. He delighted, too, in his own righteousness, and in the hope of justification on the ground of it. But now that he has become dead to the law, he ceases from these desires and delights. He no more delights in himself, nor in his legal performances; for he now sees that all such righteousness is as filthy rags (Isaiah 64:6). Nay, even if, instead of being so polluted and defective as they are, they were even perfect, yet he now takes no pleasure in justification by the works of the law as a covenant (Job 9:15, 21). On the contrary, beholding the incomparable excellence of the way of justification and salvation in the covenant of grace, he desires above all things to be found in Christ Jesus, not having his own righteousness which is of the law, but that which is through the faith of Christ; that he "may know Him, and the power of His resurrection, and the fellowship of His sufferings" (Philippians 3:9–10).

Section 3. Of the Means of Becoming Dead to the Law as a Covenant of Works

The Apostle Paul, in his epistle to the Galatians, says of himself, "I through the law am dead to the law" (2:19). The means, then, of becoming dead to the law as a covenant is the law itself. This, at first view, may

seem a very strange and unlikely means of attaining
such a purpose; but upon due attention to the subject
it will be found that no means are, in the hand of the
Holy Spirit, so well adapted to divorce a sinner from
the law in its federal form as the law itself. The law indeed is not the cause, but it is the occasion of a man's
becoming dead to it as a covenant; for it accuses, condemns, and terrifies the awakened sinner; and so it
urges him to flee speedily for refuge to Jesus Christ,
who is the real cause of one's becoming dead to the
law. "The law was our schoolmaster," says the apostle,
"to bring us unto Christ, that we might be justified by
faith" (Galatians 3:24). To bring a sinner to Christ is
no proper effect of the law, but yet it is occasioned by
the law inasmuch as the law forces him away from itself, and leaves him no ground of hope that he shall
ever be justified by his own obedience to it. The law, by
the strictness of its precepts and the severity and terror
of its threatenings, is an occasion to him of seeking
righteousness and eternal life where they are to be
found. To be dead, then, to the law through the law is,
by means of the strictness and rigor of the law, or of a
work of legal conviction and humiliation, to be driven
to Christ for justification by faith "without the works of
the law."

When the Holy Spirit sets the law home to the conscience of a sinner, the following effects of the work of
the law are means of his becoming dead to it as a
covenant of works:

1. Through the law as a covenant, an awakened
sinner attains discoveries of the infinite holiness, justice, and majesty of the Lord. Since the law is not only
a declaration of the will of God, but a transcript of His

moral image, no sooner is the understanding of a sinner enlightened than, in the glass of the law and by the light of the Spirit, he begins to discern the spotless holiness of God. He perceives, in God's forbidding the smallest degree of sin, and requiring the highest degree of every duty, and that on pain of the most tremendous punishment, that he hates sin and loves holiness in an infinite degree. And therefore His nature and will are infinitely and immutably holy. In the glass of the law, the sinner discerns also the inflexible justice of the divine nature. He sees that, in requiring perfect conformity of heart and life to His righteous law, the Lord requires nothing but what every rational creature owes Him; and that in threatening death in all its dreadful extent and duration for the very smallest sin, He threatens nothing but what is justly due to the sinner. Perceiving that God requires nothing but what is just and reasonable, and that He prohibits nothing but what is unjust and unreasonable, the sinner now sees that the strictest equity is displayed in all the precepts of the law. Discerning at the same time that every sin committed against the infinite Majesty of heaven justly deserves infinite punishment, he sees that the highest justice appears also in the penalty of the law. Through the law, he discerns likewise, the glorious majesty of the Lord. The law of the King eternal, immortal, and invisible is a royal law. The greatness and dignity of it deserve that it should be honored with perfect and perpetual obedience. It is clothed with majesty; it binds the conscience; it demands the obedience of the heart as well as of the life; and it must be universally as well as perfectly obeyed. Through the law, then, the awakened sinner discerns not only the

holiness and righteousness, but the majesty, of the
sovereign Lawgiver, who is able to save and to destroy
(James 4:12). When therefore the commandment,
clothed especially with the majesty of the Lord, comes
into his conscience, sin will revive and self-confidence
and legal hope will die (Romans 7:9). When he hears
the great and terrible God Himself speaking to him in
His law, he will be constrained to cry, "Enter not into
judgment with me; for in Thy sight shall no man living
be justified" (Psalm 143:2).

2. By means of the law in the hand of the Spirit, a
sinner is made to discern the divine authority and
majesty of the law itself. Under a convincing work of
the Holy Spirit, he begins to consider the law in its
federal form as the law of Jehovah, as the ordinance of
the one Lawgiver who is the uncreated fountain of authority and the sovereign Judge of angels and of men.
Regarding it as the law of the infinite Majesty of
heaven, he, in the light of the Spirit, begins to see that
it bears immutable impressions not only of truth and
rectitude, but of divine authority and supreme majesty.
Beholding the face of Jehovah in His righteous law,
and conscious that his provocations of Him are innumerable, the sinner cannot but be struck with remorse
and dread. When he hears the Most High God speaking to him in His fiery law, he will be ready to exclaim,
"If Thou, Lord, shouldst mark iniquities; O Lord, who
shall stand?" (Psalm 130:3). Thus, the divine authority
and majesty of the law, coming into the conscience,
destroy all expectation of life by the works of the law.

3. Through the law, an awakened sinner discerns
also the holiness, spirituality, vast extent, and perfection of the law itself in its covenant form. The Holy

Spirit opens the eyes of his understanding to see the strict conformity of the commandment to the holy nature and will of God. The Apostle Paul, speaking of himself as unregenerate, says in a passage quoted above, "I was alive without the law once; but when the commandment came, sin revived and I died"(Romans 7:9). It is as if he had said, "Touching the righteousness which is in the law, I was blameless. I imagined that I was sufficiently holy and righteous. But when I began to discern the spotless holiness of the divine law, sin revived and I died. I then was convinced that I was a sinner indeed; and so I died to all hope of justification and of eternal life by my own obedience to the law."

By the same means the sinner discerns not only the holiness, but the spirituality of the law. "We know," says the apostle, "that the law is spiritual" (Romans 7:14). No sooner are the eyes of a man's understanding opened than he sees that the law is the authoritative and binding rule of all the dispositions, thoughts, and motions of his heart, as well as of all the words and actions of his life. When he begins, under the convincing influences of the Holy Spirit, to understand the meaning, and to feel the power especially of this command: "Thou shalt not covet" (Romans 7:7), his hope of life by his own righteousness perishes. He now sees that every divine precept requires spiritual obedience—the service of the whole heart as well as of the whole life. He discerns also the great extent of the holy law. "Thy commandment," says the Psalmist, "is exceeding broad" (Psalm 119:96). When he sees that the commandment extends to all his inclinations, affections, and designs, and to all his thoughts, words, and actions, he begins to be convinced that he has no righteousness answerable to the requirements of the holy law. No sooner is his awakened conscience informed of the breadth and length of the righteousness required in the law than he is convinced that his own righteousness is a bed shorter than he can stretch himself on, and a covering narrower than he can wrap himself in (Isaiah 28:20). Thus, through his discovery of the vast extent of the law as a covenant, sin revives in his conscience, and he dies to all hope of justification by his own righteousness. Moreover, "The law of the Lord is perfect" (Psalm 19:7). It requires, on pain of eternal death, perfect and unceasing obedience as the condition of eternal life. So absolutely perfect, indeed, is this holy law that the man who offends but in one point is guilty of all (James 2:10). To disobey any one command, though in a single instance, is an insult offered to the divine authority of the whole law. When a man, then, is convinced that he has, in innumerable instances, presumed to transgress this righteous and perfect law, he cannot but acknowledge himself to be so guilty before God as to be justly condemned by the violated law to eternal death. And when that conviction is not counterfeit, but true, he cannot but renounce all confidence in his own righteousness for a right to eternal life, and so become dead to the law.

4. By means of the law as a covenant, a sinner attains the knowledge of sin. "By the law is the knowledge of sin" (Romans 3:20). In proportion as a man is truly convinced of sin, or is conscious of his having transgressed the divine law, he discerns not only the reality, but the malignancy and hatefulness of his sin. He sees that while it is a transgression of the law of God, it is directly opposite to the holy nature and will

of God. Sin now appears sin and, by the commandment, becomes in his view exceeding sinful (Romans 7:13). By the commandment, the Holy Spirit convinces him that his nature is not only destitute of original righteousness, but is wholly corrupted; that this corruption of his whole nature is not merely the consequence and evidence of his having been guilty of Adam's first sin, but is the source of all the innumerable transgressions of his life; that he is under the dominion or power of sin; and that the law, instead of having the smallest tendency to rescue him from the power of sin, is itself the strength of sin (1 Corinthians 15:56). Now, when he is enabled thus to discern the nature and dominion of the sin that dwells in him, he becomes dead to all hope of eternal life by the works of the law.

5. Through the law, he likewise attains alarming discoveries of that tremendous wrath which is revealed from heaven against him for his innumerable transgressions. Convinced of sin by the law, the sinner is made to see that by the curse of the broken law he is bound over to suffer eternal punishment. As by the precept of the law in its federal form he is convinced of the evil nature of sin, and of its desert of punishment, so, by the penalty of the law, he attains the knowledge of the dreadful consequences of sin. The law, under the convincing influences of the Holy Spirit, shows him plainly that the fiery indignation, the intolerable, overwhelming, and endless wrath of the great and terrible God, is the sure, the direful consequence of his transgression. This wrath of God is revealed from heaven to him not in groundless alarms of approaching danger, but in threatenings as certain as they are terrible. Now

when the convinced sinner thus begins to see that the
wages of sin is death, and that he in particular is justly
condemned to endure the fierceness of Jehovah's
wrath, the fury of His almighty indignation, not for an
age, or millions of ages, but forever and ever, his hope
of salvation by the works of the law will perish. He now
sees clearly that the penalty of the violated law is not to
be satisfied by doing, but by suffering. Thus his conviction of guilt and wrath by the threatenings of the law
tends to destroy his confidence in his own righteousness, and so to render him dead to the law. For he
cannot now but see and feel that he is imprisoned or
"concluded under sin" (Galatians 3:22), and that none
can say to such a prisoner, "Go forth," but He whom
God "hath given for a covenant of the people" (Isaiah
49:8–9). Knowing the terrors of the Lord, he is now
convinced that his own righteousness is but a refuge of
lies which the hail shall sweep away.

6. By the instrumentality of the law as a covenant, a
man is at the same time convinced that it would be just
in God to punish him for the very least of his transgressions with everlasting destruction. He is made to know
that sin, as it is committed against the infinitely great
Jehovah, deserves an infinite punishment, even the everlasting perdition of the sinner. Convinced of the malignity and demerit of sin by the law, he is satisfied that
God could do him no manner of injury, though He
should consign him to the place of torment, and there
punish him with all the severity of almighty vengeance.
He sees that infinite justice could not be glorified, nor
the credit of it maintained, unless infinite punishment
were inflicted either upon himself or upon a responsible Surety in his stead for the infinite offense given to

it by his transgression. He is persuaded that the Lord is righteous in executing vengeance, adequate to the infinite evil of presuming to sin against His infinitely glorious majesty. Accordingly, the Apostle Paul says, "Is God unrighteous who taketh vengeance? God forbid; for then how shall God judge the world?" (Romans 3:5–6). The sinner now sees, in the glass of the law, that it is highly proper and even necessary that divine justice should be honored by a complete satisfaction. And indeed, if he did not see damnation to be just, he could not discern salvation to be free. But discerning as he now does the equity and righteousness of God in the infliction even of eternal punishment upon him for sin, he is well pleased with the doctrine and the offer of a free salvation through the infinite satisfaction given to divine justice by Jesus Christ, and is content that the justice of God should receive a satisfaction far more complete than he himself could give, though he should suffer in the place of torment through all eternity. And so he becomes dead to the law as a covenant by the body of Christ.

7. Finally, by means of the law, a man is convinced of his great need of the righteousness of Jesus Christ offered to him in the gospel. Contemplating, in the glass of the law and by the light of the Spirit, his sinfulness and his misery; dreading the wrath of God, which he has provoked by his great transgressions; convinced of the equity of God, though He should punish him with everlasting destruction; and despairing of deliverance by his own righteousness and strength, he perceives his extreme need of the righteousness of Jesus Christ to answer for him the high demands of the law as a covenant. While he discerns by

the gospel the suitableness and sufficiency of that consummate righteousness for his justification, he discovers by the law his absolute need of it for that purpose. He sees plainly in the glass of the law that he must inevitably and eternally perish without communion with Christ in His righteousness. The consequence is that, under the renovating influences of the Holy Spirit, he is disposed to be an eternal debtor to the glorious righteousness of the last Adam for all his security from eternal death and all his right to eternal life. The righteousness which the law as a covenant demanded from Christ, the Representative and Surety of elect sinners, is not only a glass in which the sinner sees that righteousness which he must fulfill if he would enter into life on the ground of his own obedience; but in the gospel it is offered to him as a lost sinner, that by receiving the gift of it "the righteousness of the law may be fulfilled in him" (Romans 8:4). And no sooner does he receive the gift of that spotless righteousness than it is imputed to him for justification; and so he who is unrighteous in himself becomes "the righteousness of God in Christ" (2 Corinthians 5:21). Thus he becomes dead to the law of works not only in point of legal hope, but in respect to his state before God.

Section 4. The Important Consequence of a Believer's Being Dead to the Law as a Covenant of Works

The consequence or fruit of a believer's having become dead to the law as a covenant is, by the Apostle Paul, expressed thus: "Wherefore, my brethren, ye also are become dead to the law by the body of Christ; that ye should be married to another, even to Him who is raised from the dead, that we should bring forth fruit unto God" (Romans 7:4). Here our apostle informs the believers in Rome, and all believers to the end of time, that they have become dead to the law as a covenant of works so that it can neither justify them nor condemn them; and that they are dead to it by the body of Christ, that is, by the service and suffering of the body or human nature of Christ (Hebrews 10:5). As the obedience and suffering of Christ in human nature, which have answered all the demands of the law as a covenant, are imputed to them for their justification, so the law in that form, being thereby satisfied with respect to them, has nothing more to demand of them for a title to life. They have become dead to the law, and so, in its federal form, it has no more dominion over them than the civil law has over a man after he is dead.

The design, according to our apostle, of believers being dead to the law is that they should be married to another, "even to Him who is raised from the dead." So long as the law, their first husband, continued to have dominion over them, they could not justly or honorably be married to another; but when that husband is dead to them, or when they are set free from the dominion of the law as a covenant, they are at liberty to be honorably espoused to another, even to Him who is raised from the dead. The Lord Jesus, having been "raised from the dead, dieth no more." He continues always to be a living Husband to His saints. And therefore, as they can never be loosed from the bond of their union with Christ, so they shall never be released from the law of this Husband. Although, then,

they are set free from the obligation of the law as a
covenant of works, yet they are under the law to Christ,
under the law as a rule of duty in the hand of Christ;
under obligation to yield even perfect obedience to it;
and they shall never be released from that obligation.

Now the main design of their deliverance from
their first husband, and of their conjugal relation to
Christ, is, as our apostle expresses it, "That they may
bring forth fruit unto God." It is not that they may be
left at liberty to live as they please without law to God,
but that by union and communion with Christ, their
Head of spiritual influences, they may bring forth
"fruits of righteousness, which are by Jesus Christ unto
the glory and praise of God" (Philippians 1:11). As
children begotten and born in marriage are legitimate,
and all before marriage are illegitimate, so those works
only which are the fruits of union with Christ, which
are performed in faith and to the glory of God, are
genuine fruits of righteousness; whereas all that are
done before union with Christ are spurious. According
to our apostle, then, the certain consequence of believers' being dead to the law as a covenant, and of
their being united to Christ, is that they bring forth
fruit unto God. As long as sinners are alive to the law as
a covenant, which is the ministration of death, "they
bring forth fruit unto death" (Romans 7:5); but no
sooner are they dead to the law than "they have their
fruit unto holiness, and the end everlasting life"
(Romans 6:22).

In another passage, our apostle expresses the consequence of being dead to the law thus: "But now we
are delivered from the law, that being dead wherein we
were held; that we should serve in newness of spirit,

and not in the oldness of the letter" (Romans 7:6). Here the apostle affirms that believers are delivered from the law not indeed as a rule of duty, but only as a covenant of works; that they who hitherto were held fast under subjection to it as their first husband are delivered from it because it is dead to them: "That being dead wherein we were held." Although, in their unregenerate state, they were held fast under the dominion and obligation of it as a woman who has a husband is "held by the law of her husband," yet now that is dead to them, they are delivered or discharged from it as a widow is from the bond of marriage to her dead husband. They are delivered from the rigorous exaction, the dreadful curse, and the irritating power of it. But for what purpose are believers delivered from the law as a covenant? They are delivered, says our apostle, not in order that they may live a loose or licentious life, but "that they may serve in newness of spirit, and not in the oldness of the letter." To serve in newness of spirit is, in consequence of their standing in a conjugal relation to Jesus Christ, and under a new and better covenant to serve the Lord their God, "without slavish fear, in holiness and righteousness before Him"; to serve Him, under the renewing influences of His Holy Spirit, the former of the new creature in their souls; to serve Him from a new heart and a new spirit, from new principles and motives, to new ends and by walking in newness of life. It is to serve Him in a new manner, with filial confidence in Him, with reverence and godly fear, with freedom and delight, as persons renewed in the spirit of their minds, and with their minds to serve His law by yielding unfeigned and unreserved obedience to it as the only rule of their duty. Believers are also delivered from the law as a covenant that they may serve not in the oldness of the letter; not with an old covenant spirit, nor in a mere outward observance of the law as a rule of life; and not in a bare external compliance with some to the neglect of others of its injunctions. The letter kills by its bondage and terror; but they are set free from it in order that they may serve the Lord not only without servile fear, but in spirit and in truth. The consequence or fruit, then, of being delivered from the law as a covenant of works is that believers become capable of serving God in newness of Spirit, and not in the oldness of the letter.

Our apostle in another place expresses the consequence and fruit of having become dead to the law in its federal form in these very remarkable words: "I through the law am dead to the law, that I might live unto God" (Galatians 2:19). According to these words of the inspired apostle, a believer's living unto God is the native consequence and fruit of his being dead to the law as a covenant of works. As long as a man continues alive to the law, he is dead to God; but when he becomes dead to the law in point of justification, he begins to live unto God in respect of sanctification. The death of his legal hope is in order to his life of evangelical obedience. His becoming dead to the law issues in his living unto God; in his living a new, spiritual, holy life, and that to the glory and praise of God. If he did not become dead to the law as a covenant, he could not live to God in conformity to the law as a rule. His living unto God, then, is the necessary fruit, the sure consequence of his having become dead to the law in its covenant form.

The life which the true Christian lives, in consequence of his having become dead to the law, is not a life either of perfect or of imperfect conformity to the law as a covenant of works (Romans 5:6 and 9:31–32); but it is a spiritual life, the life of a spiritual man, in conformity to the law as a rule. It is the result of the inhabitation and gracious operation of the Holy Spirit in his soul (Ezekiel 36:27). It is called in Scripture "the life of God" (Ephesians 4:18), for it "is hid with Christ in God" (Colossians 3:13). God lives in Himself, and the believer lives in union and communion with Him. It is wholly in and of God, and is a living in favor and fellowship with Him. Our apostle calls it "a living by the faith of the Son of God," and he says of himself, "I live, yet not I, but Christ liveth in me" (Galatians 2:20). Christ is the purchaser, the bestower, the restorer, and the preserver of the believer's life. Christ is the principle of his life from whom, the pattern of his life according to whom, and the end of it to whom, he lives. Indeed, Christ the living Redeemer, the resurrection and the life, is all in his spiritual life. "To me to live," says the apostle, "is Christ" (Philippians 1:21). It is also called "living and walking in the Spirit (Galatians 5:25), a living in the strength of the Spirit as a Spirit of life (Romans 8:2) under the guidance of the Spirit (Romans 8:14), in the liberty of the Spirit (2 Corinthians 3:17), in the comforts of the Spirit (Acts 9:31), and in the fruits of the Spirit (Galatians 5:22–23).

Living unto God, as the consequence of being dead to the law in its covenant form, is moreover called a holy, humble, and heavenly life. It is called a "conversation such as becometh the gospel of Christ (Philippians 1:27), "a walking circumspectly" (Ephesians 5:15), and "a living soberly, righteously, and godly"

(Titus 2:12). It includes the love and practice of all
those duties of piety toward God, of sobriety with
respect to himself, and of righteousness toward his
neighbor which the believer is commanded in the law
as his rule of duty to perform, and which he is bound
to perform, under the influences of the Spirit of grace,
from the principles and motives, according to the rules
and patterns, and to the ends exhibited in the word of
grace.

To live unto God, that unspeakably important consequence of having become dead to the law of works,
comprises more particularly:

1. The believer's living suitably to the endearing relations in which God in Christ as his Covenant God
stands to him. It is his living to God as his Father, his
Redeemer, his Head and Husband, as his Judge,
Lawgiver and Sovereign, as his Portion, and as the
Object of his supreme love, of his high admiration,
and of his holy adoration.

2. It includes his living suitably to the inestimable
blessings of salvation which he has received from God.
Has God enlightened the minds of His people in the
saving knowledge of Himself and of Christ? Then to
live to Him is to walk as children of light. Has He
called them with a holy calling? To live to Him is to
walk worthy of the vocation wherewith they are called.
He has brought them into a state of grace and of rec-
onciliation to Himself; they therefore live to Him when
they live not as persons in a state of nature, but in a
state of grace; or as persons not under the law, but under grace. Has He graciously forgiven their iniquities
and justified their persons? To live to Him is to stand
fast in the liberty wherewith Christ has made them

free. Has He renewed and sanctified them according to His own image? They live to Him when they are holy in all manner of conversation. Has He given them exceeding great and precious promises, and faith to rely on them? They live to Him when, having such promises, they cleanse themselves from all filthiness of the flesh and spirit, perfecting holiness in the fear of God. Has He made them heirs of a glorious inheritance in heaven? Then to live to Him is as strangers and pilgrims on the earth, to set their affection on, and to seek those things which are above, where Christ sits at the right hand of God. In a word, has He graciously advanced them to joy and peace in believing? They live to Him when they live in peace and serve Him with gladness.

3. It also comprises his living in comfortable communion with God in Christ as his God. To live in the style of the Holy Spirit is to live comfortably. To live to God, then, is to live in delightful fellowship with Him. Believers live in such communion with God when they daily contemplate His glory in the face of Jesus Christ and sanctify Him in their hearts; when they trust in Him at all times, receiving all communications of grace from Him by the exercise of faith, and returning all to Him in grateful obedience; and when they have His love so shed abroad in their hearts as to be constrained by it, constantly to love and delight in Him. They also live to God when they live in the comfortable enjoyment of Him as all their portion and felicity, all their salvation and desire, renouncing all in heaven and upon earth as a portion but Him alone (Psalm 83: 25–26).

4. Last, it includes his living in conformity to God as

his covenant God. To live unto God is to live in conformity to His holy and perfect nature, to be holy as He is holy, and to be pressing on toward perfection of holiness. It is to live in conformity to His manner of living. God's way of living is a holy, just, good, merciful, gracious, and faithful way. His way is to have a general good will to all men and a special good will to some; and so will that of His people be in proportion to the degrees of their sanctification. It is a living also in conformity to His ends. The chief end which the Lord proposes to Himself in all His works is the glory of His infinite name, the honor of His beloved Son and His blessed Spirit, the advancement of the Redeemer's kingdom, the overthrow of Satan's kingdom, and in all the praise of the glory of His grace. To live unto God, then, is to make these the chief end of all our thoughts, words, and works. In a word, to live unto God is to live in conformity to that law of God as the rule of life which is a transcript of His holy nature and a revelation of His holy will. They who live to Him, from love as well as from conscience, study to keep all His holy commandments. They not only account it their duty, but their privilege and their pleasure to yield spiritual obedience to His holy law.

Section 5. Of the Necessity of a Believer's Being Dead to the Law as a Covenant in Order to His Living unto God

As the believer's living unto God, according to the law as a rule of life in the hand of the Mediator, is the necessary consequence or fruit of his having become dead to the law as a covenant of works, so his being dead to the law is necessary to his living unto God; so absolutely necessary that were he not dead to the law as a covenant, it would be utterly impossible for him to live unto God in conformity to the law as a rule. This will be evident to the devout reader if he considers the following particulars:

1. The man who is under the power of the law as a broken covenant is under the power of sin; for the law under that form "is the strength of sin" (1 Corinthians 15:56). Hence our apostle said to the saints in Rome, "Sin shall not have dominion over you; for ye are not under the law, but under grace" (Romans 6:14), intimating to them that if they had been still under the law as a covenant, sin would have had dominion over them. The believer's deliverance, then, from the dominion of sin, so as to be rendered capable of living to God, necessarily depends upon his having become dead to the law in its covenant form.

2. The sinner who is under the law as a covenant is without strength; and therefore he cannot serve God in a holy and acceptable manner (Romans 5:6). And the law, being "weak through the flesh," is as unable to sanctify him as it is to justify him.

The works of the law cannot sanctify him, seeing they are evil and not good works. They can render him more and more unholy, but they cannot make him holy. He must be created unto good works before he can perform them. But the new as well as the old creation is the work of God alone. Therefore, while a man is under the law as a covenant of works, and is unregenerate, he cannot perform a single holy or good work. He may do many things that are materially good, but he can do nothing that is formally good. All his works are dead works, the works of a man who is dead in sin and dead to God; and therefore it is as impossible for them to make him alive to God as it is to merit for him eternal life.

3. He who is under the law as a covenant is without Christ, in whom only quickening and sanctifying grace is to be found. They who live unto God "are sanctified in Christ Jesus" (1 Corinthians 1:2) and are saints in Him (Philippians 1:1). Their implantation in Christ, instead of being from the law or works of the law, is wholly from grace; and their sanctification, while it is wholly from grace, is only in Christ "who loved the Church and gave Himself for it, that He might sanctify and cleanse it with the washing of water by the Word" (Ephesians 5:25–26).

4. The man who is under the law as a covenant of works has no principle of holiness in him. The grand principle of evangelical holiness, or of living unto God, is the holy, sanctifying Spirit of Christ dwelling in the heart. Now a man receives the Spirit of sanctification "not by the works of the law, but by the hearing of faith" (Galatians 3:2). He becomes a partaker of the Holy Spirit not by obedience to the law of works, but by means of hearing and embracing the doctrine of faith. It is the new testament or covenant, and not the law or legal covenant that is "the ministration of the Spirit" (2 Corinthians 3:6–8). It is the glorious gospel in which the new covenant is offered and the Spirit promised that, through grace, calls a sinner effectually to a life of sanctification (2 Thessalonians 2:13–14). When the sinner is effectually called, he "receives the promise of the Spirit through faith" (Galatians 3:14).

This is through the faith of the gospel, not by the works of the law. As long, then, as a man is under the law of works, and is of the works of the law, he is destitute of the Spirit of Christ, the main principle of living to God.

5. Once more, the sinner who is under the law as a covenant has no promise of sanctification by that law. The law in its federal form promises life to him only on condition of perfect obedience to be performed by himself, and performed in that strength which was given him in the first Adam; but it promises him no quickening or sanctifying influences to enable him to obey. On the contrary, by its awful curse it bars effectually all sanctifying influence from his soul, and shuts it up under the dominion of sin. Indeed, if true holiness or ability to live unto God were to be found in the man under the covenant of works, the promises of the covenant of grace, with reverence it is said, might be altered, and that of sanctification be expunged from it. We might erase from that well-ordered covenant especially these promises: "I shall put My Spirit in you, and ye shall live" (Ezekiel 37:14). "A new heart also will I give you, and a new spirit will I put within you. I will put My Spirit within you, and cause you to walk in My statutes, and ye shall keep My judgments, and do them" (Ezekiel 36:26–27). Were it possible for a sinner, while he continues under the law as a covenant and, consequently, under the dominion and strength of sin to possess, notwithstanding, true holiness or ability to live unto God, there would be no need of these and similar promises. But suppose we had no other proof of it; the very existence of those absolute promises in the covenant of grace proves, with the highest degree

of certainty, that no man, while he continues under
the law as a covenant of works, is capable of living to
God.

Thus it is evident that a man must be dead to the
law as a covenant, in point of justification, and must be
dying daily to it, in point of temper and practice, in order to his living unto God, in reference to sanctification. The former is indispensably requisite to the latter; and the latter is not only the consequence, but the
necessary consequence, of the former. It is absolutely
necessary that a sinner be dead to the law in its federal
form, with respect to his state before God, and also
that he be dying to it, in respect of his inclination and
practice, in order to his being capable of living a holy
life. But to evince still more clearly the necessity of a
man's becoming dead to the law, in order to his living
unto God, I shall take a different view of this fundamental subject and inquire what causality or influence
his having become dead to the law as a covenant has
upon his living unto God.

In the first place, a man's being dead to the law has
a physical, or rather a spiritual influence upon his
sanctification, or his living unto God.

They who are become dead to the law are married
to another, even to Him who is raised from the dead.
And so they cannot but live or bring forth fruit unto
God. In union and communion with Christ Jesus, they
have life, spiritual and eternal life. While they were
under the law as a covenant, they were spiritually as
well as legally dead, "dead in trespasses and sins"; but
now in Christ, their Head of righteousness and life,
they have life, and have it more abundantly. Because
He lives, they shall live also. "He that hath the Son

hath life." Now that they have been divorced from the law of works, their first husband, and are united to Christ, they live and act spiritually. In Christ, their Head of influences, they have light as well as life. As long as a man is under the law as a covenant he dwells in darkness, and cannot see to work the works of holiness or be spiritually active in living unto God. He is blinded with ignorance, prejudice, and self-conceit; and as he cannot see the vanity of his legal works, so neither can he discern the way of evangelical holiness. But no sooner is he united to Christ, who is "a Light to lighten the Gentiles," than he receives "the spirit of wisdom and revelation in the knowledge of Christ"; and by this spiritual light, shining on the Word of Christ, he sees distinctly how to live to God. He discerns the beauty and amiableness, as well as the manner, of true holiness. In the Lord Jesus, they who are dead to the law have strength likewise. Sinners who are joined to the law as their husband cannot live to God; for they have no strength for acceptable obedience, and the law cannot afford them any. But believers have in Christ, their spiritual Husband, strength to enable them to perform spiritual obedience. He affords them, from His overflowing fullness, sufficient and continual supplies of grace and strength. His grace is sufficient for them; for His strength is made perfect in weakness (2 Corinthians 12:9). The consequence is that all things are possible to them who believe. When, by trusting in Him at all times, they are "strong in the Lord, and in the power of His might" (Ephesians 6:10), they can do all things through Christ who strengthens them (Philippians 4:13). In union with Christ, their Covenant Head, they also have liberty, the

glorious liberty of the children of God. While they
were under the law as a covenant which genders to
bondage, they were in bondage, severe bondage to the
command of perfect obedience on pain of eternal
death; and were also in bondage to the curse of the law
and the fear of eternal wrath. In this miserable condition it was impossible for them to live unto God; they
could not have either a heart or a hand to serve Him.
But in union and communion with the Lord Jesus, believers have liberty. If the Son shall make you free, you
shall be free indeed—free to serve God in spiritual and
acceptable manner. "Where the Spirit of the Lord is,
there is liberty." Partaking of the Spirit of the Lord
Jesus, they walk at liberty, yea, they run the way of
God's commandments; for He enlarges their hearts.
Now that they are delivered from the hands of their
enemies, they serve the Lord without fear, in holiness
and righteousness before Him, all the days of their life.
They serve Him willingly, affectionately, and cheerfully. They are now at liberty to serve Him in hope,
knowing that their labor shall not be in vain. They are
at liberty to serve Him spiritually and acceptably; for as
they are so joined to the Lord Jesus, as to be one Spirit,
so they are made accepted in the Beloved. Christ, their
Representative and Surety, satisfied all the demands of
the law as a covenant for them; they are therefore accounted in law as having answered them all in Him,
and so are accepted in Him. In union with Him, their
persons are accepted as righteous and their performances as sincere. Oh, how grateful, how cheering is
this liberty to the exercised believer! And what a delightful and powerful inducement is it to that holy and
acceptable obedience, which is a living unto God!

In the last place, a man's being dead to the law as a covenant has not only a physical, but a moral influence upon his sanctification or living unto God. The love of Christ, manifested in delivering believers from the law as a covenant of works, constrains them to live not unto themselves, but to Him who died for them and rose again (2 Corinthians 5:14–15). Men's natural way of thinking and speaking is, "We should serve God that He may save us"; but the evangelical way is, "He saves us that we may serve Him. He redeems us from the law as a covenant that we may serve Him, and so live to Him, in obedience to the law as a rule." When our apostle said, "I am dead to the law that I might live unto God," in the next verse he enlarges in these words: "The life which I now live in the flesh, I live by the faith of the Son of God, who loved me, and gave Himself for me" (Galatians 2:19–20). It is true believers only, who are dead to the law of works and are united to the Son of God, who have a true faith and sense of His immense love to them, and who are powerfully constrained by it to love and live to God. And while redeeming love to them constrains them to love God as their Covenant God, they see that they have every encouragement to live to Him. They see that their adorable Surety has, in wonderful condescension, fulfilled all that righteousness of the law as a covenant for them which they could never have fulfilled for themselves; and when by the eye of faith they perceive this, they are sweetly impelled and encouraged by it to holiness of heart and of life. If a man has no faith in the love of God in Christ, no hope of His favor as a God of grace, how can that man be pure in heart, and holy in all manner of conversation? Nay, he cannot; it is only

the man who has this hope in Him who purifies himself, even as Christ is pure (1 John 3:3). All exercised
Christians know by experience that when their souls
are most comforted, and their hearts most enlarged
with the faith of God's favor in Christ, and with the
hope of His salvation, then it is that they are most disposed and encouraged to live to His glory. And, on the
contrary, when through the prevalence of unbelief
they are most suspicious of God and His love to them,
they then find themselves most averse from the exercise of graces and performance of duties.

But that the moral influence which dying to the law
as a covenant of works has upon living unto God may
be more evident, it will be proper to show how every
part of the law itself—having been changed to believers from the form of a covenant of works into that of a
rule of life in the hand of the Mediator—constrains
them to evangelical obedience. The law in the hand of
Christ as a rule of duty, in all the commands, promises,
and threats of it, is, as it were, a chariot paved with love
for believers. It wears a smiling, inviting, encouraging
aspect to them.

1. The commandments of the law in the hand of
Christ, having been divested of their old covenant
form, discover to believers much of the love and grace
of God. The command of the law as a covenant, as was
observed above, is "Do and live"; but that of the law as
a rule is "Live and do." The precept of the law of works
is "Do or you shall die"; but that of the law of Christ is
"You are redeemed from eternal death, therefore do."
The command of the law in its federal form is "Do perfectly that you may be entitled to eternal life," but that
of the law in the hand of Christ is "He has merited for

you and given you eternal life; therefore do, by His grace, as perfectly as you can until you attain absolute perfection."

The command of the law as a rule is materially the same as that of the law as a covenant; and therefore, though as much obedience is required in it as in that of the law of works, yet less is accepted from those who have the perfect obedience of their divine Redeemer imputed to them. And as the command is materially the same, so the authority which enjoins obedience is originally the same, and yet vastly distinct; for the commandment of the law as a covenant is the command of God out of Christ; but the command of the law as a rule is the precept of God in Christ, of God as a God of grace and love in Him. The sovereign authority of God in commanding obedience is not in the smallest degree lessened in that His law is in the hand of Christ; for He, as the eternal Son of God, is the Most High God and co-essential with the Father and the Holy Spirit. But while it is not, and cannot be, in the least degree lessened, it is, notwithstanding, rendered so mild, so amiable, and so desirable to believers as powerfully to constrain them to spiritual obedience. For His design in commanding their obedience is not to require from them a righteousness for their justification, but to show them the holiness of His nature, to beautify them with His holy image, to afford them illustrious displays of His glorious grace, to do their soul good in the most effectual manner, and to favor them with daily opportunities to glorify Him, to edify their neighbor, and so to manifest their love and gratitude to Him for having redeemed them from the law as a covenant.

2. The promises of the law in the hand of Christ, having dropped their old covenant form, display to believers much of the love of God, and so constrain them to live to Him. The law in its federal form promises eternal life as a reward of debt for perfect obedience; but the law as a rule in the hand of Christ promises rewards of grace in and after evangelical obedience—especially as this obedience is an evidence of union with Him in whom believers are justified, and in whom all the promises of God are "yea and amen." The consideration that "in keeping His commandments there is great reward," that in the way of evangelical obedience there is a gracious promise of delightful communion with God and Jesus Christ (1 John 14:21, 23), and that after the course of such obedience in this world is ended there will be an eternal reward powerfully constrains and greatly encourages believers to live unto God.

3. Finally, the threatenings of the law as a rule of life are also divested of their old covenant form, and are changed into paternal threats issuing from redeeming love which powerfully incite true Christians to live unto God. There is now no such threatening to the believer as: "If you do not do this, you shall die." Now that he is dead to the law of works and delivered from condemnation, the believer has no more cause to fear its threatening of eternal death than a woman has to fear the threats of a dead husband (Romans 8:1). Believers, because they are not under the law as a covenant, but under grace, are under no threatening of eternal wrath, no sentence of condemnation to eternal punishment. The law in the hand of Christ has indeed threats of chastisement, but they are fatherly

and all from love. "If his children forsake My law, and walk not in My judgments; if they break My statutes, and keep not My commandment; then will I visit their transgressions with the rod, and their iniquity with stripes" (Psalm 89:30–35). It is as if Jehovah had said, "Although I will not send them to hell, nor deprive them of heaven, any more than I will break My covenant, or violate My oath to My eternal Son; yet, as a father, I will chasten them. I will not only visit them with the rod of external affliction, but I will hide My face from their souls. I will deny them that sensible communion with Me which they have sometime enjoyed; and I will fill them with trouble instead of comfort, with bitterness instead of sweetness, and with terror instead of hope." A filial fear of these paternal chastisements will do far more to influence the believer to holy obedience than all the despondent fears of eternal punishment can do. Accordingly, when he has gone aside, it is commonly such a reflection as this that through grace makes him return to the Lord: "Oh! How am I now deprived of those delightful interviews with my gracious God and Savior, which I formerly enjoyed!" Therefore, "I will go and return to my first Husband; for then it was better with me than now" (Hosea 2:7). And when he is enabled to see that he is delivered from the threatenings of eternal wrath, and that he is only under threats of fatherly correction, this breaks and melts his heart more than all the fire of hell could do. The slavish dread of avenging wrath disquiets and discourages him, weakens his hands in spiritual obedience, and disposes him to flee from God; whereas the filial fear of God's fatherly anger, which is kindly, is a motive of love that excites and urges him to holy living. The former works upon his remaining enmity and rouses it; but the latter acts upon his love and enflames it.

But here the attentive reader may be ready to ask, "Ought not the believer to live unto God without respect to the threats of paternal chastisement?" I answer, as long as he is in this world a body of sin dwells in him; and therefore he needs to be incited to his duty by threats of fatherly correction. He ought indeed to serve the Lord, as the redeemed in heaven do, merely from love to the command itself, and because it is his God and Savior who commands him. Still, however, as on the one hand he is perfect in Christ, his federal Head and Representative, he needs not have respect to what the law in its covenant form either promises or threatens* so, on the other, as he is imperfect in himself while here, it is his duty to have, in his obedience, regard to what the law as a rule in the hand of Christ promises and threatens—which indeed is a holy and affectionate regard tending to promote holiness in his heart and life.

Thus it is manifest that the whole form of the law as a covenant of works, having been dissolved to believers, the law as a rule of life in the hand of Christ, is all love, all grace; and so it influences and constrains them to advance, with increasing ardour, in evangelical holi-

---

* It is not here meant that believers need not regard with holy admiration and gratitude the grace manifested in the promise of the covenant of works; nor, that they need not regard with holy awe the terrible wrath revealed in the threatening of that broken covenant, but only that they need not, and should not, have respect to them, or take them into their view as motives to live unto God or to obey the law as a rule of life.

ness. Instead of affording them the smallest encouragement to commit sin, it not only requires, but like a cord of love it draws them to, the love and practice of universal holiness.

For the greater part of what has been advanced in the last two sections, I have been indebted to the substance of four excellent sermons by Mr. Ralph Erskine. If the reader chooses to receive further information respecting the highly important subject of this chapter, he may peruse Abraham Booth's treatise entitled *The Death of Legal Hope the Life of Evangelical Obedience,* Robert Hall's sermon on Galatians 2:19, and Thomas Boston's sermon on Romans 6:14.

A few reflections from what has been said will conclude this chapter.

Is it the privilege of true believers only to be dead to the law as a covenant of works? Then the law in its covenant form is, to every unregenerate sinner, as much in force as ever it was. It retains all the authority and dominion over unconverted sinners that ever it had. As it is dead to believers, and they dead to it, so sinners in their unregenerate state are alive to it, and it is alive to them. Retaining all its original authority over them, it continues to demand from them perfect obedience as the condition of life and complete satisfaction for sin. This is clearly taught us not only by the Lord Jesus, but also by the Apostle Paul (Luke 10: 25–28; Galatians 3:10); and all who continue to reject the second Adam and His consummate righteousness, shall, to their everlasting confusion, find it so. Oh, that secure sinners would believe this and flee for refuge to the great Redeemer before it is too late!

Does the law as a covenant require of every descendant of Adam personal as well as perfect obedience? Then it inevitably follows that the obedience of two or more cannot form a justifying righteousness. Righteousness for justification must be the obedience of one only. It must be the obedience either of the sinner himself alone or Christ alone. The Lord Jesus will either save sinners Himself alone or not save them at all (Acts 4:12). If a man would be justified before God, he must exhibit to the law either a perfect righteousness of his own, and have no dependence on that of Christ, or the perfect righteousness of Christ, in the hand of faith, and place no reliance on his own (Philippians 3:9). The righteousness of Jesus Christ, imputed to believers for their justification, is a righteousness without works; a righteousness wholly unconnected with works of any kind, performed by themselves. These two cannot stand together in the affair of justification. "I will make mention of Thy righteousness," says the holy Psalmist, "even of Thine only" (Psalm 71:16). Oh, let my reader take heed that in the affair of justification he does not connect his own obedience with that of Christ, nor Christ's obedience with his own; that he never presumes to make up a justifying righteousness for himself, partly of his own works and partly of those of Christ. Let him be zealous for good works and perform them as fruits and evidences of justification, but never as grounds of right to it. For it will be impossible for him to live unto God till he begins to die to all hope of justification and salvation, either in whole or in part, by his own performances.

Is it through the law that a man becomes dead to the law? It is obvious, then, that ignorance in unregenerate sinners is a principal cause of their self-righteous temper (Romans 10:3). Their ignorance of the infinite holiness, justice, and faithfulness of God; of the precept and penalty of His righteous law; of the covenant, promise, and design of His gospel; of the person, righteousness, fullness, and glory of Christ; and of their own extreme need of Christ—this willful, pharisaic ignorance is a special cause of their desire to be under the law of works (John 3:19; Galatians 3:1). Oh, that they would no longer condemn the counsel which the exalted Redeemer offers to each of them! "I counsel thee to buy of Me gold tried in the fire, that thou mayest be rich; and white raiment, that thou mayest be clothed, and that the shame of thy nakedness do not appear; and anoint thine eyes with eye-salve, that thou mayest see" (Revelation 3:18). Ah, secure sinner, how gross, how reproachful is your ignorance when you expect to become righteous in the sight of an omniscient and holy God by your own partial and polluted obedience! How blind are the eyes of your understanding when you can presume to hope that the holy and righteous law will accept your amendment and sincere obedience, your penitence and tears, instead of perfect obedience and perfect satisfaction for your innumerable sins! Alas! You do not know that the violated law demands, and cannot but demand from you, perfect obedience, and, at the same time, complete satisfaction for all your aggravated crimes; and that it will not absolve you till all its high demands are fully satisfied. Oh, continue no longer ignorant of the exceeding sinfulness of sin of your inexpressible misery and danger under the law as a covenant, and of your extreme need of the righteousness and grace of the second Adam.

Is a man's being dead to the law as a covenant the reason why he lives unto God? Then it must be admitted that the reason, or at least one reason, why unbelievers and formalists live not to God, but to sin and self and the world, is that they are not dead to the law in that form. The very reason why sin reigns in the sinner is because he is under the dominion of the law; which stands as a bar to prevent sanctifying influences from flowing into his heart. The law, especially in its condemning and irritating power, "is the strength of sin" (1 Corinthians 15:56). Every man, therefore, who is under the dominion of the law as a covenant is, and cannot but be, under the dominion and strength of sin (Romans 6:14). It is impossible for that man who continues alive to the law to be a holy or a godly man. He may have the form, but he cannot experience the power of godliness. He may take his encouragement from the law as a covenant, and delight in the works of it; but he cannot delight in the holiness and spirituality of the law as a rule. He may advance to a high degree of counterfeit virtue, but he remains an entire stranger to true holiness.

Reader, the only way in which it is possible for you to attain true or evangelical holiness is to be so convinced of sin and righteousness as to part with your legal righteousness. You cannot trust cordially in the Lord Jesus for righteousness and strength till you begin utterly to despair of being able to work out for yourself such a righteousness as the law requires. You cannot desire the great salvation offered to you in the gospel, until you despair utterly of salvation by the works of the law. Nor is it possible for you to live unto God till you die to all hope of redemption from the curse of the broken law, and from the justice of an offended God, by any righteousness of your own. Be assured that you must be dead to the law as a covenant in order to be either able or willing to yield the smallest degree of acceptable obedience to the law as a rule.

How inexpressibly miserable are they who are alive to the law as a covenant of works! They may have a name to live, but they are dead. They are dead to God—to the favor, image, service, and enjoyment of God. They are legally dead, for they are under the tremendous curse of the violated law, and are liable every moment to the intolerable and eternal wrath of Almighty God. They are morally dead, likewise, for they are destitute of spiritual life; and they have no inclination or ability to live unto God. Such persons know not what it is to live a life either of justification, sanctification, or consolation. The righteous law condemns them because they have transgressed it; and its awful sentence not only shuts them up under the dominion of spiritual death, but binds them over to all the horrors of death eternal. Oh, secure sinner, the state in which you are is that of a criminal condemned to temporal, spiritual, and eternal! Do not say, "I hope that is not my state," for you are of the works of the law; you are depending on your own works for a title to the favor of God and the happiness of heaven. And this renders it certain that you are under the curse or condemning sentence of the law: for thus said the Spirit of inspiration, "As many as are of the works of the law are under the curse" (Galatians 3:10). Oh, renounce, and that without delay, all dependence on your own works. Believe that the Lord Jesus, with His righteousness and salvation, is freely, wholly, and particularly, offered to you. And relying on His consummate righteousness alone for all your right to justification and salvation, trust in Him not only for deliverance from the curse of the law, but for complete salvation. So shall you become dead to the law of works and, in union with the second Adam, be instated into the covenant of grace.

All believers have, in the eye of the law as a covenant of works, obeyed, suffered and satisfied fully in Jesus Christ, their federal Representative and Surety. As all mankind has sinned and become subject to death in the first Adam, so all true believers have obeyed, died, and so satisfied the law and justice of God in the first Adam. Thus they have answered and completely satisfied all the demands of the law as a covenant. The consequence is that the law in that form, having received all that it had to demand from them, absolves them from guilt and declares them righteous. Hence they become dead to the law, and the law to them. The Representative and the represented, the Surety and the principal debtor, are, in legal estimation, but one person. They therefore are accounted in law to have done and suffered all that Christ, their Representative and Surety, did and suffered for them. Accordingly, they are said in Scripture to be crucified with Christ (Galatians 2:20), to be dead and buried with Him (Romans 6:4, 8), and to be raised up together in Him (Ephesians 2:6). They have obeyed and suffered, and so satisfied every demand of the law as a covenant not in their own persons, but in the person of Christ.

Although the sins which believers commit after the commencement of their vital union with Christ are not formally transgressions of the law as a covenant of works, yet they are all, by legal interpretation, sins against it. In the justification of believers, in which they have become dead to the law as a covenant, all their future sins, considered as transgressions of the law in that form, are forgiven. As sins against the law as a covenant, in the act of justification they are so pardoned that a non-imputation of them to believers is inviolably secured. "Blessed is the man," says the Apostle Paul, "to whom the Lord will not impute sin" (Romans 4:8). All the sins of believers after, as well as before, their vital union with Christ were charged and punished on Him as transgressions of the law in its federal form, and as such are, in their justification, freely and wholly pardoned. The Lord Jesus, their divine Surety, has satisfied the justice of God for all their sins committed after as well as before the act of their justification—and that by enduring in their stead the punishment threatened in the covenant of works. Though, therefore, their sins after union with Christ are directly and formally committed against the law as a rule of duty, yet, by legal interpretation, they are transgressions likewise of the law as a covenant of works.

Are believers wholly delivered from the condemning power of the law as a covenant? The guilt of sin, then, in reference to them is twofold: the guilt of eternal wrath and the guilt of paternal anger. The guilt of eternal wrath is a sinner's obligation or liableness to the avenging and eternal wrath of God as the just punishment of his sin. The guilt of fatherly displeasure, on the other hand, is a believer's obnoxiousness to the awful effects of God's paternal anger as chastisements for his disobedience.

Accordingly, the pardon of sin is twofold: namely a

removal of the guilt of eternal wrath from him in the
act of his justification, and an absolving of him from
the guilt of paternal displeasure in the progress of his
sanctification. The former is called "legal pardon," the
latter "gospel pardon." The one is the instantaneous
and perfect removal of all that guilt which was con-
tracted by transgressing the law as a covenant; the
other is the gradual removal of that guilt which is con-
tracted daily by disobeying the law as a rule. That is afforded completely and at once to a converted sinner
upon his first acting of faith, when he becomes dead to
the law as a covenant: this is vouchsafed to a believer
repeatedly upon his renewed exercise of faith and repentance. When therefore a true Christian—who is in
some happy measure assured of his justification prays
with understanding for the pardon of his iniquities—
he prays that the Lord may preserve and increase in
him his assurance of the pardon which was given him
in his justification (Larger Catechism, question 194),
and also that he may graciously remove from him the
guilt of fatherly displeasure which he is daily contracting (Psalm 51:8–12). And when he asks divine acceptance, he prays that the Lord may preserve and increase in him his assurance of the acceptance of his
person in the Beloved; and that He may favor him
daily with the acceptance of his performances.

Are believers dead to the law as a covenant, and is it
dead to them? Then it cannot either promise eternal
life or threaten eternal death to them. "What things
soever the law saith," either in its promise of life or its
threatening of death, "it saith to them who are under
the law" (Romans 3:19). But believers are not under
the law, but under grace (Romans 6:14); and therefore

the law in its federal form can say nothing to them. In their justification by faith they are delivered from condemnation to eternal death, and are accounted so righteous as to be fully entitled to eternal life (John 3:16). They are already redeemed from eternal death, and they have already the begun possession of life eternal. How, then, can the law either promise eternal life or threaten eternal death to those who, by their communion with Christ in His righteousness and fulness, have already attained the one and escaped the other? Though believers ought always to regard the threatenings of the law as a covenant with holy awe, as a glass in which they may contemplate the dreadful demerit of their sins, and their infinite obligations to redeeming grace; yet they ought not to consider those threatenings as directed to them or as denunciations of evil against them. They should regard them at all times with filial awe, but never with slavish dread.

Is every man who is justified before God, and so dead to the law as a covenant, taught to believe that his own works of obedience form no part at all of a justifying righteousness for him? It would surely be very unreasonable and unjust to infer from this that he needs not perform good works. He is indeed delivered, and wholly delivered, from the law as a covenant of works; but he is still under the infinite and eternal obligation of it as a rule of duty. To infer, then, from a believer's being directed and exhorted to place no confidence in his good works for a title to justification and eternal life, that it is not necessary for him to perform and maintain good works; would be as absurd as if a man should conclude that, because it is the ear only that hears, there is no need of the foot or the hand

(Romans 3:8; Jude 4).

Once more, are true believers delivered from the commanding, condemning, and irritating power of the law as a covenant? Let them, then, amidst all their trials, and all their conflicts with spiritual enemies, be of good comfort. Oh, let them rejoice exceedingly in that almighty, compassionate, dear Redeemer who, in His love and pity, has redeemed them from the dominion and curse of the broken law (Galatians 3:13). You, O believer, have become dead to the law by the body of Christ, and are married to another husband, even to Him who is raised from the dead, that you may bring forth fruit unto God (Romans 7:4). You are dead to the law of works; nevertheless you live. You live to God as your own God, your covenant God, and you serve Him in newness of spirit. In union with your living Redeemer, who loved you and gave Himself for you, you live a life of justification—and consequently it is your privilege as well as your duty to live a life of sanctification and consolation. Being justified by faith, you have peace with God through our Lord Jesus Christ, and, in some measure, peace of conscience. If then the law as a covenant of works should at any time enter your conscience again, and require perfect obedience from you as the ground of your title to eternal life, saying "This do, and you shall live," present to it, in the hand of faith, the perfect obedience of your divine Surety in answer to that demand. And as often as the law in your conscience repeats the high demand, renew your application of His consummate obedience, and trust firmly that it was performed for you in order to entitle you to eternal life. The righteous law, magnified and made honorable by that meritorious obedience, will, in proportion as you do so, cease to disturb the peace of your conscience. The spotless obedience of the second Adam is, as was observed above, the only obedience which you ought to exhibit to it as a rule of life.

And should the law as a covenant ever be permitted to rise again as from the dead, and to attempt exercising its condemning power over your conscience by demanding from you satisfaction for your innumerable transgressions of it; present to it, in the hand of an appropriating faith, the infinite satisfaction for sin given by your adorable Surety in answer to that demand. Trust anew that your living Head, your heavenly Husband, has given complete satisfaction for all your sins; and so, referring the law to Him, plead that if it has any charge to exhibit against you the action must lie between it and Him. Never say to the law, in answer to any of its demands, "Have patience with me and I will pay you all"; but without delay present it with full payment. In answer to its demand of perfect obedience as the condition of life, present in the hand of faith to it the perfect obedience of the second Adam; and in answer to its demand of complete satisfaction for sin, exhibit to it His infinite atonement for the sins of all who believe in Him. That is the way to honor it and, at the same time, recover and maintain peace of conscience.

Chapter 11

The High Obligation under which Believers
Lie to Yield Even Perfect Obedience to
the Law as a Rule of Life

All who are united to Christ, and justified for His righteousness imputed to them, are dead to the law as a covenant; not that they may be without law to God, but that they may be under the law to Christ; not that they may continue in disobedience, but that they may be inclined and enabled to perform sincere obedience in time, and perfect obedience through eternity, to the law as a rule of life. One design of their being delivered from the obligation of the law in its federal form is that they may be brought under the eternal obligation of it as a rule of duty in the hand of the adorable Mediator. Divested of the form of a covenant of works to believers, and invested with that of the covenant of grace, it stands under the covenant of grace as the law of Christ, and as the instrument of government in its spiritual kingdom, enforced by all its original and immutable authority. It loses nothing of its original authority by its being conveyed to believers in such a blessed channel as the hand of Christ since He Himself is God over all, and since the majesty, sovereignty, and authority of the Father, the Son, and the Holy Spirit are in Him as Mediator (Exodus 23:21).

Indeed, it behooved the law of the Ten Commandments, inasmuch as it is the substance of the law of nature, a delineation of God's moral image, and a transcript of His unspotted holiness, to be a perpetual and unalterable rule of conduct to mankind in all the possible states and circumstances in which they might be placed. Since God is unchangeable in His moral image, nothing but the entire annihilation of every human creature can divest His holy law of that office. Its being an immutable rule of duty to the human race does not in the least depend on its having become the matter of the covenant of works. Whatever form it might receive, whether that of the covenant of works or that of the covenant of grace, still it could not but continue an authoritive rule of conduct. No form, no covenant whatever, could at any time lessen its high obligation as a rule of duty on the reasonable creature. As the form of the first covenant was merely accessory to the moral law, so the law continues, and will forever continue under that form as the rule of duty to sinners, even in the place of torment. And as the form of the second covenant is also accessory to it, so it will remain eternally under this form, the rule of life, to saints in the mansions of glory.

The sovereign authority of the divine law continues eternally the same; and it can never be in the least impaired by any of the forms under which that law is promulgated to us. And seeing God the Father has so consulted the necessity of His redeemed, in subordination to His own glory, as to put His law into the hands of His eternal Son as Mediator, from these hands they receive it invested with all the sovereign authority that ever belonged to it, together with all that God the Son as their great Redeemer has added to it. That believers

ought not to receive, nay, and cannot receive, the law
otherwise than from the hand of the infinitely glorious
Mediator, is so far from being injurious to the infinite
Majesty of God, the sovereign Creator, or to the high
obligation of His holy law, that the infinite honor of
His glorious majesty and His holy law is thereby most
illustriously displayed. As the law as a covenant of
works was honored in an infinite degree by its having
been obeyed and satisfied by the eternal Son of God in
our nature, so, as a rule of life to believers, it is magnified in no less a degree by its being conveyed to them
in His hand. Their obligation to perform not only sincere, but even perfect obedience to it, is on these accounts confirmed and increased. Now the obligation
under which all true believers are to yield such obedience to the law as a rule of life proceeds chiefly from
the following sources:

1. It arises from God's being the Lord, or from His
being the sovereign, super-eminent, and supremely excellent Jehovah. The obligation under which believers
lie to yield obedience to His law arises from His universal supremacy and sovereign authority over them as rational creatures. "Ye shall, therefore, keep My statutes
and My judgments—I am the LORD" (Leviticus 18:5).
"Ye shall keep My statutes and do them; I am the
LORD which sanctifieth you" (Leviticus 20:8). Because
God is Jehovah, "the eternal, immutable, and almighty
God, having His being in and of Himself, and giving
being to all His words and works" (Larger Catechism,
question 101), all obedience is due to Him. The infinite greatness, excellence, and amiableness of the perfections of Jehovah make it the duty of all men, and
especially of all believers, to love Him supremely, to

obey Him in all things, and to make His glory the chief end of all their obedience to Him. The infinite super-eminence and amiableness of Jehovah lay them under inconceivably high obligations to love Him above themselves, and to live to Him ultimately and not to themselves. And as His greatness, excellence, and loveliness are infinite, immutable, and eternal, and as the highest possible degree of love and obedience is therefore due to Him, so the obligation under which believers lie to love and obey Him even in a perfect degree is infinite, immutable, and eternal. They are thus bound to love and obey Him with all their hearts because He is the LORD, or because He is what He is. On this account principally, and antecedently to every other consideration of Him, He is inexpressibly amiable; and therefore they are under the firmest obligation to love and obey Him, and that in the highest possible degree. This obligation, arising from that infinite greatness, excellence, and loveliness of God which result from His natural and moral perfections, is binding upon believers previously to any consideration of rewards or punishments, or even of the revealed will of God; and it is that from which all other ties to duty derive their obligatory force. It is from the infinite excellence and amiableness of the divine nature that every additional obligation under which they lie to perfect love and perfect obedience derives its binding force.

2. The obligation under which believers are to yield perfect obedience to the law as a rule flows also from God's being their Creator and their being His creatures. It is He who made them and not they themselves (Psalm 100:3). They receive life, breath, and all things from His creating hand. His right therefore to them,

and to their perfect and perpetual obedience, is not only original, underived, and perfect, but infinite. The power which He employed in creating them was infinite; and therefore He has an infinite right to all that they are, have, and can perform. By right of creation, the Lord has an irreversible and perpetual claim to their supreme love and their cordial and grateful obedience.

The relation subsisting between Him as their Creator and them as His creatures lays them under the firmest bond of subjection and obedience to Him; and the grace of the gospel, instead of diminishing, increases the force of that natural obligation. The sovereign Creator is far from having resigned His right of dominion over His saints by His having afforded them, independent of their own works, a title to eternal life. For as they cease not to be creatures by being made new creatures, so they are bound, and shall eternally continue bound, by the sovereign authority of the triune God as their Creator to yield personal and perfect obedience to His law as a rule of life. The divine law, as I have already observed, loses nothing of its original obligation by being divested of its covenant form, and conveyed to believers in the hand of Christ; for "by Him were all things created that are in heaven, and that are in earth, visible and invisible" (Colossians 1:16). And the sovereignty, authority, and all other excellencies of the Father, are in the Son; yea, "in Him dwelleth all the fulness of the Godhead bodily" (Colossians 2:9). Indeed, that high obligation cannot cease to retain its original force as long as the immutable and eternal Jehovah cannot cease to be the Creator, and the saints to be His creatures.

3. Their obligation to obey the divine law as a rule of duty arises from God's being their continual Preserver. "In Him," says the Apostle Paul, "we live and move and have our being" (Acts 17:28). And, says the holy Psalmist, "Lord, Thou preservest man and beast" (Psalm 36:6). His eyes are upon all His works, so that even a sparrow cannot fall to the ground without Him. By the word of His power, He upholds all His creatures in their being and operation. Every living creature lives upon His goodness and subsists by His bounty. His infinite power every moment upholds all; His unsearchable wisdom governs all, and His unbounded goodness cares and provides for all. "He openeth His hand, and satisfieth the desire of every living thing" (Psalm 145: 16). But in a special manner "He preserveth the souls of His saints" (Psalm 97:10). "The Lord preserveth all them that love Him" (Psalm 145:20). "The Lord shall preserve thee from all evil; He shall preserve thy soul. The Lord shall preserve thy going out, and thy coming in, from this time forth, and even forevermore" (Psalm 121:7–8). Since believers, then, are every moment dependent on God for the continuance and comfort both of their natural and spiritual life, they are bound, in obedience to His law as the rule of their life, to love Him supremely, to serve Him constantly, and to glorify Him in their body and spirit, which are His. The necessary relation in which they stand to Him as their constant Preserver obliges them to devote cheerfully all that they are, have, and do to His service and glory. Their being and their welfare are continually upheld and defended by His omnipotent arm; and therefore these ought at all times to be employed for Him. And because His manifested glory is His chief end in

preserving His saints, they are bound to make it their chief end also in all that they do (1 Corinthians 10:31).

4. The obligation under which the spiritual seed of Christ lie to perform perfect and perpetual obedience to the law of God flows also from His being their God in covenant.

He is their God in Christ, and in the covenant of grace; and this obliges them to perform universal obedience to His righteous law as it is in the hand of Christ, and as it stands under the covenant of grace.

He is also their God in grant or offer. He offers Christ, the blessed Mediator to them, in common with all the other hearers of the gospel; and He also offers Himself to them, to be, in Christ, their God. In the preface to the Ten Commandments, He says to every hearer of the gospel, "I am the Lord thy God." It is as if He had said, "I am your God in offer." And in the first commandment, as was observed above, He requires everyone to believe the gracious offer with application to himself, saying, "Thou shalt have no other Gods before Me" (Exodus 20:2–3). He commands every man to know and acknowledge Him to be the only true God, and his God, upon the ground of the unlimited offer; and He enables all His own people to believe cordially that He is their God in offer.

He is also their God in choice. In the exercise of their faith, they choose the Lord Jesus to be their Savior and God in Him, to be their covenant God, saying, "What have we to do any more with idols?" (Hosea 14:8). "This God is our God forever and ever" (Psalm 48:14). Each of them is enabled to say to the Lord, as the Psalmist did, "I trusted in Thee, O Lord. I said, 'Thou art my God' " (Psalm 31:14); it is as if he had said, "Thou art my God not only in offer, but in choice (or in preference to every other god); and I, accordingly, have trusted in Thee as my God, and placed all my hope and happiness in Thee."

He is their God also in possession. By believing cordially that He is theirs in offer, and by choosing Him for their God and portion in preference to every other god, as well as by trusting that in Christ He will perform the part of a God to them, they take possession of Him as their God. According to their faith in Him is their possession and enjoyment of Him; and in bestowing Himself on them as their God and portion, He makes over to them all that He is, has, does, and will do to be theirs in time and through eternity (Hosea 13:4; Psalm 84:11; 1 Corinthians 3:21). Seeing, then, that in amazing condescension He bestows Himself upon them as their God, they are under infinite obligations to devote themselves, and all that they are, have, and do to Him as His people. By His being their God, they are firmly bound, as well as powerfully excited, to love Him supremely, and to delight in yielding spiritual and universal obedience to Him. Because He is the Lord and their God, they are bound to keep all His commandments. And because it is of sovereign grace that He has been pleased to become their God, they are bound to obey His law as it stands in His covenant of grace—to obey it not that He may become their God, but because He already is their God. The covenant right which, according to His gracious promise, they have to Him as their God, gives Him an additional claim to them, and to all their love and obedience.

5. Their obligation to obey His law as a rule of con-

duct proceeds likewise from His being their redeeming God. In His love and pity He has redeemed them. From eternity He, according to the good pleasure of His will, has chosen them to everlasting salvation, and has devised the amazing scheme of their redemption. In the immensity of His redeeming love, and in the exceeding riches of His glorious grace, God the Father has sent His only begotten Son to purchase redemption for them, and His adorable Spirit to apply it to them. He has appointed His only Son to answer the demands of His law as a covenant for them that they might be justified, and His Holy Spirit to write His law as a rule on their hearts that they might be sanctified. As means of attaining the inestimable benefits of eternal redemption, He has moreover favored them with the doctrines, promises, and ordinances of His blessed gospel. Thus the Father, Son, and Holy Spirit, one Jehovah, stands in the endearing relation of a redeeming God to all true believers; Christ the glorious Mediator stands in the relation of a near Kinsman, an incarnate Redeemer; and the Holy Spirit in the relation of a Sanctifier and Comforter to them. And while God the Father and Christ and the blessed Spirit stand in these and other endearing relations to believers, believers stand in all the correspondent relations to them. Now from those relations an additional obligation to love and to good works arises which, instead of impairing, greatly strengthens all the other ties under which believers lie to yield evangelical and universal obedience. Because God graciously redeems them from the hand of all their enemies, and that with an infinite price and by infinite power, they are surely under the firmest possible obligations "to serve Him without fear, in holiness and righteousness before Him, all the days of their life" (Luke 1:74–75). The notion of a divine Redeemer implies that of a Creator. "Thus saith the Lord thy Redeemer, and He that formed thee from the womb, 'I am the Lord that maketh all things' " (Isaiah 44:24).

As God's being the Redeemer of His people, then, implies His being their Creator, in subordination to His glory in the redemption of them, so the obligation to obedience arising from His being their sovereign Creator is implied in, and strengthened by, the obligation flowing from His being their Redeemer. The redeeming grace of God in Christ is so far from lessening the force of the natural obligation under which believers as creatures lie to love and obey Him, that it increases this obligation in the highest possible degree. The great God who is glorious in holiness has not resigned His right of sovereign authority over His saints by redeeming them from the law as a covenant, and from their spiritual enemies; but, on the contrary, He has hereby laid them under further and stronger obligations to universal obedience to the law as a rule. The more illustrious the displays of His glorious perfections, and especially of His infinite goodness, are which He has afforded in their redemption, the greater are their obligations to obedience. When they consider that they have the righteousness of the incarnate Redeemer imputed to them to entitle them to eternal life, and His Spirit dwelling in them to make them meet for the perfection of it, they must surely acknowledge themselves to be under the firmest obligations possible to devote themselves entirely to the service and glory of their redeeming God.

In order to be satisfied of the truth of this, we need only to consider the new relations mentioned above, from which arises a set of new duties which no man is capable of performing, or has access to perform, unless he previously is a partaker of those relations. Of this class of duties are the faith, love, reverence, and worship which believers owe to Christ the adorable Mediator, to God in the relations of a Friend, Father, and God in covenant, and to the Holy Spirit dwelling in them as a Quickener, Sanctifier, and Comforter—also the duties which they owe to fellow-saints as members of Christ's mystical body. From those endearing relations, and the inestimable blessings issuing from them, believers cannot but be laid under new and peculiar obligations not only to perform these, but all the other duties required of them, in the law as a rule of life.

6. The holy will of God, revealed in His law as a rule of duty to believers, lays them under infinite obligations to obedience. The law in the hand of Christ is to His spiritual seed not only the rule, but the reason of their duty. They are bound not only to do that which is required in the law, and to leave undone that which is forbidden, but they must do what is commanded for the very reason that the Lord requires it, and abstain from what is forbidden because He forbids it. "Thou hast commanded us," says the holy Psalmist, "to keep Thy precepts diligently. Oh, that my ways were directed to keep Thy statutes!" (Psalm 119:4–5). To keep His commandments is, according to the phraseology of Scripture, to do His will. "He that doeth the will of God," says the Apostle John, "abideth forever" (1 John 2:17). And, says another apostle, "This is the will of

God, even your sanctification" (1 Thessalonians 4:3). It is the will not only of God the Father, but of God the Son: "I have ordained you, that ye should go and bring forth fruit, and that your fruit should remain" (John 15:16). It is the will also of God the Holy Spirit, whom believers grieve, and even quench, when they do not study to advance daily in the love and practice of universal holiness.

The law as a rule is not only a transcript of the infinite purity of God's holy nature, but it is, at the same time, a declaration of His holy will respecting the duty which His people owe to Him. They are, then, under the firmest ties to keep His holy commandments because it is His will that they should keep them. His will declared in His law is infinitely, eternally, and immutably holy, and therefore, in connection with the other sources of obligation already mentioned, it lays believers under the highest possible obligations to perfect and perpetual obedience of heart and life to His holy law.

7. Once more, the obligation under which believers are to obey the law as a rule arises also from the inexpressible benefit or advantage of holiness to themselves. The law in the hand of Christ is not only holy and just, but it is good. It is good in itself and good for believers. It requires nothing of them but what is good for them to perform, and to endure nothing but what is suitable and advantageous to them; nothing but what is agreeable and delightful to the new and holy nature imparted to them in regeneration. To be enabled, then, from principles of faith and love, and for the glory of God, to perform spiritual obedience to such a law is profitable, honorable, and delightful to real be-

lievers. It is profitable for them. "Godliness is profitable unto all things" (1 Timothy 4:8). "Godliness with contentment is great gain" (1 Timothy 6:6). "Charge them that are rich in this world . . . that they do good, that they be rich in good works" (1 Timothy 6:17–18). "These things are good and profitable unto men" (Titus 3:8). To love the Lord their God with all their heart, soul, strength, and mind, and their neighbor as themselves, is the very perfection of their nature, the highest advantage of which it is capable.

Holy obedience to the law in the hand of Christ is also honorable to believers. "If any man serve Me," said our blessed Lord, "him will My Father honor" (John 12:26). And again, "If a man love Me he will keep My words; and My Father will love him, and we will come unto him and make our abode with him" (John 14:23). What a high honor, what an exalted distinction is conferred on sinful worms of the dust when they are not only beautified with the holy image of God, but are advanced to intimate fellowship with Him! Conformity of heart and of life to the divine law is true honor. To resemble Him who is the brightness of the Father's glory, and the express image of His person, is the honor and glory of a man.

To yield obedience to the law of Christ is delightful also to holy souls. As they delight in the law itself, so they take pleasure in yielding spiritual obedience to all its holy commandments. Wisdom's ways are ways of pleasantness to them. Holiness is not only connected with happiness, but is itself happiness. A man is miserable in proportion as he is sinful, and happy in the same degree in which he is holy. In obedience there is a present and a great reward. True holiness is the health and happiness, the peace and pleasure of the soul. It renders the external comforts of the believer doubly pleasant and his heaviest crosses light, his life valuable and his death desirable. The holy commandments are inscribed on his heart; and therefore, he is well pleased with the purity, spirituality, and goodness of them. He delights in meditating on them (Psalm 1:2), and especially on the holiness of them; he counts them an easy yoke, and he chooses and resolves to perform spiritual and perpetual obedience to them. He knows by experience that he is happy in proportion as his inclinations, thoughts, words, and actions are holy; and that he is in his proper element only when he is exercising graces and performing duties.

Now, seeing holiness is, in subordination to the glory of God, profitable, honorable and pleasant to believers themselves, and so is highly beneficial to them, they are bound to make continual progress in the love and practice of it. As they are bound to glorify God as their redeeming God, and, in subordination to this, to advance in the enjoyment of Him, so they are under strong obligations, in obedience to His holy law, to advance in conformity to Him and in communion with Him: for they cannot glorify Him but in proportion as they enjoy Him, and they cannot enjoy Him but by such conformity to His image as is the fruit of communion with Him. Let every believer, then, endeavor diligently to advance in faith and holiness according to the law of Christ; for "blessed is the man that trusteth in the Lord, and whose hope the Lord is" (Jeremiah 17:7), and "blessed also is the man that feareth the Lord, that delighteth greatly in His commandments" (Psalm 112:1).

From what has now been said, we may warrantably
infer that all they to whom the law of the Ten Commandments is given as the authoritative rule of their
life have already received spiritual life as the beginning
of life eternal. They have all been quickened by the
Spirit of Christ, united to Him as their living Head, instated in His covenant of grace, and justified for His
righteousness imputed to them. And so they have received already the beginnings of eternal life as the gift
of God through Him. "He that believeth on the Son
hath everlasting life" (John 3:36). And again, "Whosoever liveth and believeth in Me shall never die" (John
11:26). The law as a covenant of works says to the dead
sinner, "Do this and live; do this for life." The law as a
rule of life, on the contrary, says to the living saint,
"Live and do this; do this not for, but from life already
received." All they, then, to whom the law as a rule of
life in the hand of the Mediator is given already have,
in their regeneration, received the beginning of
eternal life prior to their being capable of performing
the smallest degree of obedience to the law in that
form. They cannot obey the law as a rule of life otherwise than by working from life; but this supposes them
to have life previous to such working, and as the principle of it. Christ lives in them, and they live by the
faith of Him. Their spiritual and eternal life is the life
of Christ, life which is wholly derived from Him; and
the rule of it by which all its activity is to be regulated is
the divine law as the law of Christ (Galatians 6:2).
Regeneration and vital union with Christ are previously
and absolutely necessary to the smallest act of acceptable obedience to the law as a rule of life.

Does the law as a rule of life oblige believers to

yield even perfect obedience to its precepts? We ought not to infer from this that it can either justify them before God or condemn them. To justify or to condemn a man belongs to the law as a covenant, but not to it as a rule. To be under the law as a rule of life is the privilege only of believers who are already justified freely by grace through the redemption that is in Christ Jesus, and who are thereby placed forever beyond the reach of condemnation (Romans 8:1). The law as a rule cannot justify believers for their obedience to it, for they were perfectly justified in the sight of God before they began their course of sincere obedience; and besides, their obedience is far from being perfect. Neither can it condemn them to eternal wrath for their disobedience; for in their justification they were delivered from condemnation before they began, strictly speaking, to disobey it. It can indeed adjudge them to endure the painful effects of paternal anger, but not to suffer the direful effects of avenging wrath (John 5:24). The law as a rule can direct and bind believers even to perfect obedience, but it cannot either justify them to eternal life or condemn them to eternal death. Their title to eternal life, and their security from eternal death, have been merited for them by the obedience and death of the last Adam; and they are secured to them by His intercession. This consideration should endear exceedingly the holy law as a rule of duty to the true believer, and should constrain him to rejoice in the thought that he is bound, and in the prospect that to all eternity he shall be bound, by the authority of it to perfect and perpetual obedience (Psalm 119:77; Revelation 22:3).

Hence also it is evident that the main reason why

many true believers have but little holiness of heart
and life is that they have much of a legal spirit still remaining in them. It is only with their renewed nature
that they obey, or are capable of obeying, the law as a
rule. Their unrenewed nature still cleaves to the law as
a covenant. In proportion, then, to the degree of corruption remaining in them is that of their legal or old
covenant spirit; and the more this prevails in them, the
less holy they are. Evangelical or true holiness is a conformity of heart and life not to the law as a covenant of
works, but to it as a rule of life standing in the
covenant of grace. Although believers, as we said
above, are wholly delivered from the dominion of the
covenant of works as a rightful sovereign, yet many
times it is permitted to re-enter their consciences and
usurp authority over them. At such times it will venture
either to promise eternal life to them for their obedience, or to threaten eternal death to them for their
disobedience. Now in exact proportion to the degree
of their legal temper they are disposed to hearken to
the voice of the law in their consciences; and as far as
they regard the usurped authority of the law as a
covenant of works, they so far disregard the high authority and obligation of it as a rule of duty. Believer,
you cannot advance in holy conformity to the law as a
rule but in proportion as you, by the Spirit, mortify
your legal temper. You may be eminently strict, exact,
and uniform in your external performance of every
duty; but in as far as a legal spirit prevails and influences your performance of them, they are so far unholy and unacceptable to God. He will accept none of
your works but those which are done from evangelical
principles and in an evangelical manner. Nothing will

more effectually retard your progress in true holiness than either to hope that you shall obtain heaven for your works of obedience or to fear that you shall be cast into hell for your sins. If you trust your habits of grace rather than the fullness of grace in Christ; if you derive your comfort from your lively frames and religious attainments rather than from Christ and the promises; and if you make either the good dispositions implanted in you or the good works performed by you the ground of your right to trust daily in Him for salvation, instead of trusting in Him upon the ample warrant afforded you by the offers and calls of the gospel, by doing so you will assuredly decline from holy and cheerful obedience to the law as a rule of life. If instead of coming always as a sinner to the compassionate Savior, and placing direct confidence in Him for salvation to yourself in particular, you refuse to trust in Him except when you can bring some good qualification or work with you to recommend you to Him, you cannot advance in that holy obedience to His law which is the obedience of faith (Romans 16:26).

It is no less manifest from what has been said that the state to which believers are advanced upon their vital union with Christ is so far from being a state of liberty to commit sin that it is a state in which they are laid under the highest possible obligations even to perfect obedience. If all men are bound to keep the commandments of God because He is Jehovah, the redeemed are especially and still more firmly bound to yield all obedience to them because He is not only Jehovah, but is besides their God and Redeemer. None are under such high and strong obligations to holiness of heart and life as the ransomed of the Lord are. He is

their God in covenant, and this lays them under the
firmest ties to be His obedient, holy people. He is their
almighty and gracious Redeemer, and therefore they
are not their own, but His, and are infinitely bound to
glorify Him in their bodies and in their spirits, which
are His (1 Corinthians 6:20). Why do the saints bitterly
bewail the strength of their corruptions and the weakness of their graces, the innumerable sins of which
they have been guilty, and the want of perfect conformity to the holy law of which they are sensible? Is it not
because they feel their infinite obligations not to
merely sincere, but even to perfect obedience? And
why do they, in their exercise of evangelical repentance, loathe themselves in their own sight for their iniquities and their abominations (Ezekiel 36:31)? Do
they it not because they are enabled to account their
want of that perfect conformity to the law to which
they are bound an abominable defect? The wonderful
grace of God displayed in their justification and deliverance from the law as a covenant of works, instead of
leaving them at liberty to continue in sin, disposes and
powerfully constrains them to depart from all iniquity
and advance resolutely in universal obedience to the
law as a rule of life. There is not a true believer in the
world who does not know this by experience.

What has been advanced may also serve to throw
some light on the doctrine of vowing to the Lord, and
of the obligation which arises from a lawful vow.
Believers are far from being left at liberty to vow or not
to vow as they please. They are expressly commanded
to vow to God, and also to perform their vows. "Vow,
and pay unto the Lord your God" (Psalm 76:11). "Pay
thy vows unto the Most High" (Psalm 50:14). It is clear

from the context that the vows mentioned in this last
passage are not legal and ceremonial, but spiritual or
moral vows; vows which believers in all ages of the
Church are bound both to make and to perform.
Isaiah, when predicting the conversion of multitudes
in New Testament times, and especially in the millen-
nial period of the Church, says, "The Egyptians shall
know the Lord in that day; yea, they shall vow a vow
unto the Lord, and perform it" (Isaiah 19:21).
Accordingly, the venerable Assembly at Westminster
teaches that "vowing unto God is a duty required in the
second commandment of the moral law" (Larger
Catechism, question 108). All true converts, in every
age of the Church, dedicate themselves, and all that
they are, have, and do to the Lord; and in doing so
they either expressly or implicitly vow to Him. That is
to say, they solemnly purpose and promise that in dependence on promised grace, or that in as far as the
Lord Jesus will according to His promises, enable
them, they shall, all the days of their life, yield sincere
and increasing obedience to His holy law as the rule of
their duty. They do not engage or promise to yield perfect obedience in their present state of imperfection,
or to perform so much as a single duty in the strength
of grace already received, but to perform in the
strength of that grace which is promised, and which
they trust will be given them, all necessary duties. This
is not a particular, but a general vow. Neither is it a legal and ceremonial, but a spiritual and moral vow. It is
the believer's baptismal vow which, if opportunities are
afforded, he will be sure willingly, explicitly, and frequently to renew at the Table of the Lord.

Now, from this vow or promissory oath arises an

obligation on the believer to do as he has said. He vows
to perform nothing but what he was previously under
the firmest obligations possible to perform; and therefore, though his vow cannot add to the authority of
God in His law, nor, strictly speaking, strengthen those
obligations to obedience which are already as strong as
it is possible for them at the time to be; yet it is the
source of a new, a distinct and a super-added obligation. It is not, indeed, a primary source of obligation to
obedience like those mentioned above; but still it lays
the believer under a new and distinct obligation to fulfil his engagement. He engages or obliges himself, by
his own voluntary act, to perform sincerely all those
duties to which he is already bound by the law. And the
more often he repeats his vow, the obligation arising
from it becomes the firmer. If a lawful vow, with respect to things indifferent, founds an obligation, as
generally seems to be allowed, much more, surely,
must a lawful vow concerning necessary duties be binding. The new obligation to necessary duties, arising
from a deliberate and solemn vow to perform them, is
not in the least inconsistent with those high obligations
to them which flow from the other sources already explained. It is, indeed, associated with these obligations,
but it is no disparagement to them.

Should any still be disposed to question if a lawful
vow respecting moral duties can found a new and distinct obligation to perform them, I would only add that
it either lays the believer who makes it under a new
obligation or it does not. There can be no medium
here. If it lays him under an obligation, it must be an
obligation posterior to those considered above, and
therefore a new and distinct one. If it lays him under

no obligation, it will follow that lawful vows do not bind; if they do not bind or impose an obligation, they cannot be broken; and, if so, the saints in all ages have acted an unwise, yea, and a superstitious part when they have confessed and bitterly bewailed their breach of vows. Many professors of religion in our day seem unwilling to vow to the Lord for fear that, by the breach of vows, they should increase the number of their sins. But this discovers both a want of knowledge and a want of sincerity. Matthew Henry, commenting on Isaiah 45:23, says well, "If the heart be brought into obedience to Christ, and made willing in the day of His power, the tongue will swear to Him, will lay a bond upon the soul, to engage it forever to Him; for he that bears an honest mind doth never startle at assurances."

In conclusion, believers are under every obligation not only to obedience to the divine law, but to free and voluntary obedience. They are bound to yield such obedience as cannot be performed under the law as a covenant of works, as cannot be performed from the principle either of slavish fear or of servile hope. They are under the strongest ties to yield voluntary obedience to the law as a rule of life. They are firmly bound, but it is to free obedience; to the obedience not of slaves or hirelings, but of sons and daughters. The Lord Jesus says in His law to them, as on a particular occasion He did to His disciples, "Freely ye have received, freely give" (Matthew 10:8). With infinite willingness, He obeyed the law as a covenant for them in order that they, by His grace, might with sincere willingness and, in due time, with perfect willingness obey it as a rule. The law as a rule of life to believers has, as was said above, no threatening of eternal death, and no promise of eternal life annexed to it. No obedience, therefore, is suitable to it but that which is free and voluntary, proceeding from love to God, delight in His will, and concern for His glory. In proportion, accordingly, as the saints are enabled to believe the astonishing love of God with application to themselves, and to contemplate the infinitely free grace manifested in redeeming them from the broken covenant of works, and in bringing them under the law of the hand of Christ, they yield free and unconstrained obedience to this law. Made a willing people in the day of the Redeemer's power, they obey willingly, and that not from legal motives, but from 'evangelical ones. They study to do what the Lord requires because He commands them, and in order to please and honor Him. They hate all manner of sin because it is hateful in itself, and because He hates it. With holy abhorrence they forsake iniquity because He forbids it, and in order that they may not displease or dishonor Him. And though their obedience will not be absolutely free till it is absolutely perfect, yet the freeness of it will always be in exact proportion to the strength and frequency of their actings of faith and love. When a man is habitually attentive to the manner as well as to the matter of every act of obedience, it is a good evidence that he is dead to the law as a covenant, and is brought under the obligation of it as a rule; that the law as a covenant has begun to be erased from his heart, and the law as a rule to be written on it.

Chapter 12

The Nature, Necessity, and Desert of Good Works

Good works are such actions or deeds as are commanded in the law of God as a rule of life. An action is a good work in the view of men when it is materially good; that is, when the matter of it appears agreeable to the letter of the law, and when it is profitable either to the individual himself who performs it or to any other. But nothing is a good work in the sight of God unless it is formally as well as materially good. While the matter of it must accord to the letter, the form must, in some degree, correspond to the spirit of the holy law. No man, while he is under the law as a covenant of works, can do a single action that is formally good. He must be a true believer, justified by faith, dead to the law as a covenant, under the law as a rule, and "created in Christ Jesus to good works" before he can perform the smallest action that will be good and acceptable in the sight of God (Romans 5:6). Good works cannot be done but in obedience to the law in the hand of the Mediator as an authoritative rule of conduct; and they cannot be performed but by persons who are vitally united to Him as the last Adam, and who have communion with Him in His righteousness and fullness (John 15:5). In order to perform the smallest good work, a man must be justified on the ground of the perfect righteousness of Christ imputed to him; and therefore his good works arrive too late to form any part of his justifying righteousness. As it is impossible for a man to be justified in the sight of God by the works of the law before conversion, so it is equally impossible for him to be justified by his good works after it. Good works will, indeed, justify the believer's profession of faith before men, but not his person before God. Such works, not being performed under the law as a covenant, and at the same time not being perfect, cannot enter into the ground of a sinner's justification; but they manifest him to have true faith, and to be already justified by faith; and so they evidence his profession of faith before men to be sincere (Galatians 2:16; Philippians 3:9; James 2:24). As good works are strictly enjoined in the law of God, and as it is of the highest importance to the honor of God, and also to the advancement of holiness and comfort in believers themselves that they understand well the nature, the necessity, and the desert of such works, I shall here consider briefly, each of these in order.

Section 1. The Nature of Good Works

Holiness of life, or the constant practice of good works, proceeds from that holiness of heart which is imparted to elect sinners in regeneration and sanctification. It consists in their conformity of life to the law as a rule of duty. The habitual and constant performance of good works is the same as holiness of life; and it is the distinguishing character of every adult person who so believes in the Lord Jesus as to have the beginnings of eternal life. Here it will be necessary, briefly, to point out what it is that constitutes an action, a good work in the sight of God, the omniscient and sovereign Judge of all.

Much more is required for this purpose than merely a good intention. A man may, in his actions, propose to himself a good end, or may have an apparently good intention to serve, while yet he is ignorant of the holiness and spirituality of the divine law (1 Timothy 1:7). Many, with what has appeared to them to be the best intention, have done and still do things which are expressly forbidden in the holy law of God (1 John 16:2). The sovereign authority of God in His law obliges men to regulate not only their ends of acting, but their principles, inclinations, and the matter and manner of their actions by that divine standard (Deuteronomy 12:32; Mark 12:30–31). The following things especially are requisite to constitute our works of obedience as good works:

1. They must be such as are required in the law of God, and are performed in obedience to His holy will, expressed in the precepts of His law. "He that keepeth the commandment keepeth his own soul" (Proverbs 19:16). "He that doeth the will of God abideth forever" (1 John 2:17). The law of God is the revelation of His sovereign will, and therefore it is the authoritative rule of our obedience. No action, then, is a good work unless it is performed agreeably to His will, and as an act of obedience to His commands.

2. They cannot be accounted good works unless they are raised on a good foundation. Our works cannot be good unless they are works of new and evangelical obedience; and this they cannot possibly be unless they are built on a new and evangelical foundation. Good works cannot stand but on a good or an evangelical ground, namely the doctrines, offers, invitations,

and promises of the gospel, and especially, the glorious doctrine of justification only for the righteousness of Christ imputed and received by faith; as also the holy law, in consequence of the second Adam's fulfilling of it, divested of its federal form to believers, and in and by Him given to them as the only and immutable rule of their new obedience. "If ye know these things," said our Lord to His disciples, "happy are ye if ye do them" (John 13:17). And the Apostle Paul wrote, "These things," namely the things mentioned in the immediately preceding context, "I will that thou affirm constantly, that they which have believed in God, might be. careful to maintain good works" (Titus 3:8).

3. It is also requisite that they flow from evangelical principles. They cannot be spiritually good or acceptable to God unless they proceed from good principles of action. But no principles are good unless they are evangelical. It is not sufficient for this purpose that our performances be barely moral, as many of the actions of heathens were; they must be evangelical and holy also. They must flow from such evangelical principles as these: a soul regenerated by the quickening Spirit of Christ; a mind enlightened with the saving knowledge of Christ, and of the truth as it is in Him; union with Christ, and with God in Him, by a living faith; communion with Christ in His righteousness and fullness, and with God in Him; a conscience sprinkled with His justifying and peace-speaking blood; and a heart sanctified and comforted by His Holy Spirit (Ezekiel 36:25–27; Matthew 12:35). They must proceed more immediately from principles and habits of faith, hope, and love in a sanctified soul. "Without faith, it is impossible to please God" (Hebrews 11:16). "Every man that hath this hope

in Him purifieth himself, even as He is pure" (1 John 3:3). "This is the love of God, that we keep His commandments" (1 John 5:3).

4. We must be excited to the performance of them by evangelical motives only. To render our works spiritually good, it is not enough that they proceed from good principles; they must, moreover, be influenced by good motives, deeply affecting and determining our hearts, such as: the astonishing love and grace of God manifested in His gospel (1 John 4:19); the sovereign authority and will of God as our Covenant God and Father, declared in His law as the rule of our duty (1 Thessalonians 4:3; Exodus 20:2-3; 2 Corinthians 5:14); our deliverance from condemnation, and the ample security from eternal death which the blood of Christ affords us (1 Corinthians 6:20; 1 Peter 1:17-19); the promise and the hope of "eternal life as the gift of God through Jesus Christ our Lord" (Titus 1:2; Romans 6:23), and the perfect pattern of good works, which Christ has proposed for our imitation (1 Peter 2:21; Hebrews 12:1-3).

5. Another requisite is that they be performed in a special manner. It is necessary that the manner as well as the matter of our works be spiritually good and acceptable to God. The manner of performing them must be evangelical, suited to the state, the privileges, and the prospects of believers. They cannot be good works unless they are performed inwardly as well as outwardly; for the law is spiritual, and it requires the obedience of the whole heart as well as of the whole life. They must, in order to their being good works, be performed in the exercise of trusting with firm confidence that Christ will, every moment, afford us grace

to enable us to perform them acceptably (1 Timothy 1:5; Philippians 4:13; Hebrews 11:6); in the exercise of a lively hope (1 Peter 1:3–4); in the exercise of supreme love to Christ, and to God in Him (1 Timothy 1:5; Romans 13:10); in the exercise of adoring gratitude to the Lord for all His benefits bestowed and promised (Psalm 116:12–14); and in the exercise also of evangelical contrition and humiliation, counting ourselves utterly "unworthy of the least of all His mercies" (Genesis 32:10), and indebted wholly to His sovereign grace for all our salvation (Ephesians 2:8–10). They are good works only in proportion as they are performed in the exercise of spiritual graces and in the strength of promised grace.

6. Once more, it is no less requisite that we propose to ourselves good ends in performing them. The ends which we propose to ourselves in the practice of them must be evangelical, as well as our principles, motives, and manner. They cannot be accounted good works, except our chief or ultimate end in doing them, be the glory of God in Christ, as our God (1 Corinthians 10:31). Nor is it sufficient for this purpose that in them we virtually and habitually intend the glory of God; it will be necessary that, in performing each of them, we actually aim at the glory of His holy name as our highest end. It is also requisite that in our practice of them we have it ever in view, in subordination to the manifested glory of God, to advance in conformity of heart and of life to our great Redeemer (1 Peter 1:15–16; Philippians 3:10–14), to embrace every opportunity of doing good to all around us (Matthew 5:16), and to prepare for the full and everlasting enjoyment of God—Father, Son, and Holy Spirit—as our infinite

portion (Psalm 73:25–26).

Now the performances of real Christians have, in a higher or lower degree, all these requisites; and therefore they are, strictly speaking, good works. The depravity that remains in the hearts of believers hinders, indeed, their works from being perfectly good; but it cannot prevent them from being truly or spiritually good and "acceptable to God through Jesus Christ." The good Spirit of God dwells in all saints, and "works in them, both to will and to do of His good pleasure" (Philippians 2:13). He has begun, and He promotes, a good work of grace in their hearts; and from this proceed all good works of obedience in their lives (Philippians 1:6). But, seeing their best actions are not yet perfectly good, they ought so to increase and "abound in every good work," so as constantly to press on toward perfection in holiness. They are commanded to increase more and more in the strength and liveliness of their spiritual graces, and in the zealous and diligent performance of their necessary duties (2 Peter 3:18; 1 Thessalonians 4:1).

Section 2. The Necessity of Good Works

In this section, I shall, first, endeavor to show for what purposes good works are not necessary, and, next, in what respects, or for what ends, they are necessary.

In the first place, I am to show for what purposes they are not necessary.

1. Good works are not necessary to move God to be merciful and gracious to us. They are not needful to recommend us so to the favor of God so as to excite

His compassion and good will to us, or to produce the
smallest change in His intentions concerning us. The
change to be promoted by the continual practice of
good works will be only in ourselves; it cannot be in
God. "He is in one mind, and who can turn Him?" He
is Jehovah, and He changes not. Our holy performances, do not render God more willing than He is already to show mercy or give grace to us; but they are
means of rendering ourselves more and more willing
to receive His mercy and grace. We must, then, never
depend on our own good works, but always on the
spotless righteousness of Christ, and on the gracious
promises of God, for all the effects of His mercy and
favor.

2. Our good works are not necessary to afford us a
right to trust in Christ for salvation. They cannot obtain for us a right to believe in the Lord Jesus; nor is it
requisite that they should. The commandment of the
law to believe in the name of Jesus Christ (1 John
3:23), together with the offers, invitations, and
promises of the gospel, affords us all the right or warrant that is requisite to come as sinners to the Savior,
and to place the confidence of our hearts in Him for
His whole salvation. These afford to us, in common
with all the other hearers of the gospel, a full right as
sinners of mankind to approach, and, with the firmest
confidence, to trust in Him. And therefore we have no
need to procure by our performances the smallest degree of right to come to Him (Isaiah 55:1; Revelation
22:17). Our good works are necessary for other purposes, but not for this. "Christ Jesus came into the
world to save sinners," and "not to call the righteous,
but sinners to repentance." We must, therefore, ap-

proach and trust in Him as sinners utterly unworthy of Him, and that without looking for any good qualities or works of our own either to recommend us to His regard or to entitle us to trust that He will save us. How can our good works be necessary to afford us a right to trust in the Savior when we must begin to trust in Him before we can perform the smallest good work?

3. Neither are good works necessary to acquire for us a personal interest in Christ. So far are they from being requisite to merit, or so much as to obtain for us a saving interest in Jesus Christ, that our being previously interested in Him is indispensably necessary to our being capable of performing so much as the very smallest of them (Ephesians 1:6; John 15:5). Good works, then, can have no place in procuring for us a personal interest in the Savior. It is necessary to qualify us for them, but they are not necessary to confer on us a right to it. They are indeed an evidence of it, but not a procuring cause; they follow upon it, but do not go before it. They can have no existence before it; and therefore, they can neither entitle us to it nor qualify us for the reception of it. A personal interest in Christ must either be received as a gift of sovereign grace, by faith only, or not received at all. Many convinced sinners err greatly in this matter. They hope that their reformations, their frames, and their performances will so recommend them to God as to procure for them a saving interest in the person and work of Christ. Thus they themselves try to begin the work of their salvation, and then to trust that the Savior will help it forward. But this is to "seek righteousness not by faith, but as it were by the works of the law, and to stumble at that stumbling stone" (Acts 15:9; 1 Corinthians 6:11;

Colossians 2:12). No man can attain a saving interest in
Christ until he is made willing to receive it as a gift of
infinitely free grace.

4. Good works are not requisite to acquire for us a
right to increasing degrees of sanctification. We ought,
indeed, to employ them diligently as means of growing
in habits of grace; but we must not hence conclude
that they are needful to procure for us a title to those
influences of sanctifying grace which are every moment requisite for increasing our habits of grace and
exciting them to exercise. They are necessary as means,
and also as evidences, but not as procuring causes of
progressive holiness. It is not the good fruit that makes
the tree good; but, on the contrary, it is the good tree
that produces the good fruit. It is not the good works
of believers, but the infinitely perfect righteousness of
the second Adam, that entitles them to increasing holiness both of heart and life. And therefore, while they
ought to be diligent and zealous in performing all
good works, they must not presume to place the least
dependence on their performance of them for a title
to continued supplies either of sanctifying or comforting grace. Instead of trusting to their own endeavors
for a continued increase of inherent holiness, their
duty is to rely on the righteousness of Jesus Christ for
their whole title to it. They ought to rely on His surety-
righteousness as much for a title to sanctification as for
a right to justification. It is by faith in the Lord Jesus as
their righteousness and strength that they are sanctified as well as justified (Acts 15:9; 1 Corinthians 6:11;
Colossians 2:12). While then they trust constantly in
Christ Himself for continual supplies of sanctifying
grace, they must, instead of depending on their own

works, rely daily on His righteousness alone for all their title to those supplies. Though good works are indispensably necessary in those who are sanctified, yet they are so far from being requisite to procure for the saints a title to progressive sanctification that these could not perform so much as one of them till after they began to be sanctified.

5. Once more, good works have no place in obtaining for the saints a right to eternal life in heaven. Eternal life is the gift of God through Jesus Christ our Lord. It is a purchased possession, purchased for all His spiritual seed by the obedience unto death of the second Adam. It is an inheritance which He, "the heir of all things," bequeaths to them, and of which they attain possession not on the ground of their own good works, but by union and communion with Him. It is not their own good deeds, but His righteousness that is meritorious of eternal life for them. "Not by works of righteousness which we have done," says the Apostle Paul, "but according to His mercy He saved us" (Titus 3:5). It is Christ only who "hath obtained eternal redemption" for believers (Hebrews 9:12). They are accepted as righteous in the sight of God, and entitled to eternal life, not for their own good works, but only for the righteousness of Christ imputed to them, and received by faith alone. It is "by the righteousness of one" that grace, or "the free gift, comes upon all men who believe, unto justification of life"; for "by the obedience of one shall many be made righteous" (Romans 5:18–19). Were the good works of believers to entitle them in the smallest degree to salvation, their salvation would, in the same degree, be of debt to them and not of grace. But it is not by any merit of theirs, but by the

sovereign grace of God that they are saved (Ephesians
2:8–9).

Besides, if their good works afforded them a right
claim to eternal life, it would inevitably follow that they
could not have a right to it till after they had performed them all. But the infinitely perfect righteousness of Jesus Christ gives them in their justification a
complete right to life eternal, and that before they begin to do one good work (Romans 4:4–6). Indeed, believers, even if they could perform perfect obedience,
could yield no degree of obedience but what they
owed to the Lord; and therefore even their perfect
obedience could not merit the least favor from Him.

And as their good works can give them no meritorious right to eternal life, so neither can they afford
them a pactional title to it; for by the consummate
righteousness of Jesus Christ imputed to them they
have already both the one right and the other, and
that in the highest possible degree. Though good
works, then, are not necessary in order to procure or
obtain a right to eternal salvation; yet they are the necessary duties of all who are justified and entitled to that
salvation. They are the consequences of salvation already procured; and they are the antecedents which
prepare believers for the salvation to be still attained.
At the same time, however, they are not causes of obtaining the possession either of the beginning, the
progress, or the consummation of salvation. They are
indispensably necessary in all adult persons who shall
be saved, but not necessary to obtain or acquire salvation. Believers are saved not *by* their good works, but *to*
them, as effects and evidences of their salvation already
begun. These words of the Apostle Paul, "They do it to

obtain a corruptible crown, but we, an incorruptible," will not prove that good works are necessary to obtain eternal salvation; for the verb in the original properly signifies "to receive or apprehend" (1 Corinthians 9:25); and it is so rendered by our translators in the verse immediately preceding. Believers are not saved either by their works, for their works, or according to their works.

We are not saved by them. "Not by works of righteousness which we have done, but according to His mercy He saved us" (Titus 3:5).

We are not saved for them. " 'It is not for your sake do I this,' saith the Lord God, 'be it known unto you' " (Ezekiel 36:32).

We are not saved according to them. "He hath saved us, and called us with an holy calling, not according to our works, but according to His own purpose and grace" (2 Timothy 1:9). Men are, indeed, to be judged according to their works; but are not to be saved according to them. The rule of judgment will be the law; but the rule of salvation will be the gospel.

I proceed now, as was proposed, to show in what respects or for what important purposes good works are indispensably requisite.

1. They are necessary as just acknowledgments of God's sovereign authority over believers, and as acts of obedience to His righteous commands. "For this is the will of God," said Paul, "even your sanctification" (1 Thessalonians 4:3). The infinite Majesty of heaven has not laid aside His right of dominion over believers by affording them deliverance from condemnation and a right to eternal life; but on the contrary He has, in that wonderful way, laid them under additional

obligations to holiness in all manner of conversation.
The glorious liberty to which He has called them is
given them for this purpose: "That they may serve Him
without fear, in holiness and righteousness before
Him, all the days of their life" (Luke 1:74–75). He has
delivered them from the law as a covenant for this very
end: that according to the law as a rule "they might
serve Him in newness of Spirit" and "be careful to
maintain good works." The sovereign will of God as the
supreme rule of duty is expressed in His commands;
and therefore universal and perpetual obedience to
them is necessary.

2. Good works are indispensably requisite as being
one special end of the election, redemption, regeneration, and effectual vocation of the objects of God's everlasting love. They are one design of the election of
sinners. "The God and Father of our Lord Jesus Christ
hath chosen us in Him," said the Apostle Paul, "that we
should be holy, and without blame before Him in love"
(Ephesians 1:4). They are also one end of the redemption of elect sinners. For the same apostle said, "Christ
gave Himself for us that He might redeem us from all
iniquity, and purify unto Himself a peculiar people,
zealous of good works" (Titus 2:14). They are one of
the designs too of the regeneration of God's elect. "We
are His workmanship," said our apostle, "created in
Christ Jesus unto good works, which God hath before
ordained that we should walk in them" (Ephesians
2:10). Good works are the native and necessary opera-
tions of a regenerate and sanctified soul. Grace in the
heart is a living, operative principle of holiness in the
life. Good works are likewise one of the ends to be attained by their effectual vocation. "As He which hath

called you is holy," said the Apostle Peter, "so be ye holy in all manner of conversation" (1 Peter 1:15).

3. Good works are also necessary inasmuch as they are one great design of the gospel, and of the ordinances and providential dispensations of the Lord. As for the gospel, it is "the mystery of godliness" (1 Timothy 3:16), "the doctrine which is according to godliness" (1 Timothy 6:3). The doctrine of the gospel is not speculative merely; it is also transforming and practical. It is not only the instrument of enlightening the mind, but also of renovating the will, and of rectifying the affections of the soul. In the hand of the Holy Spirit, it is a fire which penetrates, warms, softens, quickens, purifies, and comforts the heart. It is a light which assimilates (2 Corinthians 3:18) and truth which sanctifies (John 17:17). It is also "the law of the Spirit of life in Christ Jesus" which, by making believers "free from the law of sin and death," brings them "under the law to Christ" (1 Corinthians 9:21). The design, too, of the ordinances of the gospel is that sinners may be converted to the love and practice of holiness, and that saints may be enabled to abound more and more in every good word and work. This is the design likewise of all providential dispensations to the children of God. If they are favored with prosperity, it is that the goodness of God may constrain them to "bring forth fruits meet for repentance"; or, if they are visited with adversity, it is "that it may yield the peaceable fruit of righteousness to them" (Hebrews 12:11).

4. It is indispensably requisite that believers perform good works as expressions of gratitude to their God and Savior for all His inestimable benefits vouchsafed to them. They are bound to always be grateful

and thankful to the Lord for His great goodness to
them in creation, in providence, and especially in redemption. It is He who has made them and not they
themselves. He has preserved them amidst innumerable dangers, and has liberally supplied their various
wants. He has distinguished them from all others of
the sons of men by the greatness of their privileges and
the inestimable value of their enjoyments; by the innumerable instances of His kindness and the rich
abundance of His favors. He has also, in the immensity
of His love, sent His only begotten Son to redeem
them to Himself by His blood, and to merit for them
the full and endless fruition of Himself in the mansions of bliss. Moreover He has sent His Holy Spirit to
dwell in them, to apply redemption to them, and, by
His sanctifying and comforting influences, to prepare
them for every good work and advance them to the full
enjoyment of eternal life. How boundless, then, how
inexpressible, is the debt of adoring gratitude which
they owe to the Father, to the Son, and to the Holy
Spirit! Now, what does the Lord require of them in return for all His benefits? Nothing but that they should
"be ready to every good work," and be "zealous for
good works." Having been bought with a price of infinite value, they are no more their own, but are indispensably bound to glorify God in their body and in
their spirit, which are His, by a spiritual, universal, and
cheerful obedience to Him. It is the will of their
sovereign Benefactor that they express their gratitude
to Him for the inestimable blessings of His grace by
taking pleasure in keeping all His commandments,
and by showing themselves patterns of good works
(Titus 2:7).

5. Good works are no less necessary as they are our walking in the way which leads to heaven. Jesus Christ is the way (John 14:6). Faith and holiness are our walking in Him as the way. This way, accordingly, is called "the way of holiness," or "the holy way" (Isaiah 35:8), inasmuch as none can walk in Christ other than by faith, and by that holiness of heart and life which is "the obedience of faith." As no man can arrive at heaven but by Christ, so "without holiness," or walking in Him, "no man shall see the Lord" (Hebrews 12:14). None is in the way to heaven but he who, by a life of faith and the practice of those good works which are the fruits of faith, is advancing toward perfection of holiness. It is the order immutably fixed in the everlasting covenant that a man be made holy in heart and in life before he is admitted to see and enjoy God in His holy place on high. The love and practice of good works, then, in one who has an opportunity of performing them, are necessary as appointed means of disposing or preparing him for the holy enjoyments and employments of the heavenly sanctuary. The redeemed, therefore, who are in the way to the celestial city, are zealous for good works and "fruitful in every good work" (Colossians 1:10).

6. Good works are also indispensably requisite in order to evidence and confirm the faith of the saints. Wherever a living and a saving faith is, good works are, in every adult believer, the native fruits and proper evidences of it. "Show me," said the Apostle James, "thy faith without thy works, and I will show thee my faith by my works" (James 2:18). Sincere obedience is the necessary consequence, and therefore a necessary evidence, of justifying and saving faith. Good works are

works of faith, works performed in faith, and proceeding from it as the living principle of them. Whatever seeming evidences of true faith, then, a man may have, they are all to be regarded as counterfeit and delusive if he does not, at the same time, love and practice good works. Such works not only evidence a living faith, but they also encourage the believer resolutely to persevere in renewing his exercise of faith; and so they prove to be means of confirming his faith.

7. Good works are necessary to believers for making their calling and election sure to them. Although such works afford a man no right to eternal salvation, yet they are an infallible proof to him that he has a personal interest in it and a sure title to it. They, under the witnessing of the Holy Spirit, supply the believer with arguments, which not only serve to confirm his assurance of faith, but to increase his assurance of personal interest in Christ and His great salvation. "Hereby we do know that we know Him," said the beloved disciple, "if we keep His commandments. . . Whosoever keepeth His Word, in him verily is the love of God perfected; hereby know we that we are in Him" (1 John 2:3, 5). To the same purpose the Apostle Peter says, "Giving all diligence, add to your faith, virtue; and to virtue, knowledge; and to knowledge, temperance; and to temperance, patience; and to patience, godliness; and to godliness, brotherly kindness; and to brotherly kindness, charity. . . Give diligence to make your calling and election sure; for if ye do these things, ye shall never fall" (1 Peter 1:5–7, 10). Without the diligent performance of good works, no believer can attain assurance of his personal interest in eternal salvation, far less establishment in that assurance.

8. Good works are indispensably requisite for the maintenance or continuance of peace and joy in the Holy Ghost. Though such works are not procuring causes of spiritual peace and joy, yet, as fruits of righteousness imputed and fruits of faith, they always accompany that peace and joy which issues from the lively exercise of faith (Psalm 119:165; 2 Corinthians 1:12). The consolation which flows from the vigorous exercise of an appropriating faith, and from cheering discoveries of personal interest in the covenant of grace, cannot be retained without unwearied diligence in the exercise of spiritual graces, and in the performance of good works. If believers would know by experience that "wisdom's ways are ways of pleasantness, and all her paths are peace" (Proverbs 3:17); and if they would enjoy a continued sense of redeeming love, and a sweet foretaste of heavenly felicity; they must be habitually careful not only to maintain, but to be rich in good works.

9. Good works are no less needful in order to adorn the doctrine of God our Savior, and our profession of that holy and heavenly doctrine. The Apostle Paul gave this charge to Titus: "Exhort servants to be obedient unto their own masters, and to please them well in all things; not answering again; not purloining, but showing all good fidelity; that they may adorn the doctrine of God our Savior in all things" (Titus 2:9–10). Believers cannot otherwise be a credit to the gospel, and to their holy profession of it, than by a cheerful and diligent performance of every good work. It is only by the love and practice of universal holiness that they can strike a conviction of the holiness, excellence, and efficacy of the gospel of God our Savior on the con-

sciences of hardened sinners around them. No other practice than that of good works in all their variety becomes the gospel of Christ. It is only "the beauty of holiness" that is suitable and ornamental to His glorious gospel. If believers, then, would not afford occasion to the enemies of the Lord Jesus to blaspheme His glorious name, to speak evil of the way of truth, and to conclude that all who profess faith and holiness are hypocrites and imposters, they must diligently follow every good work. If, while men seek to be justified by Christ, they themselves also are found sinners, this reflects much dishonor on our great Redeemer, and makes Him "the minister of sin" (Galatians 2:17).

10. Good works are also requisite to stop the mouths of wicked men and to prevent offense. "For so is the will of God," said the apostle, "that with well-doing, ye may put to silence the ignorance of foolish men" (1 Peter 1:15). They are necessary likewise to gain over unbelievers and other enemies of the truth, and to recommend faith and holiness to their esteem. It is, by the faithful and cheerful performance of every good work, that believers commend the Lord Jesus, and the way of truth and holiness to the consciences of all around them.

11. They are necessary, moreover, for the edification and comfort of fellow Christians. Our blessed Lord, therefore, gave His disciples this high command: "Let your light so shine before men that they may see your good works, and glorify your Father which is in heaven" (Matthew 5:16). And the Apostle Paul informed the believers at Corinth that their zeal, in contributing readily and seasonably for the poor saints at Jerusalem, had provoked many (2 Corinthians 9:2).

The same apostle informs us that the doctrines of grace, and the good works to which they tend, "are good and profitable unto men" (Titus 3:8). Such works are highly necessary not only for the edification and comfort of individual believers, but also for the peace, security, and glory of the Church.

12. Finally, good works are indispensably requisite for promoting before the world the manifested glory of Christ, and of God in Him. The Apostle Paul prayed for the believers at Philippi that they might be "sincere, and without offence till the day of Christ; being filled with the fruits of righteousness, which are by Jesus Christ, unto the glory and praise of God" (Philippians 1:10–11). The Lord Jesus said to His disciples, "Herein is My Father glorified, that ye bear much fruit" (John 15:8). Believers, then, must endeavor, whatever they do, to "do all to the glory of God" (1 Corinthians 10:31). To this purpose it is requisite that they care for the things of the Lord, "that they may be holy both in body and spirit, diligently following every good work" (1 Corinthians 7:34), and that they "follow not that which is evil, but that which is good" (3 John 11).

These appear to be the leading purposes for which good works are necessary; and so indispensably requisite are they to subserve those designs that, according to the order unalterably fixed in the covenant of grace, it will be impossible for the latter to be attained without the former. Though good works, as has been observed, are not necessary out of their proper place, yet, in the place assigned to them and for the purposes intended to be served by them, they are absolutely indispensable. No man can warrantably conclude that he is instated in the covenant of grace unless he finds that he is disposed and enabled daily to perform them.

Section 3. The Desert of Good Works

Although the good dispositions and actions of one fellow creature deserve to be commended and, in some cases, to be rewarded by another, yet no good qualities or works of mere men can merit the smallest blessing or good thing from the infinite Majesty of heaven.

With respect to the works of unregenerate persons, they are destitute of every thing which can render an action good and acceptable in the sight of God. They are not done from true faith as a principle (Titus 1:15; 1 Timothy 1:5; Hebrews 11:6), nor are they performed from a principle of love (Romans 8:7 and 13:10). Neither are they done by persons who are "accepted in the Beloved" (Ephesians 1:6). They are not performed in obedience to the will of God expressed in His holy law (Zechariah 7:5; Romans 8:7–8), nor are they done to His glory as the chief end of them. All unconverted persons are said in Scripture to be sinners or workers of iniquity (Psalms 53:1–4; Romans 3:9–19) and their works, however advantageous many of them may be to themselves or others, are all, notwithstanding, represented as sins in the account of an infinitely holy God (Proverbs 21:4; Isaiah 1:13–14), for although many of them may be materially good, yet all of them are formally evil; and therefore they are an abomination to Him (Proverbs 15:8 and 21:27). Consequently, the very best works of unregenerate persons, instead of deserving the favor of God, deserve His wrath and curse, both in this life and in that which is to come. Such works deserve eternal death, and cannot surely, at the same time, merit eternal life (Romans 6:23); and yet so deplorably ignorant and self-righteous are unregenerate sinners that they all rely, either wholly or partially, on their own works for a title to the favor of God, and even to endless felicity. Nay, so gross is their ignorance of themselves, and of the righteous law of God, and so inveterate is their pride, that they depend on such works not only for a title to eternal life, but even for security from that eternal death which is already due to them for their innumerable sins, and to which they are already condemned.

As for the good works of regenerate men, these also cannot merit from the high and holy One the smallest blessing, much less eternal life. So far as they are spiritually good, they do not, indeed, like the works of the unregenerate, deserve the wrath of God; but still they do not merit the smallest favor at His hand. Merit of condignity, or merit strictly so called, necessarily requires that the works which can merit from God such a reward as would, in strict remunerative justice, be a reward of debt be performed in our own strength; that they are more than we owe to God or more than He requires from us; that they be at least absolutely perfect, and that both in parts, degrees, and continuance; that their value be equal to that of the promised reward; and that the reward be, according to the strictest rules of justice, due for them. Hence it is manifest that the very best works of the holiest of men can merit no favor, no benefit for them at the hand of God. The perfect works of Adam in innocence could not merit any good thing at the hand of the Lord; much less can the imperfect works of holy men now.

These works cannot, by their own intrinsic value, merit the smallest blessing from God. For, first, all the performances that are spiritually good proceed from the almighty agency of the Spirit of grace in believers (Philippians 2:13; 1 Corinthians 4:7). Second, according to the precepts of His holy and righteous law, believers owe perfect and perpetual obedience to the Lord (Romans 8:12; Matthew 5:48). Third, the very best of their works in this world are far from being answerable to the high requirements of the holy law of God (Isaiah 64:6; Galatians 5:17). And, fourth, their best actions, suppose they were perfect, could bear no proportion to any divine blessing, especially to the inestimable blessing of eternal life. The former are the works of finite creatures; the latter, being endless felicity, or the eternal enjoyment of God and of the Lamb, is an infinite reward (Romans 8:18 and 11:6). It is evident, then, that to believers it is wholly a reward of grace, and in no degree a reward of debt. "The gift of God is eternal life through Jesus Christ our Lord" (Romans 6:23).

As the good works of believers cannot, by their own intrinsic value, merit eternal life, or even the smallest blessing from God, so they cannot, by paction, procure the smallest right either to the one or to the other. For, first, the law as a rule of life, under which believers are, is a perfect law of liberty; and therefore it cannot contribute to or admit of pactional merit. The man "who looketh into that perfect law of liberty, and who is a doer of the Word, shall indeed be blessed in his deed"; but he shall not be blessed for it (1 Corinthians 9:21; James 1:25). Second, the good works of believers, during their state of imperfection, are never correspondent, in a perfect degree, to the law as a rule of life (Matthew 22:37–39 and 5:48; Ecclesiastes 7:20). Third, the principles of faith and union with Christ, from which all the good works of believers do flow, imply that the infinitely perfect righteousness of Jesus Christ is imputed to them, which alone merits for them a complete title to the progress and consummation of eternal life (2 Corinthians 5:21; Galatians 2:16, 20; Romans 5:21). The infinitely spotless and meritorious righteousness of Christ, therefore, which is placed to their account, as well as the infinite grace of God which abounds toward them, leaves no room for the pactional merit of their own works (Ephesians 2:7–9; Romans 5:16–19). And, fourth, we read nowhere in Scripture that God ever makes a covenant or pact with believers in which He promises to them eternal life, or even the smallest favor, in consideration of their own sincere obedience. The only covenant that He makes with them is the covenant of grace, according to which every spiritual and temporal blessing is wholly a gift of free and sovereign grace (Ephesians 2:8–9).

The good works of believers, then, do not, either by their own intrinsic value or by paction, procure for them a right to the smallest favor at the hand of God, much less to eternal life. It is only the surety-righteousness of Jesus Christ, imputed to them and received by faith alone, that merits and so procures for them a complete title to the beginning, progress, and perfection of eternal life (Romans 5:21).

It is evident from what has been said that Christ, who lives in believers, is the only source of all their good works. Having in regeneration entered by His

Spirit, He dwells in their hearts by faith as the only fountain of holiness and the sole cause of good works. If adult persons, then, are vitally united to Christ, they will certainly be renewed in the spirit of their minds after His holy image, and will perform good works as the necessary fruits of holiness implanted in their hearts. Where vital union with Christ is, good actions, by persons capable of them, will be the certain consequence; and where it is not, such actions cannot be performed, and it will be in vain to pretend to the practice of them. All the performances of believers that are spiritually good flow from Christ dwelling in their hearts by His Spirit as a spirit of faith; and whatever works proceed not from this principle have nothing more than the mere appearance of good works. "Without Me," said our blessed Lord, "ye can do nothing" (John 15:5). No works are good and acceptable to God but those which have the Spirit of Christ for their main principle and the glory of God for their chief end. And no man is "careful to maintain good works" but the man who has the Spirit of Christ in him, causing him to walk in His statutes, to keep His judgments, and do them (Ezekiel 36:27). It is from the gracious work of the Spirit of Christ in the saints that all their good works proceed. If He did not work in the heart "both to will and to do," they could not work in the life; and if He did not "rest upon them as the Spirit of glory and of God" (1 Peter 4:14), they could not perform a single action to the glory of God. The only way, then, in which either ministers in the gospel or private Christians can effectually promote the interest of good works among others around them is not only to exhibit a bright example of them in their own conduct, but to endeavor diligently to be instrumental in conducting sinners to Jesus Christ, and in teaching them how to "walk in Him."

Can a man perform no good works till after he is justified in the sight of God? Hence it is manifest that they who rely on their own obedience for a title to justification are strangers to good works. Their continued and avowed dependance on their own works for a right to justification is a sure evidence that they have never performed a single good work; it demonstrates them to be totally destitute of that "holiness without which no man shall see the Lord" (Hebrews 12:14). To pretend to sanctification, and then to rely on it for justification, is to derive the fountain from the stream, the cause from the effect, and so to invert the order of the blessings of salvation. It is necessary that our sins are forgiven, and our persons accepted as righteous in the sight of God, in order to our being capable of yielding the least degree of acceptable obedience to Him. As long as a man is not justified, he is under the curse of the law; but how can a man who is under the condemning sentence of the law, and consequently under the dominion of sin, perform good works? The Apostle Paul informs us that "as many as are of the works of the law, are under the curse" (Galatians 3:10). It is evident, then, that as long as they rely on their own works of obedience to the law for justification, they are utterly unable either to love or perform the smallest good work. It is the distinguishing property of all good works that they are performed from, and not for, justification. Oh, that secure sinners and self-righteous formalists would believe this, and flee speedily to the compassionate Savior for righteousness and strength!

The notion of a sinner's justification before God by his own works is an absurdity; it is contrary not only to Scripture, but to reason. Every condemned sinner, being under the dominion of sin, is, as was already observed, unable to perform the smallest good work; yet he flatters himself either that his ability is so great, or that the conditions of his justification and salvation are so easy, that he can, especially with divine assistance, fulfill them. "If righteousness cometh by the law, then Christ is dead in vain" (Galatians 2:21); and yet, while the self-righteous formalist seeks righteousness by the works of the law, he professes to believe that the death of Christ has satisfied divine justice for his offenses. If righteousness is by the works of the law, then remission of sins is unnecessary (Romans 4:6–7); and yet, while he is establishing his own righteousness for his justification, he professes to pray for the pardon of all his sins. He expects justification for the merit of his own works, and, at the same time, he professes his belief that they who are justified are justified by grace. In a word, he professes to believe that good works follow justification, and that "without faith it is impossible to please God" (Hebrews 11:6), and after all, he depends on his own works for his justification, as a blessing which he expects will follow them. Ah, how inconsistent, how irrational is the conduct of a self-righteous professor of Christianity! How plainly does it appear that his understanding is darkened, and that he himself is under the dominion of the prince of darkness!

Are we never to perform good works in order to recommend ourselves to Christ, or to afford us a right to trust in Him? Then how dreadful is the condition of multitudes in the visible church! There are many, very many, alas, who, if they grow remiss in performing duties, or fall into open sins, begin to suspect that Christ will not accept them! But when they labor to mortify their lusts and reform their conduct, they then presume to hope that He will receive them, and that God, for His sake, will accept them. Now what is this but to hope that they shall procure the favor of Christ and an interest in His salvation by their own performances, and that His merits will render their own works so valuable as to recommend them even to the acceptance of God. They suppose that if they themselves but begin the work of their salvation, they may warrantably trust that the Savior will carry on and finish that work. Thus they proudly and sacrilegiously presume to divide the work and the honor of their salvation between Christ and themselves. This legal temper is a sure evidence that they are under the dominion of the law of works, and that they are totally destitute of evangelical holiness. It is an infallible proof that they have no part in that salvation of the Lord Jesus, the glory of which is to be ascribed wholly to Himself, and to God in Him.

We also learn from what has been advanced that good works are to be considered as the fruits of a believers being already saved, and, at the same time, in subordination to the glory of God as the end for which he is saved. They are the fruits of his being already in a state of salvation. "Not by works of righteousness which we have done," said the Apostle Paul, "but according to His mercy He saved us by the washing of regeneration and renewing of the Holy Ghost" (Titus 3:5). Here our apostle argues against salvation by our own works of righteousness on the ground that our good works are the fruits or effects of salvation already begun in our

souls. He shows that inherent holiness from which all
our good works spring is an essential part of our salvation; for, he says that we are saved by the washing of
regeneration and renewing of the Holy Ghost. Holiness of heart, then, is a necessary part of salvation by
Jesus Christ; and holiness of life, or our being careful
to maintain good works, is the necessary fruit springing
from that salvation (Luke 1:74–75). Good works are
also the end for which believers are saved. They are
"created in Christ Jesus unto good works" (Ephesians
2:10). The great end, in subordination to the glory of
redeeming grace, for which they have been saved or
created in Christ Jesus is that they might perform and
persevere in the practice of all good works. Such
works, then, are so far from being grounds of title to
salvation that they are the fruits, or consequences of
being already in a state of salvation. True saints are actually, though not completely, saved—and their fruits
of righteousness are the evidence of it. They are not
saved by their good works, but they are saved to them;
nor are they sanctified in order to be justified, but are
justified in order to be sanctified.

The reader may hence learn how to understand
aright this proposition: "Good works are necessary to
salvation." If the term salvation is, by some, and that
without any warrant from the Scriptures, restricted to
the perfect blessedness of saints in heaven, then good
works, in the case of persons capable of them, are necessary to or toward salvation. They necessarily exist before it, not indeed as procuring causes or federal conditions, but merely as antecedents of it. They must of
necessity go before it inasmuch as that which, according to the covenant of grace, is first imparted to the

spiritual seed of Christ must with its genuine effects precede that which is last of all, conferred on them. Personal and progressive holiness is necessary to perfect holiness; and happiness begun is requisite to happiness consummated. At the same time, I dare not say that holiness either of heart or of life is necessary to procure or obtain the felicity of heaven. But if the word "salvation" is taken in its large and scriptural sense, as comprehensive both of a state of grace in time, and of a state of glory in eternity, then good works are, properly speaking, not necessary *to* it, but necessary *in* it. As imperfect, they are indispensably requisite in a state of grace; and as perfect, they are necessary in a state of glory. They are needful in progressive as well as in perfect salvation. They are indispensably requisite in every adult person who is justified and saved. That the term "salvation" ought to be taken in this comprehensive meaning is evident from this, among other passages of Scripture: "I endure all things for the elect's sake, that they may also obtain the salvation which is in Christ Jesus, with eternal glory" (2 Timothy 2:10). Here the salvation which is in Christ Jesus is distinguished from eternal glory.

What has been advanced may serve to show us the difference, or rather the opposition, between a reward of debt and a reward of grace. In the law of works, eternal life is promised to the man who yields perfect obedience. If man had yielded this obedience, that would have been a reward of debt (Romans 4:4), a recompense due by stipulation for the work done. In the gospel, the reward of eternal life is promised to the obedient believer not for his good works, but considered as united to Christ in whom he has righteousness for his justification, and in whom all the promises of God are "yea" and "amen." This is, indeed, a reward of debt to Christ, to whom the believer is united, and in whom he is justified; but it is a reward of infinitely free grace to the believer himself. It cannot be a reward of debt to the believer and at the same time to Christ. A reward of debt is promised to the act or work; but a reward of grace is promised only to the agent or worker. The former is adjudged as a recompense for the work performed: the latter is awarded in and after the work. If the reward is given to a man for his works of obedience, then it is not of grace, otherwise work is no more work; but if it is given him of grace, then it is not for his works, otherwise grace is no more grace (Romans 11:6). If the reward corresponded to the exact value of the work done, and if it followed upon work to which man was not bound, or which was more than he owed to God, and which he performed in his own strength, independent of God, then it would be a recompense strictly merited by him, and so would, in the highest sense of the phrase, be a reward of debt to him. Or even if the value of the work done bore no proportion to that of the reward, and though it were work which man previously owed to God, and which he performed in strength received from Him, yet, if God had made a covenant with man in which He promised to him the reward of eternal life for the perfect performance of that work, then eternal life would be a reward of pactional debt to man upon his complete performance of the work. On the other hand, when the reward is given, not according to the intrinsic worth, but according to the spiritual nature or quality of the work, and of the work as already due to the Lord; and when it is conferred not in consideration of the work done, but because of the free favor of God to the believer who has done the work, it is in that case a reward of grace. Although eternal life is given to the true Christian not as a recompense for his good works, but only as a gift of infinitely free grace, yet, in the Scriptures, it is called a reward to him because it is conferred on him in and after his works.

While the gospel teaches us that good works are unnecessary to the justification of a sinner before God, it affirms that they are necessary in the life of a saint. It, indeed, excludes them from being federal conditions or procuring causes of salvation; but it includes them in salvation both as parts and as consequences of it. We are not saved on the ground of them; but we are careful to maintain them because we are saved, and "saved by grace through faith." The grace of God exhibited in the glorious gospel enables as well as teaches us "to deny ungodliness and worldly lusts, and to live soberly, righteously and godly, in this present world" (Titus 2:11–12); nor have we truly discerned or received that grace which brings salvation if it has not effectually taught and enabled us to do so.

Reader, let it be your diligent endeavor to trust at all times in the Lord Jesus, for that great salvation which He has brought near to you in the offers and promises of the glorious gospel, and to trust in Him for it in order that you may thereby be enabled to perform good works. You can do nothing that is spiritually good unless you trust and pray daily for grace to enable you. Let the life, then, which you live in the flesh, be by the faith of the Son of God; and in this way you shall so die to the law in its federal form as to live unto God. Rely on His consummate righteousness, and on that only, for all your title to salvation; trust His overflowing fullness for all supplies of grace necessary to make you advance daily in the love and practice of every good work.

Faith in the adorable Redeemer is the first act of acceptable obedience, and the root of all other spiritual graces. Implanted by the Holy Spirit in the heart, it is the principle and primary means of that evangelical "holiness without which no man shall see the Lord" (Hebrews 12:14). Trust, then, and trust with all your heart in the compassionate Savior for justification by His spotless righteousness, and for sanctification by His Holy Spirit. Come to the Lord Jesus and, upon the warrant afforded you by the unlimited offers and calls of His glorious gospel, place the confidence of your heart in Him for that holiness which is the beginning and the very essence of salvation by Him. Instead of being the proper condition of salvation, this is salvation itself.

Thus, by grace derived from His fullness, you shall become "zealous of good works"—zealous for performing them, and equally zealous for placing no dependance on them for a title to divine favor. And so you shall "be filled with those fruits of righteousness, which are by Him, unto the glory and praise of God" (Philippians 1:11). United by faith to the second Adam as your Head of righteousness and life, you shall live a life of progressive obedience in time, and of perfect obedience through eternity. Oh, be persuaded that union and communion with Christ as your righteousness and strength are indispensably requisite to your being capable of performing such works as will be good and acceptable to an infinitely holy God. You yourself must, in union with Christ, be accepted as righteous, and have a right to eternal life, before any of your works can be accepted as sincere. The great Redeemer is in the gospel freely offered to you that you may have a warrant so to believe in Him as to be united to Him; and it is to your peril if you reject the gracious offer. Do not say, "I cannot believe in Him, and why should I be doomed to more dreadful destruction for not doing what I cannot do?" You cannot believe in the Savior because you *will* not; just as Joseph's brethren could not speak peaceably to him because they hated him. Were you really willing to believe in Christ and yet were not able, you could not be an object of blame. But it is quite the reverse with sinners: they are not able because they are not willing (John 5:40), and they are not willing to come to Christ because their carnal mind is enmity against Him (Romans 8:7). Their inability is moral and, therefore, sinful impotence. Nothing renders them unwilling but the sin that reigns in them. If you are willing to come to the Savior, you will, in the same proportion, be able. No sinner was ever willing to come to Him and yet was not able. In order, then, that you may be made willing to come, you ought, without delay, to trust and plead this absolute promise which, in and with Christ Himself, is graciously offered to you: "I will take away the stony heart out of your flesh, and I will give you an heart of flesh" (Ezekiel 36:26), and also this one: "In His name shall the Gentiles trust" (Matthew 12:21).

If Christ is the way to God and to glory, and if He is the way of holiness, or the holy way, then you who have believed through grace ought to take heed that you walk constantly in that way. "As you have, therefore, received Christ Jesus the Lord, so walk in Him" (Colossians 2:6). In union with Him, go forward daily in the exercise of faith and love, and in the practice of holiness. Depending on His grace and strength, advance with holy diligence and with increasing ardor in the daily practice of those good works which are works of faith and labors of love. Make constant progress in your exercise of faith, and by sanctifying and comforting influences from the fullness of Christ, walk on with cheerfulness and resolution in Him as your way to the perfection of holiness and of happiness.

To walk in Christ is, in consequence of union with Him, and by communications of grace from Him, to walk in the unwearied exercise of trusting and hoping in Him; to "walk in His commandments" (2 Chronicles 17:4), and to walk in the love and practice of all good works (Ephesians 2:10). Having, then, become dead to the law as a covenant by the body of Christ, apply and trust the promises of His gospel; and in the faith of the promises, walk in all the commandments of His law as a rule. In the humble confidence that He performs the promises of His glorious gospel to you, and so "worketh in you both to will and to do," keep the commandments of His holy law. Keep them diligently, and whatever you do in word or in deed, do all in His name, and to the glory of God in Him. Thus shall you "walk worthy of the vocation wherewith you are called" (Ephesians 4:1), and "worthy of the Lord unto all pleasing, being fruitful in every good work" (Colossians 1:10). Thus you shall both adorn the gospel of God your Savior in all things, and honor His righteous law.

Oh, believer, much depends on your behavior! The men of the world around you will always be ready to spy out every blemish in your conduct, in order to justify their contempt of you and their disapprobation of your sentiments. Others may commit many sins and escape censure; but if you do anything wrong, or discover inconsistency even in a single instance, every mouth will be open—not against you merely, but against your principles, and all who profess them. Take heed, then, that you give no occasion to the enemies of the Lord to speak reproachfully; but rather, on every occasion, study "with well-doing, to put to silence the ignorance of foolish men" (1 Peter 2:15). You are one of the children of light: "Let then your light so shine before men, that they may see your good works, and glorify your Father who is in heaven" (Matthew 5:16).

In conclusion, from what has been said we may see how good works are related both to the law and the gospel. Four things are to be remarked concerning such works: obligation to them, assistance in them, acceptance of them, and reward according to them. The first proceeds from the law as a rule of duty in the hand of the Mediator; and the other three proceed from the gospel in its strict acceptance. The obligation to perform them arises from the sovereign authority of God our Savior revealed in the law; assistance in performing them is afforded by His strength, promised in the gospel: the acceptance of them flows from His righteousness, revealed and offered in the gospel; and the reward according to them proceeds from His boundless grace, displayed and tendered also in the gospel.

Much more, therefore, is requisite to the performance of good works than merely to know that they are enjoined in the law. That, indeed, is requisite to the right performance of them; but it is far from being all that is needful.

Many think it sufficient for them only to know their duty: and no sooner do they seem to themselves to know it than they immediately and inconsiderately attempt the performance of it. But all they who have the spirit of wisdom and revelation in the knowledge of Jesus Christ, and so are made wise unto salvation through faith which is in Him, know that much more is requisite to the right performance even of the smallest duty than to know that it is commanded in the law. They not only look, therefore, to the law as a rule for authority to oblige them to the practice of good works, as well as for direction in performing them, but they look also to the gospel, and to the Savior offered in it, for strength to perform them, for merit to render them acceptable to God, and for a reward of grace to crown them. If the true Christian, then, would be ready to every good work, he must be excited and resolved not only to receive the law of Christ as his rule of direction, but to believe with application to himself the gospel of Christ, and, in believing it, to trust with firm confidence in Him for assistance, acceptance, and a gracious reward. Thus he will be enabled, while he sojourns in this valley of tears, to serve God acceptably; and at length he will be graciously rewarded with the inexpressible honor of serving as well as enjoying God and the Lamb forever and ever in the holy place on high. There, His servants shall serve Him, and they shall see His face.